DEAR
MR. FANTASY

DEAR MR. FANTASY

Diary of a Decade

Our Time and Rock and Roll

Text & photographs by
Ethan A. Russell

HOUGHTON MIFFLIN COMPANY BOSTON 1985

Library of Congress Cataloging in Publication Data
Russell, Ethan A.
Dear Mr. Fantasy.
1. Rock music — History and criticism. I. Title.
ML3534.R87 1985 784.5′4′009047 85-10890
ISBN 0-395-34421-2

Printed in Japan by Toppan Printing, Ltd.

Design: Nancy Donald and Tony Lane

This book is dedicated with love to my mother

Alice Allen Russell

and in loving memory of my father

Charles Howland Russell

To the memory of

John Lennon

and

the spirit that moved us all

#9 DREAM

So long ago.
Was it all a dream?
Was it just a dream?

I know. Yes, I know.
It seemed so very real.
It seemed so real to me.

— John Lennon, 1974

PREFACE

When we welcomed Mr. Fantasy into our lives in the mid-sixties, it was with a sense of joy and celebration. In a time when one pill made you larger and another made you small (and the ones that your mother gave you didn't do anything at all), the set of realities we had believed in all our lives was discarded with gleeful abandon. Indeed, Mr. Fantasy could have been said to be our mascot. "Further!" we would call with all the fervor of a crusade. Because real, or not real, what did it matter? We had experienced the line between real and not real to be very thin. And on that very thin line we set up camp, held a rally, gave a concert, and proposed to change the world. (For those who didn't feel actually motivated to "do" anything, we had a neat twist: they could simply "be." If the "being" were peaceful and loving, that, too, would change the world.)

We were convinced that we had a grasp on something much more substantial than these questionable realities. We had Truth. And the Truth was "Love is All and Love is Everyone." It was a persuasive call that seemed to demand allegiance, reverberating back and forth from San Francisco to London and in expanding circles to many corners of the planet.

In retrospect people often seem embarrassed by that time — the late sixties into the seventies — as if suddenly confronted with some lunatic member of your family, once revered, now disgraced. Even John Lennon, who would hold on as much as anybody, would at one point have to declare, "Don't give me no more brother, brother."

I shared this uneasiness, a vague sense of disappointment, even failure. So when my long-standing friend, and editor of this book, Gerard Van der Leun (who was the only other person who knew of the boxes of disorganized slides and negatives gathering dust in the basement of a house in California), first approached me about publishing a book of my photographs, I declined. I didn't want to publish yet another book of Famous Faces.

On the other hand I had been privileged, through a series of accidents recounted here (the catechism of the sixties, of course, doesn't credit "accidents"; everything happens for a reason), to work with many of the phenomenal performers, singers, songwriters — artists — whose work and lives had so affected "us." So the book inevitably becomes the story of me, as one fellow who believed with the rest of us but just got lucky enough to encounter what would later be called "the principals": John Lennon, the Beatles, Mick Jagger, the Stones, Pete Townshend, the Who.

For "us," the music began with rock and roll (Elvis, Little Richard, the Everly Brothers), shifted to folk (Joan Baez, Bob Dylan), then fused (Dylan meets the Beatles meet the Walrus), passing from the popular to the traditional to the political to the evangelical. The music changed our lives. We were first most clearly visible in all our numbers at Woodstock. But it didn't last. Something didn't work. Starting with Altamont (so soon after Brian Jones's death) it (whatever "it" was) started to disappear, as a fantasy.

I had been as zealous as any, had called passionately for Peace and Love, had taken it into my personal life and seen it falter. I was as entertained and transported by the music as any, for it seemed impossible not to be caught up with a music that proclaimed, "All you need is love." We were *so* certain.

When things began to go wrong, when we realized we were not going to be able to, could not, deliver all our promises, as we saw so many die (famous and obscure) in what came to be an endless, grisly procession, we seemed to lapse into an uneasy silence.

But, really, so much was accomplished, so much changed (and, even less noticed, a lot held on to), that it seems inappropriate to be quite so uncomfortable with our past. For by refusing to accept the world as we were told to (most pointedly the war in Vietnam) we held on to many of the traditional values we had been taught, not the least of which was to demand accountability from our government. We shouldn't forget that a lot *had* to change. For America couldn't forever remain the child of the Hula-Hoop with the arsenal of Armageddon.

So, back when I was a college kid and Bob Dylan was singing, "You threw the bums a dime, in your prime, didn't you?" I always used to say I wanted to be a writer. Instead, for years, I was a photographer. ("Whatever happens.") Now there is a book. With the writing comes a sense of trepidation at the power a writer has to say what he feels. In reaction I am reminded of a scene from *Lawrence of Arabia*. Lawrence (Peter O'Toole), then a young lieutenant in the British service, is called before the commanding officer. "Lawrence," booms the officer with the resonance of the Empire. "They tell me you are insolent."

"It's my manner, sir," says Lawrence, bowing from the waist, unable somehow to master the military demeanor.

"What?" commands the officer, astounded by the remark.

"It's my manner, sir. It appears insolent, but it isn't, really." ⊹

It seems as one becomes older,
That the past has another pattern. . . .

We had the experience, but missed the meaning,
And approach to the meaning restores the experience
In a different form, beyond any meaning
We can assign to happiness.

— T. S. Eliot,
"The Dry Salvages"

1

HOLLYWOOD HILLS, OCTOBER 1980.

In show business, it always seems to start with a phone call. "Congratulations, and don't say I never do anything for you," says Jo Bergman. Jo ran the Rolling Stones' office in London for many years; now she is director of film and video for Warner Brothers Records. "John and Yoko have chosen you for their new film."

From my house on the hillside I gaze through a break in the trees. Below I can see the flatlands of Hollywood stretching off into the smog. My latest career has involved the production and direction of short, musical films. A reel of these films had been sent to John and Yoko, and they have chosen me to act as producer, or filmmaker, for the promotional film they intend to make for their upcoming album, *Double Fantasy*. I am to call Yoko on the thirteenth of November at 1:45 P.M., not before.

I am told that Yoko had a chart done to determine the most astrologically opportune time to commence the filming, and that turned out to be a date still about two weeks hence. In the meantime, I am told to go to the record company and listen to the single.

Sunset Strip in the 9000s is a very good address in show business. Tucked away in little château-like offices are major deal makers. Deals worth millions of dollars are frequently put together by people who look like they have a lot of trouble getting out of bed in the morning.

Double Fantasy is John's first record in more than four years. Intermittently we have heard of his "lost weekend" in Los Angeles, his return to Yoko, his sojourn as a "house husband."

The secretary ushers me into the office where the operating head of the company sits behind his desk. He wears a beard, appears intense and very preoccupied.

"Here's the single," he says, and punches the start button of the cassette player. Over the speakers comes the sound of three chimes, followed by a slow introduction, John singing: "Our life together / Is so precious together . . ." and then the tempo shifts and breaks into the loping cadence of "(Just Like) Starting Over." John is singing in true rock idiom, sounding like the stuttering Elvis in "Heartbreak Hotel," sounding like John Lennon, and it is *so* good to hear him, so good to have him back again.

As I'm listening, the record company executive seems agitated, as if somehow this meeting is taking place against his will. When the song is over he takes out the

Left: John Lennon with Salvador Dali's "eye," Montague Square, London, 1968.

cassette and hands it to me. The album is not due for release for another two weeks. The record executive fixes his stare on me and says, "You know, if somehow one of those songs were to make it onto the radio before the release of this album, *kill* would not be too strong a word for what I would do to that person."

Out on the Strip the sun is bright and hot in that insistent L.A. way. Walking to my car, the cassette in my pocket, I once again pause to reflect upon the amazing behavior of these people. In the absolutely normal course of business, at the request of the artist, I go into a record company to pick up a cassette so I can listen to the music and prepare for a production. In that process, the executive, who has never met me, assumes that I have the morals of a pirate and threatens my life. There really is no business like show business. And in 1980, rock and roll is certainly show business.

And, though the executive didn't know it, I had worked with John and Yoko many years before.

Above and below right: John Lennon.

LONDON, ENGLAND, 1968.

Jonathan Cott and I are in a pub next door to my flat on Peel Street near Holland Park. I'm having a drink to calm my nerves, but my stomach is still an anxious knot. Jon and I are due shortly to leave to meet John Lennon, Jon to interview him, and I to do the photography.

In 1968 I am twenty-two, living in London, not clear what I am going to do with my life, but attempting to write, and working part time with autistic children in St. John's Wood. Jon is in London on a Guggenheim fellowship and is the London correspondent for *Rolling Stone*. When Jon was first introduced to me, I was told that he once interviewed Bob Dylan at a press conference in Berkeley.

As it turns out, Jon is a kind, self-effacing man in his mid-twenties whose mother will, within a month, give him a haircut while he sleeps. "How do you deal with that, Ethan?" he asks me. Jon is always in a state of perpetual wonderment about the business of this world. A New Yorker to his marrow, Jon lived briefly in the San Francisco Bay Area before coming to London in the swinging sixties, as they're being called. He's always saying, "Did you see *that,* that's incredible," and always about women, "She's beautiful. But she's crazy."

Some months earlier, Jon had come by the flat I was then renting in Kensington Court. I'd shown him some of my writing, which he said was good. This was a great compliment to me. I'd also shown Jon some photographs I had taken before I left California. They were almost entirely of children, innocent portraits, unposed and in black and white. But interspersed among those photographs, peering out at you through masses of unkempt hair, were the distinctive faces of an early heavy metal group, Blue Cheer. They were later to be managed by my brother, and before I left San Francisco to come to London I had taken pictures of them.

Jon liked the pictures, too. He told me he was scheduled to interview Mick Jagger in a couple of weeks. "Do you want to do the photographs of Mick when I interview him?" he asked.

Photograph Mick Jagger? Why, I remember in college, driving down the California highways in my VW bus, hair just beginning to grow over my collar, the bell and the feather hanging off the rearview mirror, and the dashboard painted light purple polka dots, the color I was into then, singing at the very top of my voice, "Hey, hey! You! Get off of my cloud!"

"Why sure, Jon," I said.

Now, I'm waiting to go and meet John Lennon. Jon and I rendezvous with Robert Frazer, owner of the Robert Frazer Gallery, which hosted John Lennon's first art show, "You Are Here." Frazer takes us to the basement flat where Lennon is staying. To get to it we pass through iron gates and then down stairs that wind their way to the front door. We ring the bell.

John answers the door. He is wearing jeans, a black shirt, and tennis shoes. He turns and leads us into a cluttered living room, piles of records scattered about the floor. John kneels down and puts on the first track of the Beatles' new record. The sound of screeching jet engines plays over the speakers, followed by a squeak and then the pounding of McCartney's bass. "Flew in from Miami Beach, B.U.A.C. [*sic*] / Didn't get to bed last night . . ." (It's "Back in the USSR.")

John says, "Really, I just like rock 'n' roll."

Though I'm amazed at how friendly and enthusiastic Lennon is ("There's nothing more fun than talking about your own songs. . . . It's your bit, really"), he still seems entirely too famous to be real.

I go to work. Very little daylight is able to find its way into the basement flat. There are one or two standing lamps in the room, but all in all it is really quite dark. Since nobody has ever bothered to ask me the extent of my experience, nobody knows that I have never had any reason to actually light anything. Most of my previous "sessions" had been outdoors in the California sun. Now I find myself in a dark London basement. The needle on my light meter barely registers.

If, at this time, I can be said to have any photographic approach at all, it is to be as invisible and quiet as possible, to photograph as candidly as I can. The very thought of being in the presence of John Lennon is daunting enough. It would never have occurred to me to have arrived with a lot of lights and gone "pop, flash" through the interview, though the truth was, at the time, I didn't know how to use them anyway. But there are certain adjustments that can be made in a low-light situation, and I did what I could.

Meanwhile, John is talking, answering Cott's questions. John is intrigued with this new American magazine, *Rolling Stone.* In America, after the release of *Sgt. Pepper,* the Beatles, the Stones, and rock music in general were being taken very seriously indeed. Unbelievably, in Britain the music press still seemed to be stuck in the fifties,

its attention eternally hypnotized by such critical questions as "What's your favorite color, Teen Throb?"

Lennon's wit is never far away. Jon asks, "Is there anybody you've gotten something from musically?"

John answers, "I'm still trying to reproduce 'Some Other Guy' sometimes, or 'Be-Bop-A-Lula.' . . . We're influenced by whatever's going . . . Little Richard, Presley."

Cott: "Anyone contemporary?"

Lennon: "Are they dead?"

The interview lasts an hour or so, and then John announces that he has to leave for EMI, the studio where the Beatles record. I sit in the back of the station wagon with John, as we crawl through the afternoon London traffic. John reclines, his knees resting against the back of the front seat. I look out at the other drivers, wondering if anybody will turn and look, notice, have some reaction. But, in sleepy London town, no one does.

EMI's main studio is a huge, high-ceilinged box. John says good-bye and disappears. My sense of excitement is still running at flood level. Inside that studio are the Beatles! I peek in, glimpsing George and Paul. In the booth upstairs I make out George Martin, their producer. I take a furtive snap of Ringo, a long distance away, almost hidden by a sound baffle.

Meanwhile, Jon Cott is talking to a Japanese woman. They are seated in a canteen area with beige walls, beige tables, cups of tea, and bright overhead lighting.

The woman is animated, talking, explaining. At the time I have no idea who she is. Nonetheless, I take pictures. Yoko Ono's relationship with John Lennon is not yet public in Britain, and so the massive wave of resentment has yet to set in. When Jon is finished speaking with Yoko, we leave.

Above left: The wall of the Montague Square flat.

Below: Ringo inside the EMI studios.

Right: Yoko Ono at EMI.

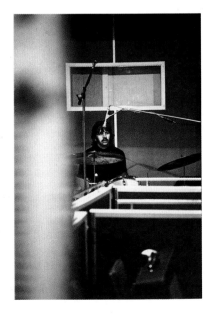

When the film and contact sheets come back from the lab the following day, the lack of light in the basement apartment can be seen to have had serious consequences. John's black shirt is a hole in the negative; there is no depth of focus, very little detail anywhere. I have the lab pull a couple of prints. No improvement.

I don't know how long I sit there stunned, but like a teenager who has just wrecked the car, I realize it doesn't matter — sooner or later the truth will be known, and there is no way I can will it to be different. Not enough light is not enough light, and now what? With great trepidation, I call John and tell him. His reaction is immediate and kind. He says to come by tomorrow. We'll shoot again.

I rush out and buy lights, flood lamps like you see in photo magazines. I ask the salesman(!) behind the counter how to use them. The next day I arrive at Montague

Square. I've brought with me the contact sheets, and enlargements of my photos of Yoko. In the canteen there was plenty of light, and Yoko looks good. She gestures, her eyes wide. She appears thoughtful.

John loves them, and pins them immediately onto a wall that is already covered with Beatle memorabilia: a circular Sgt. Pepper crest, the Beatles on the cover of *Time* magazine. With good pictures of his girlfriend, it seems as if John couldn't care less about the ones of himself.

I place the lights and shoot. This time, there is no interview, just John and me. He holds a quartz and crystal rock about the size of a baseball, with an eyeball set in it, courtesy of Salvador Dali.

This is awfully heady stuff for a boy from California who three months earlier was sitting in his one-room flat trying to write, and four days a week working in a children's hospital. Heady stuff for a boy who a few years earlier could be seen in his madras jacket and button-down shirt singing the Kingston Trio's version of "This Land Is Your Land" in St. Mark's Square in Venice.

Still, before the Kingston Trio, I could be caught singing "You Ain't Nothin' But a Hound Dog" along with Elvis Presley, just like a lot of other kids — probably just like John Lennon. ✢

Above: Yoko at EMI.

Below left: John and Yoko.

CHAPTER

2

SAN FRANCISCO, 1956.

Before Elvis, I used to lie in bed at night with the lights off, and listen to country music very low on the radio, the tiny orange lights of the tube amplifier shining through the slits in the radio's back.

My room was tucked away at the top of a three-story house, past even the attic room where the suitcases were kept. My brother and I would roam the top floor, our plastic flintlock rifles cocked, and ambush each other. On television Fess Parker as Davy Crockett, the strong, serene American hero, told us, "Be sure you're right. Then go ahead."

I was ten when Elvis came along. I used to sing his songs in front of the mirror. I imitated his smile, raising the corner of one side of my mouth. I tried to move like him, rotating one leg from the hip. And I tried to comb my hair like him. I used Vitalis, Butch Wax, Brylcream, pulling the comb through my hair and seeing little white globules of grease ooze between the teeth. I dove into a swimming pool, swam the entire length underwater, and surfaced at the other end without a hair out of place. Hair.

One day my father, vexed beyond endurance, took my brother and me to the local barbershop and told the barber to give us both crew cuts. Crew cuts! Prickly hair that grew from your skull like a ten-day stubble. Itchy, uncomfortable, and leaving you no place to hide, as if you found yourself suddenly naked in a roomful of strangers.

Elvis was the King, with his smile and small hip-shake that would reduce the girls to cream, but there were also the others: Jerry Lee Lewis (with his thirteen-year-old bride; these boys really *were* southern), the Everly Brothers (with their mellow harmonies), screaming Little Richard pounding the piano, and the duck-walking Chuck Berry.

My parents hated the music I found so exciting. In turn, I found an afternoon spent in the car with them listening to Tony Bennett was more than I could endure. Their music — Cole Porter, Benny Goodman, wonderful music, really — made no sense to me at all.

Then Elvis was drafted. He was taken to boot camp and his hair was shorn. It was awful to see him lose *his* hair. But it never occurred to me that Elvis wouldn't go into the army. Why would it have?

("Elvis died in the army," John Lennon later said. "The difference between Elvis

Above: The author "raising the corner of one side of my mouth," like Elvis.

[23]

and us is Elvis died and his manager lived. Our manager died, and we lived.")★

Shortly after Elvis was drafted, I was sent to boarding school outside Santa Barbara. As soon as I was able I grew my hair back, smothered it with grease, and combed it into as close a version of a duck tail as a prep school would allow. I donned Roy Orbison glasses. With Elvis out of circulation, I was now listening to Bobby Vee. Vee looked like a cross between Fabian and Sandra Dee. On his record cover he was wearing a powder-blue cashmere sweater with puffy balls on it, like a girl.

In 1960 I was fifteen. Eisenhower was president and Nixon vice-president. Gary Powers, flying a high-altitude reconnaissance plane, was blown out of the sky, and Eisenhower had to admit, embarrassedly, to the American people that the United States did, well, spy in peacetime. This admission reverberated through the American system like a shock wave, for it was unheard of at that time for America to do such a thing. We *fought* the countries that behaved that way.

"The employers will love this generation," said Clark Kerr, president of the University of California (who was to be discredited and later resign in the wake of the Free Speech Movement). "They aren't going to press many grievances. They are going to be easy to handle. There aren't going to be any riots."

In my room at prep school, Bobby Vee's voice is replaced by that of Joan Baez, swelling in nasal perfection. She sings "folk music." It is different from rock, but simple, affecting. It reaches inside you. She makes it into *Time* magazine.

Outside the window of my dormitory room, the California sun shone upon the well-manicured lawns and brick pathways. The Cate School was a world of blue blazers and ties, an ordered life of small classes, study halls, and chapel. I was absorbed reading *On the Road,* caught up in the world Kerouac describes: the manic Cassady, careening across America, his injured thumb wrapped in an unraveling bandage. It was all very exotic. When I read *On the Road* it was the first time I had ever heard of marijuana. ❧

★Still, this didn't stop Lennon or the rest of them from — when they finally met Elvis in Los Angeles in 1965 — gazing, speechless, at Elvis like the most star-struck fan until Elvis was forced to say, "Look, if you damn guys are gonna sit here and stare at me all night, I'm gonna go to bed." (See *The Love You Make: An Insider's Story of the Beatles,* by Peter Brown and Steven Gaines. New York: McGraw-Hill, 1983.)

CHAPTER

3

PEBBLE BEACH, CALIFORNIA, 1963.

On the back of the sofa in the large living room, Joan Baez sat, still and peaceful. Her black eyes shone, her long hair fell over her shoulders, and she smiled happily, as if she was having a wonderful time in the houses of the rich. The occasion was a fund raiser for a proposition on the California ballot to forbid discrimination in housing on the basis of race, religion, or sex.

I sat on the floor and watched, along with my high school friend Charlie Osborne, whose father, Richard, was hosting this affair. There were a lot of people in conservative Pebble Beach who felt that Richard had no business inviting a known radical singer into his house to raise money for a measure seen by them as a threat to property values. That Joan Baez was concerned and political was no secret. She sang at concerts, at political rallies, at sit-ins, and over American radio the lyrics of a new American songwriter, Bob Dylan. "How many roads must a man walk down / Before you call him a man?" As she sang, she tilted her head, her brow furrowed, and her eyes took on a questioning look. "How many times can a man turn his head," she asked, "and pretend that he just doesn't see?"

To Charlie and me, of course, Baez's presence seemed magical. We listened to what she had to say, and it seemed sensible to us. How many roads *did* a man have to walk down, after all? But we were soon shunted upstairs, where we no doubt worked on perfecting our cigarette habit. Downstairs Baez continued to sing with her strong, lifting voice. I was drawn to Baez and this "folk music," as to Kerouac's *On the Road* and things "bohemian," though my idea of it at the time was to buy a pair of sandals and a scarf, kind of like Dobie Gillis.

Twenty-six miles south of Pebble Beach, where I sat listening to Joan Baez, lies the Big Sur, known as "the Coast" to locals. I had heard it vaguely referred to as a place where "artists" and "nonconformists" lived, but I had never been there, until, one day, Richard Osborne took Charlie and me for dinner. Before we left I heard Richard ask someone, with a grin on his face, "Do you think he's ready for it?" And so I stared out the car window, wondering about the mysteries of this strange place.

We drove down Highway One past the pine forests that grow in Point Lobos; then the trees cleared, and the road paralleled the ocean, shortly to start a steep climb, winding up the mountainside. The hills were brown, dried by the summer sun. Mountain lions still lived there, I was told. Streams ran down through the hills, collecting at places into pools. Redwood groves grew in the canyons. In the sky, hawks circled endlessly.

Out the car window, I could see waves crashing against the rocks below. As the evening approached, the sky took on a pink cast and the waters of the ocean turned a darker blue. The sun was low and the sunset had turned orange by the time we reached Nepenthe. There we sat outside on the restaurant's deck, in front of an open fire, and gazed down the coastline that stretched twenty miles before us. Greek music played over a loudspeaker.

We were joined by people who lived in Big Sur: Caryl, who was a poet; Al, a jazz guitarist, who played with Nina Simone; LaVerne, an older woman who wore purple lipstick and ran an art gallery farther down the Coast. Later in the evening, sitting inside around a wooden table, next to another fire, I looked up and in the dim light saw a dark-haired woman arrive, carrying a baby on her hip, followed by a man with a drooping mustache and chestnut hair that grew to his shoulders. I looked over at Richard, whom I called "Mr. Osborne," to see if he noticed. Then I looked back. The stranger nodded to the people he knew and stayed at the edge of the crowd, gazing into the fire. He looked to me like "Wild Bill" Hickok, a living icon of the American past. In a way I couldn't explain I felt completely identified with the way the man looked, as if there was more reality in his distillation of the past than in the whole world I'd grown up in. I said nothing at the time, but it sparked in me an attraction. I would go down the Coast again and again, seeking out people who were artists, who were different.

Above: Big Sur.

These people from Big Sur later became my friends. Part of that summer I lived there, a good deal of the time naked, watching from their terraces the Pacific waves roll in hundreds of feet below, the clouds form in the sky and settle against the coastline, the almost imperceptible movements of the kelp and the currents. I was through with high school. In the fall I was bound for college. I slowed down so much that going into the small town of Carmel felt like stumbling into Manhattan in the middle of the Thanksgiving Day parade. One day my mother called. I said, not recognizing her voice, "Who's this?"

"It's your *mother*," she said (as only a mother can), a mere thirty miles but behavioral light years away.

I would stay briefly with a woman painter on Monterey's Cannery Row. The canneries lay empty, like ghosts. No other humans lived nearby. In the evening the fog rolled in off the ocean, and it would be perfectly quiet, except for the rise and fall of the sea against the rocks. ❧

DAVIS, CALIFORNIA, 1963.

Davis, home of a campus of the University of California, is a flat town, a quiet town, out in the middle of the Sacramento Valley. It is a town with street names like A Street and D Street. It was in a house on D Street that I listened to the radio as President Kennedy was taken to the hospital.

I didn't believe that he would die. It was impossible to imagine that an American president could be killed by a simple bullet. I might die, or you might die, from a bullet wound, but not President Kennedy. Surely, someone would take the bullet out, patch him up, and send him back to the Oval Office while the assassin was efficiently gunned down. Then Kennedy died.

Over and over I watched the shaky 8mm home movie showing Jackie Kennedy reacting in shock, crawling back over the trunk of the open limousine while confused Secret Service men rushed to help. All too late. *Life* magazine published blowups from that film, the images almost indecipherable from grain, pictures of Mrs. Kennedy in her pink suit stained with blood. Descriptions were broadcast: "The President was leaning forward slightly, his wife aware that he'd been the victim of a bullet. She . . . was looking at his face when a bullet struck the President in the head, exploding in a pink-red glow of blood, brain matter, and skull fragments. . . ."

I felt empty. None of this was supposed to be able to happen here, and nothing, of course, could now bring him back. And then the best America could do was to arrest some guy "they" said did it, who was then killed by some other man who, in turn, died so nobody was ever to know exactly what happened.

LAKE TAHOE, 1964.

As it grew dark, the white MGA convertible roadster I drove slipped and slithered on the snow-covered mountain road. I was with a friend, and we were late getting back to campus. Still, I pulled into a roadside diner where a television set hung up in one corner, because I really did not want to miss this new group from England on *The Ed Sullivan Show*.

Ed Sullivan, swaying from side to side, says to the audience, "Yesterday and today our theater has been jammed with newspapermen and hundreds of photographers. These veterans agree with me that the city has never witnessed the excitement stirred by these youngsters from Liverpool who call themselves the Beatles." And as Sullivan swings his arm in an arc to welcome them, the screams rise from the audience, overtaking everything.

On television they were unmistakably exciting. I didn't really know their names yet. Ringo wore the rings, right? And John was the "leader," Paul the "cute" one. George was "serious."

The first time I heard "I Want to Hold Your Hand" it had come wafting across a lawn somewhere on campus. It sounded great. But it was a little disconcerting, since I had always thought that great rock 'n' rollers were individuals, not groups. I went to the supermarket and bought the album, *Meet the Beatles*. On the cover four heads stared out from a black space. I played the record a lot. What was it about them?

On the black and white screen in the roadside diner Ringo shook his head, his hair bobbed. The girls screamed. Paul wiggled and smiled. The girls creamed. John Lennon bobbed up and down, singing into the mike, thin-lipped. Each young girl called out her favorite: "JOOHHHNNN!!!" "PAAAAUUUWWWLLL!!!"

"Aren't those Beatles cute," say the Moms.

"Paul's *my* favorite," says Sis.

Maybe even Dad likes them, though with some reservation. After all, there's that hair. But then he would add, hopefully (remembering the fifties and "juvenile delinquents"), "Well, at least they're clean."

The Rolling Stones, just around the corner, weren't so clean. And they didn't smile or wag their heads, either.

In a few years, Sis would be going out with a young fellow who had hair to his shoulders, whose eyes were often bloodshot. Sis would come home, when she came home at all, with her eyes bloodshot as well.

"There's something happening here, but you don't know what it is. Do you, Mr. Jones?" sang an insolent and snarling voice over the radio.

But, too early, still too early for that. It was only the winter of 1964.

New Jersey, 1974.

There was this guy named Ron whom I met through a fellow who worked at Warner Brothers Records. Ron was a Beatlemaniac. When I met Ron in 1974, the Beatles had been broken up for four years. Ron lived in New Jersey with his brother and his parents. Both Ron and his brother were fanatical collectors: Ron of Beatle memorabilia, and his brother of Trini Lopez posters. *Every square inch* of Ron's bedroom was covered with items from his Beatle collection: the ceiling (Beatle posters), the bed (Beatle bedspread, Beatle pillows), and the walls (record jackets and photographs). In one corner there hung an eight-by-ten black and white publicity photo of the Beatles accepting a Mersey Beat award for their song "Love Me Do." Below the publicity photo Ron had the award itself, slightly dusty.

He also had the most movie footage of the Beatles that I had ever seen, and I had sat around in the offices at Apple and seen a lot of their library. Ron had film of the Sullivan shows, the Beatles in Japan, the Beatles at Shea Stadium, and the Beatles at the Washington Coliseum in D.C., filmed the same week as *The Ed Sullivan Show*.

Ron screened the Washington, D.C., film for me, and I watched as the Beatles performed on a stage that appeared to be no more than thirty feet square. Each Beatle had one Vox amplifier and speaker. Ringo had a small drum set. Every fifteen minutes the Beatles would stop and move their microphones, the drums would be shifted, and they would turn ninety degrees and play to a different quarter of the audience, which swayed all around them in a lunatic frenzy. The screaming *never* stopped, peaking wave after wave. It was the single most intense display of energy I'd ever witnessed.

Ron made his living through Beatle memorabilia. When I last saw him he was leaving for Paris to screen one of his Beatle movies. He would (no doubt) go to Paris, spend most of his time in the projection booth, and never let the print of the film out of his sight.

Ron drove a winter-wasted American car of a completely nondescript nature, probably a Plymouth. His parents' home was in Passaic, New Jersey. The houses there were working- to middle class, almost completely drab, but nonetheless larger than their counterparts in Liverpool, England. With Ron's room completely covered with Beatles, and his brother's room completely covered with the Hollywood colorings of Trini Lopez's publicity, this was nothing other than what the Beatles successfully exported: the story of a working-class lad in a black and gray England who had dreams of gold. As in *Yellow Submarine,* where the gray-drabness of the opening gives way to the color and adventure of the film, the Beatles brought sound and color into our lives.

And although California (where I lived) could not compete with the sodden, brick grayness of Liverpool, all of the U.S.A. — the land of crew cuts and pushups, where the masculine ideal was to be a marine — could use a little lightening up, a little more play. The Beatles were just good, clean fun.

LOS ANGELES, 1979.

Years later, I was sitting in a movie theater in Los Angeles waiting for the matinee, stoned out of my mind. Time, not surprisingly, seemed to move very slowly. Shortly, I became aware of the Muzak. It was horrible, cloying. Then I thought, "What if it doesn't stop? What if, after the movie starts, it's still there?" So I pursued this thought as if it were a horror movie: A man goes to a movie, has the experience I was having, and when the movie starts the Muzak doesn't stop, but weaves its way through the soundtrack, distracting his attention (and, of course, he would look around to see if anyone else heard it, and they did not), and when the man leaves the theater, the Muzak follows him, into the shower, into his dreams, jamming his senses. Innocuous, emasculated elevator music takes over his life and eventually drives him mad.

Music can be very insinuating.

———————◆———————

The music came into the sixties like that. At first it was *Meet the Beatles,* but shortly it was "Have you seen the Stones?" Staring out at you were five Englishmen, even stranger than the Beatles. Brian Jones! with blond hair to his shoulders. Jagger lips. Their music was a lot less accessible, less "There were bells all around," more "My, my, my, said the Spider to the Fly / Jump right ahead in my web." It was soon to be called the British Invasion.

While the Beatles were singing: "Love, love me, do," Peter, Paul, and Mary — along with Joan Baez — were spreading the word according to Bob Dylan. While they paved the way with the, in retrospect, surprisingly gentle "Blowin' in the Wind," Dylan went on to write and sing increasingly angry and passionate songs: "The Times They Are A-Changin'," "With God on Our Side," and "Masters of War."

Accompanied only by his guitar and harmonica, Dylan sang, "You that never done nothin' / But build to destroy / You play with my world / Like it's your little toy."

Dylan hit a nerve. I had grown up with *Fail-Safe* and *Dr. Strangelove* and had lived through the endless grade-B Japanese horror films where *everything* was mutated from some form of radiation. The fact is, I was frightened by it all. Now it was being put to me that there were people out there who were responsible for this. I started to get angry.

Dylan sings on, his voice raspy and aggressive, "You've thrown the worst fear / That can ever be hurled / The fear to bring children into the world."

Dylan was right, and I got angrier. (There's more power in these lines sung than read.) Someone out there was lining his pockets creating weapons that could incinerate continents. And this had been going on all my life.

Inexorably, it was getting to be our turn. I was born in 1945, right after Hiroshima. When I was almost seventeen I got to live through the Cuban missile crisis, just one teenage American, terrified that I, my whole family, and my country would soon be a pile of dust. I was nineteen when I first listened to "Masters of War." It seemed a reasonable age to start to protest having one's entire life pre-empted. ⌀

5

DAVIS, CALIFORNIA, 1964.

Bruce Feldman never danced. Bruce was serious and short, with close-cropped hair and a beard. He was a political science major, and old, too. Maybe even thirty. Bruce told me the United States was involved in a war in Indochina. Bruce said that the country of Vietnam had been arbitrarily divided in half by the French and Chinese at Geneva. That the government in the South — which we supported — couldn't even muster the support of its own people. That Ho Chi Minh, the leader in the North, had asked for U.S. support and quoted the American Declaration of Independence when establishing the government of the Democratic Republic of Vietnam. The United States refused its support.

Of course, I didn't know where Indochina was. Somewhere across the Pacific?

Bruce and I would argue. Bruce seemed irritatingly certain of himself. I would not accept what he was telling me: that the United States was involved in an illegal war. To me it was simple. If that's the way things appeared to Bruce, he simply couldn't have all the facts. I refused to believe that the United States would behave in anything other than a righteous manner. I had even joined ROTC in the first semester of my freshman year. I was certain that at some point I would be in the army. Smart planning: be an officer. I came in last in my squad and was given a D. The army wasn't going to flunk anybody.

I had spent hours shining my shoes, spitting on a rag, rubbing it in polish, and making tiny little circles, a "spit shine." I lined up my tie with my belt buckle. Thursday afternoons I went to class. There I stood at attention. I saluted the sergeant. At the front of the classroom he held an M-1 rifle in the air with one hand and his crotch with the other. "This is my rifle. This is my gun. One is for fighting. One is for fun," said he.

By the end of the semester, a variety of things growing in conflict, I told the sergeant I didn't think I would be staying in ROTC. He tried to convince me to continue, despite the fact that I was his worst student. He said I "owed it to my country." This concerned me, so I told my father. My father said the only thing I owed my country was to be the best person I could be.

EARLY 1965.

I spent all day with the used-car salesman. It did not make sense to me that I could be trading in my sexy little MGA convertible on a used Volkswagen half-bus half-pickup and not get any money on the deal. I think used-car salesmen feel that if they can't fleece some college kid they'll lose their self-respect, and their wives will stop

Right, top to bottom: Students and professors from the University of California, Davis, 1965. Miles Forst. Barbara Migdal. Ellen Van Fleet. Bruce Nauman, William Wylie, and Dan Welch as the band Moving Van Walters & His Truck.

sleeping with them. He out-waited me, and I sputtered out of the car lot into a California storm, not realizing that I was soon to be one of an army of long-hairs in VW buses drifting along the California highways, in no hurry at all, man; in direct contradiction to the honcho, hunkered-down cars from the fifties, when power and speed were everything.

The bed of the pickup/bus permitted me to transport the canvases I had begun painting. (I would soon paint the inside of the bus purple: purple dashboard, purple cab. This prompted my father to reflect that this might hurt the resale value of the bus. What resale value?) At the university I had switched from the English Department to Art. Davis had a great Art Department: William Wylie, Wayne Thiebaud, Bruce Nauman. My paintings were big — eight by ten feet, high gloss, orange and purple, black and yellow. About the same time I dropped ROTC, I moved out of the dormitory. I lived in five places in one year. In a one-room shack by the railroad tracks. Noisy. In the basement of a farmhouse in the country. Damp. Three other houses. The Beatles' first film, *A Hard Day's Night,* came out. I could barely understand their accent.

Pursued everywhere by screaming fans, the Beatles never stopped running.

In the United States in 1965 the Beatles release *four* LPs. *Fifty-seven* songs. (The albums are *The Early Beatles,* March; *Beatles VI,* June; *Help,* August; and *Rubber Soul,* December.) By the time you were familiar with one record, another had been released. The Beatles tour Britain, Europe, and America. Eight days a week, indeed.

From England now came word of Carnaby Street, swinging London. "Ferry 'cross the Mersey," the Dave Clark Five, op art, miniskirts, the Yardbirds, and, of course, the Rolling Stones.

Hair starts to sprout on people's heads like mushrooms after a rain. In Davis, we're all making stuff. Make a painting, make a photo. Make each other. It's all stuff. Make stuff. People are talking about Wylie. Someone comes up with the phrase "funk art." Dan Welch makes Zen paintings. Huge canvas chairs. Artists in a cow town, the California sun beating down on us. Welch drifts off to a Zen monastery. Miles Forst, gentle, rambling madman artist from the Bowery in New York where people sleep on fire escapes in the winter, says, eyes bulging, "Look at all you beautiful people out here, whew!" People paint with meticulous craftsmanship, people paint with cans of Day-Glo. People paint each other.

Every weekend there's a party where the music is played. Dance. Smoke a little marijuana. Dance. "Love, love me, do." Beautiful, beautiful college women. John Lennon howling. Mick Jagger singing, "Time is on my side. / Yes it is."

The Beatles release their second movie, *Help!* I see it at least three times. The Beatles are as captivating as ever, and it's in color. The music is great, getting even better. John Lennon lying on the couch in the Beatles' common house sings, "Here I stand, head in hand / turn my face to the wall . . ."

It seems as though every album — from every artist — is a major creative leap

further. In 1966 Bob Dylan releases *Bringing It All Back Home*. He's on the cover with
an unnamed woman in a red dress; he's holding a cat and looking like the head of
SPECTRE in a James Bond movie. When I get the record home, I rip the shrink wrap
off and put the needle in the groove. Right away it's obvious something very bizarre
is up: drums, electric guitar, and "Johnny's-in-the-basement-mixing-up-the-medi-
cine / I'm-on-the-pavement-thinking-about-the-government / Man-in-a-trench-
coat-badge-out-laid-off / Say's-he's-got-a-bad-cough-wants-to-get-paid-off / Look-
out-kids-it's-something-you-did / God-knows-when-but-you're-doing-it-again /
you'd-better-duck-down-the-alleyway-looking-for-a-new-friend / Man-in-a-coon-
skin-cap-and-a-pig-pen-wants-eleven-dollar-bills / you-only-got-ten . . ."

The words pile on top of each other, pouring out of Dylan's mouth in an incredible rush, accelerated, surreal. Where was all this coming from? Did it matter? ✤

CHAPTER

6

Everybody must get stoned.

— Bob Dylan

DAVIS, CALIFORNIA, 1966.

When you smoked marijuana, time slowed down, and ice cream tasted better than it had ever tasted before. If you listened to music, and closed your eyes, the notes would elongate, stretch, and the music would carry you away, make you move like kelp in the ocean. Your eyes got red. Your tongue got dry. But, unlike being drunk, you didn't stumble around, get sick, wake up with a hangover.

I was so scared of marijuana that the first time I smoked it, I didn't even know what it was or I never would have touched it. A joint was offered to me by a guy with a huge, drooping mustache, who used to spend half his time in Mexico and always smoked roll-your-own tobacco. I thought he was offering me a cigarette. As I lay in a hammock, I suddenly noticed the shadows in the room growing longer, and time seemed to move eerily slow.

When I bought my first couple of joints I hid them in a can and buried them in the back yard. But when my friends and I got together and smoked them, what would start out as a smirk would soon become uncontrollable peals of laughter, everybody holding their stomachs and rolling on the floor.

I began to wonder why I'd been led to believe that marijuana was so harmful, addicting. Marijuana just seemed to make things *better.* Simple things. If you liked apple juice, it tasted better with marijuana. *Sex* was better. The great sunshine days of California seemed better. Marijuana was a good time. *Alice in Wonderland?* You thought you understood *Alice in Wonderland?* Read it again.

William Blake? Why, all these guys must have been stoned! *All* the time. There was no other explanation; it was the undeniable conclusion — the conspiracy of the stoned, the fraternity of the stoned.

Since marijuana seemed harmless to us, all our elders could finally say was that it was against the law. So? Stupid law, guys.

Then came LSD. I first heard about LSD through the media. Then one day a friend of mine said he'd tried it and it was great. "It's a trip." (A phrase we'd soon hear a lot.) There was no reason not to believe this. I'd been told that marijuana was dangerous and that had been proved false.

I took LSD in a little house in Davis. I sat around and waited for something to change. It seemed to take a long time. After a while I began to wonder whether anything at all was going to happen. I started to play darts with a friend. Then I noticed that the darts were not distinct objects as I'd always known them, but instead they left a little trail of their image after they'd left my hand. For that matter, my arm left a trailing image as it followed through. Something was up here. Me.

I went upstairs and drew for what seemed like a long time, though of course I had no sense of time. I drew very slowly and concentrated very hard. I wrote in a childish scrawl, "It's all so simple."

Then a rainstorm broke and I went outside. It was dusk and I watched a tall, leafless tree swaying against the darkening sky. Every limb, every twig, of that tree was outlined by a thin violet line. It seemed as if it were swaying under water, like something you would see if you went scuba diving. Every so often one of the violet lines would break off and go spinning into the night sky, out into the stars. It was indescribably beautiful. I had an intense sense of the connectedness of life, of how things big and small were the same. The air was the ocean was the air.

My friend came to get me. We drove by a movie theater. People were buying tickets and going in.

"What are they going in the theater for?" I asked. The theater just seemed like a shoe box. Outside was Everything. The Storm. The Night. "Can't they see? It's all out here!" I said. "Everything's out here."

"Sure. And I believe you're Jesus," said my friend, vaguely disgusted.

I tried to think what he meant, although I was sure there was some truth in it.

At the next intersection two cars collided in front of us. Then they backed up and ran into each other again. And then again. The two drivers, both men, raised their fists at each other. It was exactly like two bull elks butting in a forest.

Then I got scared. I can't remember what scared me, but suddenly I wanted to see my girlfriend, who wasn't around. To calm myself, I went home and lay in the bath. But when I looked at myself I looked unbearably skinny. It was like looking at my own skeleton. I became acutely uncomfortable. I couldn't lie there. I got out of the bath. A musician friend came by. I told him I was having a bad time. He said, "If you smoke a joint you'll go right back up again."

I said no, I really didn't want to do that. I wanted to come down.

The next day I walked around with a somewhat eerie feeling, although the hallucinations had stopped. I felt as if the entire world I lived in was somehow changed. Distinctions that I had known as reality had been dissolved, and their dissolution seemed to provide insights into truths that were greater. Spirit was visible, manifest in everything around me.

◆

When I decided to become a conscientious objector, it seemed as if I should have known all along that that's what I was going to do. It was one of those decisions that just felt right. I had spent an entire summer reading Gandhi, inspired by the power (and success) of his nonviolent movement. In the American South, Martin Luther

King, Jr., had led similar nonviolent demonstrations to correct what seemed to me to be obvious wrongs. More fuel for the fire. And still Joan Baez sang at concerts and rallies. I went to tell my father of my decision. I thought he would be delighted.

My father exploded. For the first time in our lives we fought. I couldn't believe that he was so violently opposed to my decision. After all, wasn't he the one who had said that the best thing I could do for my country was to be the best person I could be? To my mind, this was exactly what I was doing. I felt certain that all I had been taught clearly led to this choice.

My father insisted that I *absolutely could not do* what I intended to do. He said it would ruin my life. He felt I might be branded as a traitor or coward, and possibly jailed. I said that I would gladly serve wherever I was sent, that I was in no way attempting to avoid service in the army, or even battle. I felt that conscientious objection was an avenue open to me, a choice that the rules of our society permitted.

My father extracted from me a promise not to do anything right away, to think about it, not to be hasty — the advice of a caring parent. And so I departed, upset, leaving behind a worried father and a no doubt bewildered mother. In the end, there was no choice, of course, and shortly thereafter I notified the Selective Service Commission that I intended to register as a conscientious objector. ("Be sure you're right. Then go ahead.") I filled out the forms and mailed them off.

◆

In Berkeley there was a rumbling. It called itself the Free Speech Movement. When I first heard of it, it seemed preposterous. Certainly *I* had free speech. It was a given. But, as was to happen with so many things, a little examination uncovered some disturbing information: the university was in fact monitoring the political activity of the students on campus, and would shortly attempt to constrain that activity, saying that it was not the province of the student. Why my status as a student should somehow strip away my rights as a citizen seemed a mystery to me, so I chose to protest.

I got in my bus and drove to Berkeley and attempted to get arrested in Sproul Hall. But by the time I arrived, all the demonstrators had been locked inside, so I returned to my bus and drove down the coast to Monterey. Driving along, I envisioned frustrated educators saying, "Where did they get the idea they could behave like this?" "Why, from you," we would respond.

◆

In August 1966, the Beatles play their last live concert at Candlestick Park in San Francisco. That same month, *Revolver* is released. From *Revolver* the single is "Eleanor Rigby."

"Eleanor Rigby" has *no* guitars and *no* drums on it. The track appears to be made up entirely of strings: violins, bass violins. It ignores all the previous basics of rock and roll, instrumentally and lyrically. "Eleanor Rigby . . . lives in a dream," sings Paul.

"Eleanor Rigby" is the first of a series of Paul McCartney portrait songs — "Penny Lane," "She's Leaving Home," "Lovely Rita" — that draw on some part of English society to tell their story, though at this stage people are not differentiating between a "Paul" song and a "John" song. It was all the Beatles. And the Beatles are already bigger and better than anything we'd ever known. The Beatles are, by now, bigger than rock and roll. They had taken all that rock and roll had to offer and fed it back to us in their own way. Now they were growing beyond that, going further. But how much further? Lennon would shortly proclaim the Beatles "more popular than Jesus," and sing, "Love is all and love is everyone. / It is knowing, it is knowing."

Like the creature erupting from the astronaut's breast in *Alien,* like a mammoth ocean liner released from its moorings, we (the "love generation," later to be demoted to the "me generation") were launched. ☙

7

SUMMER 1966.

So the Beatles took us "further." It wasn't just further, though, it was better. The music was better, the playing was better, the lyrics were better. The Beatles (and Dylan and the Stones) were becoming the writers, the voices of our time. There were no politicians, no statesmen, and no other writers who even remotely echoed where we were at the way these singers did. And that they both wrote *and* performed their songs created a union of remarkable power. For, as entertainers, they had already won our hearts; as writers they would get our minds. So when John sang, his performance had behind it all his strength as a writer, all his personal commitment, *and* it was delivered with the musical backing of the best band of our time. It was like a tuneful Invasion of the Body Snatchers.

DAVIS, CALIFORNIA.

In an attic room of an old school administration building, I sit nursing a case of undergraduate angst: what am I doing with my life? Should I drop out? Get a job? Hair grows over the collar of my shirt. Outside the night is hot and sweaty, like summers in the South. A pall settles over everything. In the corner a small AM radio plays softly. I hear a sharp crack and then a drum, organ, electric guitar, harmonica, and the voice of Bob Dylan:

> *Once upon a time, you dressed so fine*
> *Threw the bums a dime in your prime*
> *Didn't you?*
> *People'd call, say, "Beware, doll, you're bound to fall"*
> *You thought they were all kiddin' you . . .*

My ears perk. Dylan's voice is, as usual, snarling. But what is this backing? I rush across the room and crank up the volume. Dylan's voice rides over the sound of the organ.

> *You've gone to the finest school all right, Miss Lonely*
> *But you know you only used to get juiced in it.*
> *Nobody's ever taught you how to live out on the street*
> *And now you're gonna have to get used to it . . .*

As I'm walking quietly along a country road, a car screeches past and a beer bottle careens toward me, barely misses, and shatters on the street. "Get a haircut!" Hands

are thrust out the window, the middle finger erect. "Asshole!" Voices yell. "Faggot!"

Dylan sings,

> *You say you never compromise*
> *With the mystery tramp, but now you realize*
> *He's not selling any alibis*
> *As you stare into the vacuum of his eyes*
> *And ask him do you want to make a deal?*

I walk into a restaurant where a group of five jocks sit in a booth. Silence at first. Stares. Then, in a stage whisper, one of them asks, "Hey. What's that? A boy or a girl?" Gales of laughter. They slap each other on the back. Dylan snarls:

> *You used to be so amused*
> *At Napoleon in rags and the language that he used.*
> *Go to him now, he calls you, you can't refuse*
> *When you got nothing you got nothing to lose . . .*
>
> *How does it feel*
> *To be on your own*
> *With no direction home*
> *Like a complete unknown*
> *Like a rolling stone?*

Harmonica wailing into the distance: the Lone Ranger never made such an impression with a single visit. On the record cover Bob Dylan sits holding dark glasses, wearing an open neon-bright shirt and underneath a T-shirt with a motorcycle on it. On *Highway 61 Revisited* there are no folk or protest songs as we had come to expect.

Recently Dylan had been booed off the stage at the Newport Folk Festival for appearing with his electric band. He clearly doesn't care. On the back of *Highway 61* he writes, "your rooftop — if you don't already know — has been demolished." If there were signs (like the booing at Newport) that all this was not going to be easy, it didn't matter. If later Dylan sang, "Everybody said they'd stand behind me when the game got rough. But the joke was on me, there was nobody even there to bluff," we didn't know it then. Whatever this was (and I wasn't completely sure, though I felt that I knew), I definitely wanted part of it. If I was going to join any army, it would be the ragtag crowd Dylan sang about. (Did Dylan mean a rolling stone like the Rolling Stones? Did these guys all know each other? No matter; the impression was they did.)

———◆———

The truth was obscure,
Too profound and too pure.
To live it you had to explode.

— Bob Dylan, "Where Are You Tonight?" 1978

Above left: The author as an emerging head.

Below: Valerie, and Valerie and Ethan playing dress-up.

Valerie had blond hair that hung to her shoulders and was cut in a flat bang across the front. She looked like Marianne Faithfull, or Françoise Hardy (certainly the look of the time). Like almost every boy who sees a girl who looks like something he's always dreamed of, I was certain that she wasn't going to have anything to do with me, so it came as a great surprise when we ended up in bed together, almost immediately.

Now when the crew-cutted fraternity boys would hang their heads out the window, yelling, "Is it a boy or a girl?" I felt I really had the girl on my arm, and they could yell all they wanted. So for a while we went out together, taking for granted all the good times. There were mornings lying in bed, the famous violet-rimmed tree out the window, when it seemed like heaven. I was falling in love. It was the best of times.

Six months later, after we had traveled California together, gone into the mountains, gone to the ocean, and spent many more mornings in bed together, Valerie and I went shopping for some new sheets. The little old lady in the store looked at us, a glow of delight on her face, and said, "Oh, are you two getting married?" I looked at her expression and couldn't bear to break her heart. "Yes," I said. Valerie freaked, decided this was all entirely too serious, and disappeared. It quickly became the worst of times.

Still, I knew where to turn. Love would be the answer here. It was simply a matter of its application. So with the same intense and painstaking commitment that I brought to my study of Gandhi, my commitment to pacifism, I turned all my attention to trying to save this love affair. I quickly became obsessive. Valerie, in turn, retreated, becoming silent in the face of this intensity.

I turned to my friends. I turned to anybody. What was I doing wrong? I loved this girl and love was all-powerful, that was a given. So there *must* be a way to turn this around. I would just try harder.

My studies, which had been slipping anyway, became completely irrelevant. Though I went back to the university in the fall of my junior year, I soon dropped out. Now I would lose my student deferment. This meant that I could be reclassified and probably drafted. I was as determined as ever not to fight in Vietnam.

I had not known I was so in love with Valerie while we were together, only that I was very happy. I didn't realize how happiness can become the air that you breathe until, of course, it was no longer there.

I became very depressed. It was as if everything I believed in about love was being put to the test, and it was failing. Or *I* was failing. Love couldn't fail, of course. I became more depressed.

Now I was no longer in school. I didn't have a job. I didn't know what I was doing except that I wasn't going to fight in that war, and that I loved Valerie. I did a lot of driving.

I also smoked a lot of marijuana. On a typical morning, I would wake up without any idea of what I might do that day. I'd smoke a joint, listen to music for a while. Then I'd get in my VW bus and drive. If I was in Davis, I might drive to San Francisco. If in San Francisco, I might drive down the coast to Monterey or Big Sur. Then back to Davis.

There was a lot of music now. An American group called the Byrds released their first album, *Mr. Tambourine Man*. They took a lot of Bob Dylan songs and made them electric, with harmonies. I must have listened to that record two hundred times. I would listen to the last track, "The Bells of Rhymney," where Jim McGuinn, the lead guitar player, played the instrumental break, picking high notes over the backing of the band, jumping one octave so that the notes seemed to suddenly release, spiraling off like birds. Music.

By now my hair was heading toward my shoulders. Even in San Francisco there would be daily remarks, mostly hostile. If I walked into a shop or restaurant, everyone would stare at me. It felt like a lot of pressure. With the innocence of a young man I had completely given myself to Valerie, and it was as if, when she went away, she had taken me with her. So now what was left? One evening, feeling as low as ever, hunched in a corner, I mentioned suicide to a friend. He called my father. Perhaps I should go see a psychiatrist, it was suggested.

The psychiatrist who was recommended to my father (and so to me) had offices on a high floor of a medical building on Post Street in San Francisco. I entered and sat down. The walls were bare of decoration. The doctor sat behind a massive, 1940s desk. As I looked up at him, he turned away. For the rest of the hour, he sat with his back to me.

Confused thoughts made their way into words and cascaded from my mouth.

All the pain and feelings of failure of the previous months were spilled before this man's back. I thought this back-to-the-patient idea was bullshit, so I let him know it, quite directly. At the end of the hour, the doctor turned in his chair and looked at me. Maybe, he said, it would be a good idea if I went away for a while?

The idea of going to a hospital was initially shocking, but in a funny way, it calmed me down. Maybe there was something that could be done. Anything that might give me some peace. I felt *so* gone.

And so my father made a few inquiries and a hospital was suggested: the Silver Hill Foundation, in New Canaan, Connecticut.

Before I leave for the East, I discover that my older brother smokes marijuana. Jerry is the athlete, the guy with the Corvette, four-on-the-floor, dual carburetors. This is pretty amazing. Jerry and I listen to music together. I soon discover that it's not only Jerry who is smoking, but all his friends are, too — all the athletic crowd. Jerry's best friend, Roy Buell, nicknamed Hoppy, who used to be the terror of the neighborhood when we were kids, is getting high and listening to music. Though at this point everybody has short hair, and they're wearing madras shirts, they seem to be going after this marijuana/music/drug bug, with both hands.

In the winter of 1966 I arrive in New York en route to the hospital. I am wearing my father's overcoat, purple pointed-toe Beatle boots, and long hair. Walking in Greenwich Village, I'm stopped by a French film crew. They're doing a show on what's happening with American youth. They interview me for French television. What is going on? I tell them (in French that had consistently earned me a D in college) that love is all, love is what it's all about, love will save the world.

I receive a call from a friend of my father's who is going to take me to the hospital. He says he thinks it would be a good idea if I got my hair cut before we go up. In a cold apartment somewhere in the Village, a strange girl I'd never met before cuts off all my hair, as short as I can stand it. Short. Hair.

When I arrive at the hospital door, two women walk by and one of them says, under her breath, "Is it a boy or a girl?" I get another haircut.

When I first sit facing the doctor (Dr. White, a good man with a love of living), he asks me, "What do you want to get from your stay here?"

I say I want to learn how to love. ✦

CHAPTER

8

CONNECTICUT, 1966.

"Turn off your mind, relax, and float downstream," indeed. My mind was like a rain forest full of Methedrine-crazed monkeys. Chittering voices that never shut up, that kept me awake at night.

Dr. White and I didn't talk about love as much as anger.

"But I don't want to be angry," I said to Dr. White.

"Once you're angry, it's already too late," he responded.

"But it's not *creative*," I said.

"Tough," said Dr. White.

After weeks of therapy, the voices in my head kept repeating circular questions with no answers about why Valerie and I had split up, why love had failed. I told Dr. White. He reached into his desk drawer and said, "Take these."

The music told you that one pill makes you larger and another makes you small. These pills smothered your brain like wet sandbags; size was not the issue. I took 250 milligrams of Thorazine four times a day. They made me feel better, and the fact that *anything* could dull the voices gave me some degree of hope.

The Silver Hill Foundation sat in a rich area of Connecticut. The buildings were white clapboarded and green trimmed. In the morning we ate oatmeal, eggs, kippers. In the evening people read or played bridge. Scattered about the grounds were smaller houses for patients, the woodworking shop (for men), the weaving shop (for women). I wove.

There was only one rule: you could not talk to another patient about your problems. Those were reserved for your doctor. I saw Dr. White five times a week, two hours at a time. In the beginning, even two hours seemed too short. But, as the months passed, I couldn't always fill the two hours, and they were reduced to one. Then, sometimes, even one hour seemed too long.

One night, as I fell asleep, I realized that I was tired from a walk I had taken that day, and that it had been months, maybe more than a year, since I had fallen asleep from anything other than nervous exhaustion. Slowly the great issues drifted away, replaced by the simple facts of living.

Occasionally I'd hear from my brother out in San Francisco. He had moved into a house on Fillmore with a bunch of other people, mostly musicians. They were forming a band.

Spring came. Summer passed. By autumn I was an out-patient. I roomed with a kind family in Wilton. It came time to think about getting a job. I applied at the personnel office of a discount department store. It squatted, low and unappealing, in the middle of a massive parking lot. All the merchandise in the store consisted of "seconds."

I was interviewed and given a job in the shoe department. Mothers would come in with their young children and I would fit the shoes on their feet, feeling for their toes as had always been done to me.

"Are they all right?" the mother would ask.

"Yes, certainly," I would say.

The mother looked at me as I have looked at salesmen all my life who clearly know nothing.

I went to talk to the manager of the shoe department. He looked to be in his early twenties.

"I don't think this is quite right for me," I said.

"But you're *great* at it," he said. "Look, I'm going to be leaving soon, and then they'll probably make you manager." I looked around: rows and rows of shoes, each and every shoe with something wrong with it.

"There's a good future in it," he said.

◆

In Westport, Connecticut, I walked into Klein's department store on Main Street because Klein's had the largest book department in the area. I had been an English major. I thought that might qualify me to sell books.

I said to Stanley Klein, the son of the owner, "I was wondering, do you need any help in the book department?"

Mr. Klein: "No."

I said, "Ah. Do you think there'll be any openings coming up?"

Mr. Klein: "No. But do you know anything about photography?"

"Well, yes, I, uh, studied some in college. I know how to take pictures and develop them."

Mr. Klein: "We're opening a camera department. Go talk to Gene."

In Klein's camera department I sold a lot of little 35mm Agfa cameras to people who came in wanting to buy Instamatics, explaining to them that the Agfa had a glass lens (the Instamatic's was plastic) and a pressure plate to hold the film flat (the Instamatic's cartridge didn't). Gene taught me to do that.

Every morning I'd drive to work and every evening drive home. It was a routine, and it brought in a paycheck. At lunch I would borrow a photography magazine and read about the newest lenses and films. It was soon clear that I was no salesman. Since I had taken pictures in the past, and the need for a career seemed pressing, I thought I might try my luck as a photographer. I wrote to an old friend in California and asked to borrow the money I'd need to get started.

With my father's help I had bought a white Buick station wagon with eighty-five thousand miles on it and I set out across the country. I'd get up at four in the morning and drive into the night. I drove across Pennsylvania, through St. Louis, down to the Southwest, where I saw mesas outlined against the setting sun, along Route 66, made famous by the song, across the great California Central Valley, into the foothills now green in the winter. On the road (like Kerouac), back to California, back to San Francisco, where all of a sudden *everybody* had long hair. And not just the straight, hanging hair of the Beatles, but great, curling masses of unkempt hair, sideburns that grew down men's jaws, hair that was parted and just grew straight out from there, sometimes parallel to the ground.

And everyone seemed to be getting high. My sister, still in high school, told me, describing her experience with a stop sign, "I just sat there forever, waiting for it to turn green."

In Haight-Ashbury, Victorian houses were being taken over by long-hairs called "hippies." In rambling houses people created one-room homes, placing multicolored tie-dyed sheets over the windows. Peacock feathers sprouted from jars. Layers of Oriental carpets covered the floors. Beds were set on the floor in the middle of the room, blanketed with Indian paisley bedspreads and mounds of tasseled pillows. Wicker baskets overflowed with copies of *Rolling Stone* and *The Oracle,* the Haight newspaper. *The Oracle* was printed with swirls and colors, trying to escape the linear logic that newspapers were said to represent. Posters advertising local bands were thumbtacked all over the walls, each poster an image overprinted with the swirling lines of psychedelia.

In the windows, prisms hung from thin threads, casting rainbows against the walls when the sunlight struck them. Incense burned. Boxes of beads, with endless little compartments, were kept for stringing, beads bought from the local head shop, which also sold cigarette papers, roach clips, hash pipes, and black lights. Under these lights patterns of violet would shine from anything painted with luminous paint.

And in every room there was a phonograph so that the music, which held all this together, promoted it, and urged it further, could be played.

At night people gathered at the Fillmore Auditorium to hear Jefferson Airplane, Big Brother and the Holding Company (with Janis Joplin), the Quicksilver Messenger Service, or the Grateful Dead. The bands stood on stage playing long, long songs, loud. On the walls all around them giant projections of various colored dyes, mixed together, swirled, merging into each other, like finger paints, like ever-reforming mandalas. The music moved and the images moved and people on the dance floor moved, throwing their arms above their heads and swaying, all together. It was all very, well, kind of . . . liquid. Almost everybody was high on one thing or another. Those who weren't high soon would be.

Right: Blue Cheer with a Hell's Angel in the Haight, 1966.

Because of all the attention the Haight began to attract, the Gray Line bus company initiated a tour down Haight Street. Tourists from Kansas, Oklahoma, Los Angeles (who knows?), would stare out of tinted windows, cruising through the Haight looking for hippies. On more than one occasion a man with hair hanging to his shoulders is seen running alongside the bus holding a mirror aloft, reflecting these sightseeing faces directly back at them.

The band my brother lives with gives itself a name: Blue Cheer. Jerry, who does not play an instrument, is designated their manager. At first, there's six of them and various people who hang out with them or who are planning to work with them. There's Gut, ex-president of the San Bernardino chapter of the Hell's Angels. It's never quite clear what Gut is going to do for the band. He looks like an Italian Renaissance Jesus, with black, slightly curling hair past his shoulders. Gut has a little sign by his bed that says, "WELCOME TO MY CLOUD."

Inside Blue Cheer's house all the windows are covered so that the light is murky. Each room has plywood bunk beds, built up five feet off the floor. The house keeps a pet monkey, which lives on a dead tree branch in one corner of the living room. The monkey swings off it, free to roam about the house. I am told to be careful, as monkeys could be mean.

On the stove in the kitchen there's a pot of purple stew. "It's been there for five days, man," says Leslie, a dark-haired girl wearing a shapeless muumuu. "We keep adding to it, and it just keeps getting better. Yesterday we put food dye in it. Far out, huh?"

One day Blue Cheer plays a brief opening set for Timothy Leary, who's in San Francisco to give the faithful his version of the word: "Turn on, tune in, drop out." Later, Leary goes back to Blue Cheer's house, already famous in the Haight for consuming more drugs than any other. Leary wants them to chant "Om." They tell Leary to forget it. They're not into it. Leary leaves. No searching spiritual pathways here, just a bunch of inner-city boys who like to get high.

Left: Blue Cheer in rehearsal.

Reeford, a friend who now lives in Carmel Valley, recalls: "I was living in Big Sur in the sixties, and I picked up this sailor hitchhiking up the coast from San Diego. He told me he'd gone AWOL and was on his way to San Francisco to see what was happening up there. He asked me to hold on to his duffle bag and said he'd be back to get it in a few days. So I said sure.

"A couple months later he reappears, totally blissed out. He's got this card from his girlfriend, which is painted, you know, with swirls, green pastures, a pink sky, and a purple moon. And she's written a note that says, 'There's acid in the purple moon so all you have to do is lick it.' But by that point he couldn't remember what the color purple was so he just ate the whole card."

———◆———

The people of the Haight staged the Be-In. A "be-in" was different from the more political "sit-in" or "lie-in"; you weren't there to *do* anything (sit, lie), you would just show up and "be." Though the value of "being" was supported by a wealth of Eastern writing, LSD convinced most of us. In any conflict, after all was said and done, both sides were the same. Good/bad, love/hate, inside/outside. All the distinctions were superficial.

On the day of the Be-In thousands of hippies gathered in Golden Gate Park, clustered under banners of their own making, tie-dyed pennants looking like the markers of an ancient crusade. Flowers were in abundance everywhere. A lot of people were obviously tripping. One couple danced, totally engrossed, with their arms held out in front of them and each of their fingers extended toward the other's, almost touching, waving like tentacles. I could almost envision the little LSD energy waves flowing off each finger. On this day, Golden Gate Park totally lived up to its name, with the sun streaming through the trees, shedding a golden light over everyone and everything. People were smiling and dancing. It was completely possible, even probable, that a stranger would smile at you, and you would smile back, and that fleeting exchange might catapult the two of you into bed together for at least one night of love, only to move on the next day, following whatever was happening. (It seemed so much more sensible, so much more human, than having to grope in the back seat of a car or neck in the back row of a movie theater.)

As the day ended, Allen Ginsberg suggested walking to the ocean and watching the sun set. So the "gathering of the tribes" set off slowly through the afternoon glow, carrying flags and flowers, playing guitars and singing. They stood on the edge of the continent, feeling (no doubt) like so many before them, that they had come this far, here was the edge of America, and they were pioneers, come to watch the holy sun set into the vast Pacific.

———◆———

But in the real world, as it were, things were not quite so sunny. More than 5000 Americans had been killed in Vietnam by 1966. According to the Pentagon, there were 380,000 troops there as 1967 began. Martin Luther King, Jr., was to propose that the civil rights movement merge with the antiwar movement. In April, the largest antiwar demonstration to date took place in New York City. It was estimated as 400,000 by the organizers and as 100,000 by the police. Which one did you believe? It was like body counts. These had become the fiction of Vietnam, repeatedly shown to be incorrect, one of the many ways that Americans were discovering they were being lied to.

I had been drafted while in the hospital. Dr. White read me the draft notice one day. He said not to worry; he had written the draft board a letter. I was then classified 1-Y, a six-month medical deferment. It was clear I could be drafted at any time after the deferment was up. I still had no intention of going.

Most of the people I knew in San Francisco just intended to get too fucked up to be draftable. If you were called to report, you'd start taking drugs about a week before the appointed date, staying up day after day, purposely warping your mind beyond recognition so that when you were finally called you would be incapable of recognizing a question much less having the ability to answer it.

Some decided to take heroin, to become addicted, "just for the physical. When that's done, I'll kick. Beats going to Vietnam, man, and having your fucking brains blown out." Some never kicked. Some died.

———◆———

He blew his mind out in a car
He didn't notice that the lights had changed.

— John Lennon, "A Day in the Life"

Roy Buell was my brother's closest childhood friend. His family nicknamed him Hoppy because as a child he had so much energy that he hopped around all the time. Roy was blond, good-looking, and did whatever he wanted. All through the fifties, it seemed like what he wanted to do was all that fifties stuff: get a fast car, drive it fast, drink beer, and make out with as many girls as he could.

Because he was my older brother's friend, I saw him from that younger-brother distance, watching as he and Jerry went out and cruised. Hoppy was a little wild, but Hoppy had it made, like the fighter pilot who acts crazy and uncontrollable but who would, in the end, down more Zeros than the rest. When I left for the hospital, Hoppy was smoking dope. That was a little different. You could go out and be crazy on grass just as well as beer, but sooner or later it was going to turn you inward.

When I came back to California, Hoppy was dead. It seems he'd stolen his mother's Porsche and gone to Mexico. There he had taken a shotgun and blown his brains out. I was told that he'd gotten into a lot of acid and didn't know who he was anymore, that he was afraid he might be a homosexual.

He lost it, people would say.

One day I was tagging along with my brother as he went to visit some people he knew up the street on Fillmore. Jerry preceded me up the stairs. Again, though it is the middle of the day, all the windows are covered. A fellow in the corner with very long hair looks at me suspiciously and says, "Who's that?"

Jerry says, "It's my brother."

"Looks like a narc to me, man," says the guy. ("Narc," too, is a word we'll come to hear a lot.)

The Buffalo Springfield sing, "Paranoia strikes deep / Into your heart it will creep."

Little pockets of darkness in the Haight.

But, for a very large number of people, this darkness was entirely peripheral. They were embarking on their own journeys, starting from the rooms they had set up, listening only to the word of music and what it promised. And the promises were big promises, promises of not less than everything. Martin Luther King had a dream, *we* had a dream, and it was, almost literally, a dream of a return to the garden of Eden. It was a dream reinforced by visions, visions made immensely real through LSD. Because these were shared visions, there seemed little reason to doubt their authenticity. The dream, the vision, was golden; it invoked God in all His (Her) forms; it required that we love one another, as we had always been told we should. And so we all met, and ate, and loved, and traveled, and got high together.

If all this seemed too magical, we would remind ourselves that magic was merely another, older science, and that, in any event, we lived in a universe where nothing happened by chance.

In our enthusiasm and excitement we welcomed back all the forgotten or discredited dreamers, from William Blake to Lewis Carroll, from the American Indian to Walt Whitman. Out of the overwhelming materialism of the fifties we tried to establish the overriding power of the spiritual, and we were not talking about going to church. "On the brave and crazy wings of youth," Jackson Browne later sang about what, by then, seemed brave and crazy, we set out to try and fulfill the vast promises we imagined. Sometimes this was political and sometimes it was a journey back to nature. If it seemed daunting, no one was alone. "In [our] hearts [we] turned to each other's hearts for refuge," sang Browne, capturing the magic in "Before the Deluge." We were all, most decidedly, in this together. By our vision we were already — whether we chose it or not — part of one great family, the family of man. We would affirm this. We would reject the life of the suburban nuclear family. We would reject the "reality" that rejected our "dream." And we never questioned which was the more powerful. For it was (indisputably! unarguably!) the dream that inspired reality, not the other way around. Reality was the corpse after life had passed from it. The dream was the waking body.

As everyone stood on the edge of the Pacific after the day of the Be-In, watching

Below: Blue Cheer in Golden Gate Park.

the sun go down, a single parachutist could be seen skydiving through the air. It was reputed to be Owsley, the Bay Area's most infamous manufacturer of LSD.

◆

On July 24, 1967, the Beatles release "All You Need Is Love."

If somehow, somewhere there were some promotional-director-in-the-sky who took care of these things, if somehow all of this were being done on purpose (as we were sure it was), it could not have happened with more effect, nor at a more opportune time. The Second Coming could hardly have been more convincing.

The song begins with a blast of horns and a snare drum, sounding every inch like the Queen's guard announcing her arrival. Then John and Paul, double-tracked in harmony, sing: "Love, love, love / Love, love, love / Love, love, love." Then bass violins enter in a descending progression, and then John (once again it's John) singing,

> *There's nothing you can do that can't be done.*
> *Nothing you can sing that can't be sung*
> *Nothing you can say but you can learn how to play the game*
> *It's easy.*

The song has strings, drums, choruses of horns like in burlesque houses. The song bounces along:

> *. . . There's nothing you can know that isn't known.*
> *Nothing you can see that isn't shown*
> *There's nowhere you can be that isn't where you're meant to be*
> *It's easy.*

As the song closes, the melody diminishes as high-pitched strings, classical oboes, swing trumpets, whistling, yelling, all are mixed together into what is becoming a classic Beatle ending. The strains of "Greensleeves" are mixed up and then John sings, "She loves you, yeah, yeah, yeah," an early Beatles hit. It's always been the same, John's saying. It always will be the same. It's always been love. Throughout all of this the line "Love is all you need" is endlessly sung. . . . "Love is all you need, love is all you need. . . ."

As it turns out, the Beatles had been asked to represent Britain on a show called *Our World,* the first worldwide live television broadcast. For this, they composed "All You Need Is Love." More than 200 million people saw that broadcast.

Pictures of the Beatles at the time show them as having changed once again. No longer are they the four jolly moptops. Now all have mustaches. John appears with his distinctive glasses. Film of them at the time shows them walking down a Liverpool street following the release of "Penny Lane." They are all wearing capes. They move with the bearing of indisputable royalty in a land where royalty is an establishment long closed to them. Could it ever get any higher (the word that has come to replace "better") than this?

That same summer, the Beatles release *Sgt. Pepper.* On the cover they are dressed in bright satin costumes and holding musical instruments; they're surrounded (in collage) by Marilyn Monroe, Karl Marx, Jayne Mansfield, Marlon Brando, and a host of others, placing themselves among, and in the center of, the major cultural influences of our time.

As an album, *Sgt. Pepper* is applauded by *everybody.* Once again it surpasses everything in popular music that had preceded it, including the Beatles' own work. It ends with a song called "A Day in the Life." The first time I heard it was over the radio as I was driving through Haight-Ashbury. The disc jockey had been hyperventilating for the previous twenty minutes. "I have here the latest from the Beatles! Stay where you are! This is going to *Blow! Your! Mind!!!*" And over the airwaves came John: "I read the news today, oh boy . . ."

John sings about a man who "made the grade," who "blew his mind out in a car." The news was sad, but "I just had to laugh . . ." The second verse ends with "I'd love to turn you on," the words sung with vibrato as if they were spinning; then the guitars drop out and the surge of an orchestra comes in, but it sounds strange, somehow different (it's the tape being played backward), like a maddened swarm of bees that suddenly accelerate as if backed by some jet engine, and this sound just grows and swells until it peaks some thirty long seconds later with a high note, and then an alarm clock rings. Paul sings:

[53]

Woke up, fell out of bed,

Dragged a comb across my head . . .

Found my way upstairs and had a smoke

And somebody spoke and I went into a dream . . .

("Had a smoke and went into a dream." Right!) Then John's voice again, after the word "dream," singing in falsetto, high and drifty. Behind John an orchestra plays, all drifting. Out There. Then John sings the last verse, ending, "I'd love to turn you on . . ."

And here comes that maddened swarm of bees for an encore, growling, growing, surging (this is every bit the musical predecessor to Lucas's leap into hyperspace in *Star Wars*), peaking until it totally explodes, then . . . silence for one beat, then . . . one note is played, a low drone that is sustained for a further twenty seconds, until it diminishes to nothing.

For once, a disc jockey is right. It does totally blow my mind. This comes as the last song of the album, the experience you're left with. It's almost exhausting.

To paraphrase Joan Baez ("Speaking strictly for me / We both could have died then and there"), speaking strictly for myself, it was as if all of music (as "music" then meant to us, the explosion of talent, and hope, and belief that somehow all of this was going to transform and make better the entire world) climaxed at that moment, rising as high as it was going to go. The Beatles, seeming to live the most magical of lives, were giving it all back to us. They were holding out this promise and hope if we would just pursue it.

Remember, there's nothing that you can do that can't be done. It's easy.

Of course, as the drone faded into silence, and I marveled once again at what these guys could do, the workaday world (even in San Francisco) came back. I was living in Berkeley, near the ghetto. I had set up a darkroom next to the kitchen. I was taking photographs.

Then I went to see Michelangelo Antonioni's movie *Blow-Up*. It is the story, set in "swinging London," of an immensely successful English fashion photographer, played by David Hemmings. He drives a Rolls-Royce and is surrounded by beautiful models and musicians smoking hashish. Unsuspectingly, Hemmings gets caught up in a murder, or so we're led to believe. In the end, despite photography's ability to depict the "real," Hemmings is uncertain of what he's seen. The closing shot is a group of mimes (who have wandered through, though always on the edge of, the movie) playing a game of tennis, with all the shots: serves, volleys, lobs, and slams, people scrambling to get the ball, only: there is no ball. Hemmings walks slowly by.

Who should be the star of this very popular movie but a photographer! Suddenly this "business" of mine was catapulted into hip respectability. So, for a while, I would wander Golden Gate Park, as Hemmings had wandered the parks of London, my camera always with me, peering into the bushes.

As all bands ultimately do, Blue Cheer decided that it needed some pictures. So I took my cameras and we all walked through San Francisco. We went to Potrero Hill, walked through the Haight, into Golden Gate Park.

Hippies are everywhere. More are coming. The announcement of the "Summer of Love" has City Hall threatened. (Interestingly, the summer of 1967 was called the Summer of Love *before* it happened.) Over the airwaves Scott McKenzie sang, "If you're going to San Francisco, be sure to wear some flowers in your hair." Tens of thousands flock to San Francisco and the Haight, each with his or her own vision of hope and expectation. The *San Francisco Chronicle* worries, "Where will they sleep? What about drug use?" Undaunted, the kids arrive in endless numbers, talking about love, looking for love.

Bolstered by *Blow-Up* to think that there was some radical edge to the work I was doing, I also started to think, too, about making movies. Why not? Painting, photography, whatever — it was all making things. Of course, to make movies you have to have, at least, a movie camera. So once again I pored through magazines, reading, learning. Armed with a set of answers about costs versus features, I went to speak to my father about a loan.

My father listened patiently to me as I set forth my plans. When I was done, he asked me, "Do you think you're spending your time as wisely as you can?"

"Short of going around the world, yes," I replied.

"Well, then, why don't you do that?" said my father. ☙

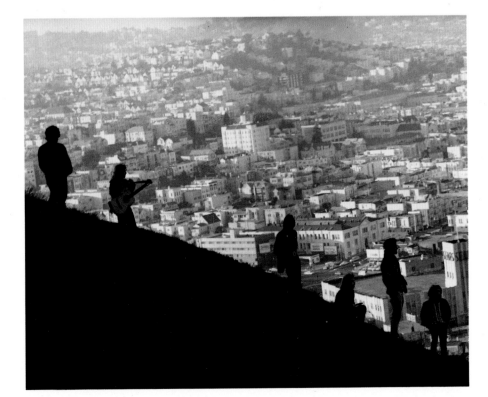

Right: Blue Cheer with San Francisco in the background, from Potrero Hill, 1967.

CHAPTER

9

SUMMER 1967.

At New York's Kennedy Airport, the cabbie took the tip from my seventeen-year-old sister, Linda, counted it, counted it again, and then hurled it violently to the floor in disgust. New York. It was a hot and muggy evening, and we gladly boarded the Scandinavian Airlines jet bound for Stockholm. Over the Arctic, the aurora borealis shimmered outside the window.

Early the next morning the plane made a brief stop in Oslo, and Linda and I deplaned. The dawn light seemed somehow different, very clear, and we wandered into the terminal, wide-eyed, with that sense of expectation of the new traveler.

Inside, standing not fifteen feet from us, stood four citizens of the People's Republic of China. They were dressed identically in black, facing each other, bothering no one. For an American who had grown up in the fifties, seeing a Red Chinese was like gazing upon some exotic creature, something almost other-worldly. In a way, they were. So completely had America cast them as the extraordinary foe, the modern Mongol, that I couldn't believe they could inhabit the same space as other human beings. I nudged Linda in the ribs. "Look at that, will you?" We stared, newly aware of the whole world out there. "Bet they've never heard of Big Brother and the Holding Company." So I thought, "One good revolution deserves another."

Soon the plane departed, taking us to Stockholm, where the late summer sun gleamed on the rivers and buildings, making the city look brand-new. We strolled through small, winding streets, peering into tiny, leaded windows, and became increasingly excited by the foreignness of it all, thinking: Jesus! The dogs speak Swedish. The cats speak Swedish. For all we know, the fish speak Swedish. Still, not really to our surprise, outside our hotel there was a poster glued around a lamppost, saying, "Long Live the Grateful Dead."

The next day we depart for Göteborg, where a brand-new green Volvo 122S waits for us at the factory. My sister and I drive off and arrive in Copenhagen, searching out a woman friend of a friend from Berkeley.

That night, we climb a long circular stairway and are greeted by Birgit. Birgit is thin, blond, Danish, and utterly exotic. In her small room are about ten people, talking quietly, standing around a table covered with food. Birgit soon offers us a hashish joint and asks if we would like some. Do hippies have long hair? The joint is lit and passed around as music fills the room. The dream is real, people are high, and music is everywhere.

Above: Ethan and Linda, Switzerland, 1967. Photo by Gerard.

Birgit and I talk about San Francisco and what is happening there. Later we are dancing thigh to thigh as heavenly visions of Danish coitus fill my mind. We smoke a little more hash. Then, in the corner of my vision, there appears a sallow-complexioned girl with a long, dark braid and a very serious expression. "Hello," she says. "They say you are American, yes? Well, I am from Russia." And she thrusts out a hand.

"You tell me what it is like in America?" she asks.

"America or San Francisco?" I respond, smiling.

She does not smile, but begins to catalogue the sins of the U.S.A. She says we exploit our working class, keep our blacks imprisoned in ghettos, are military expansionists. Her questions seek only their own answers. All I want to do is dance. How could I explain *Let's Make a Deal* or "Eight Miles High"? I have a Haight-Ashbury reaction, figuring her problem is she's straight. I offer her some hash. She refuses.

"It is an escape from reality," she says.

"Which reality would that be?" I say, smiling again.

"Stop that. Be serious."

She is intent. I am her first American. She, in turn, is my first Russian. She is not to be shaken off. How can I be like this? What about our two countries? What of the war in Vietnam? Of course she is right, but now is not the time.

In the end, she shrugs. Bourgeois capitalist. If I have no time for the Revolution, she has no time for my flickering realities. Where does she get her certainties from? They could be entirely ephemeral. It's all just the wink of an eye.

To me she seems entrapped in a nineteenth-century gloom, gray rooms filled with grim men eating potato soup. San Francisco has become the city of the flowering mandala. Relax, I say. Turn off your mind and float downstream, I intimate. It is Russia versus America on a new, unexplored level.

And so, internally, I react as the Beatles have taught me. "Though she feels she's in a play, she is anyway."

———◆———

Outside Amsterdam, driving along a flat dike, there is a looming gray sky overhead, the slate Atlantic on our right. Linda and I pass almost no one else on the road. The presence of England, just across the water, is suddenly made real by a crackling of the radio and the voice of a BBC announcer. We can barely hear him as the signal drifts in and out. But how he speaks! The accent is incredible. And *no* commercials!

Linda and I take a ferry that docks in Southampton. We drive off in the dark, headed toward London, our copy of *Europe on $5 a Day* close at hand. We find a room in a boarding house on Old Brompton Road, a tree-lined street of three- and four-story homes converted into flats and rooming houses. We are but a few blocks from

the South Kensington tube station, which I know from the Donovan song "Sunny South Kensington." That means we must be near the right place. A peppery-haired, stout lady of some European extraction lets us in, takes our money.

For Linda and me, there is no question what we intend on our first night: we're going to go out and *Find the Music*. Since we know nearly nothing, we decide to go to Piccadilly Circus. The name, at least, is familiar, and it sounds like fun. So, we read the instructions in our tour book and take the tube to Piccadilly, fully expecting to surface into the English Haight-Ashbury.

As we emerge, it is raining. The buildings are drab brick or fronted with wet, gray stone. Piccadilly Circus reminds us of Broadway in San Francisco: tourist shops sell buttons, teacups, postcards; on the back streets are strip joints, Wimpy Bars, pubs. No music, no hippies; if it feels like anything, it feels like a scene in every British war movie you've ever seen. Linda and I go to a Wimpy Bar and order a burger. What arrives is a gray patty slightly larger than a silver dollar centered on a cold bun with a limp pickle. We walk around some more, but no place seems inviting. All evening the rain keeps falling. Where could the music be?

The next day, getting our priorities in order as we had been taught, the first thing we do is buy a stereo and a copy of Jimi Hendrix's *Are You Experienced?* To be "experienced" is to understand purple haze, amplified feedback, and the extension of time. From the album cover Hendrix, flanked by two white British musicians, peers back at us wearing a cape, like a magician. "'Scuse me while I kiss the sky."

The next day Linda and I find our way to Carnaby Street, tucked in a corner behind Regent Street, a wide avenue of major department stores, Carnaby Street reveals itself to be minuscule, one clothing boutique jammed next to another. Music blares over hidden speakers. The clothes are colorful. The walls are combinations of op art and psychedelicized posters. And the young Englishmen selling the clothes are

Above: Tower Bridge, London, 1967.

Left: The rooftops of Kensington Court.

Below right: A chemist's shop on the Old Brompton Road.

uniformly rude, abrupt, and condescending. There is absolutely no revolutionary fervor. Linda and I leave, slightly puzzled.

If what you were looking for in London was the new, there were endless disappointments. It was in the traditional that London was such an exciting town. The numerous parks were vast — great avenues of trees shady in the summer: Hyde Park, Regent's Park, Green Park, Battersea Park, Hampstead Heath.

There was the grandness of royalty and the Empire: the memorial to Prince Albert (from Victoria) across from the Royal Albert Hall, the Houses of Parliament, Westminster Abbey, the Tower Bridge, the Victoria and Albert Museum, Buckingham Palace, St. James's Park.

Then there were the many small mews, originally stables, now converted into small houses. The pubs with varied English beers, with small-paned windows and inviting yellow lights inside. Even the rows of classic English housing, as in Bill Brandt's photographs or *Coronation Street,* were wonderful to me.

I was completely taken by all the endless discoveries of a new place. No free matches (what!?). Gas was called petrol. Aluminum was pronounced al-yoo-MIN-ee-um. Apartments were flats. If you wanted warm water or heat in your little room, you had to put a shilling in the meter. The policemen didn't carry guns (it seemed so civilized). They were called "bobbies" and were said to be friendly.

I was surrounded on all sides by the English, who spoke so wonderfully, saying "sorry" constantly when they meant "excuse me," saying "in fact" or "in actual fact" in every fourth sentence. The letter *z* was an entirely different animal, pronounced "zed." "How terribly interesting," they would say, meaning it was utterly unremarkable. They were unfailingly polite. I decided to stay.

For a short time, Linda and I rented the basement room of a house in St. John's Wood. Soon after, we moved to a flat in South Kensington. We went to an antique

market where I bought (for two pounds) a four-by-six-foot black and white photo of a decaying mummy's face, which we called "Charlie" (weird was in). Charlie sat on our wall staring down at us. "No flies on Charlie," we would say. Since Charlie had cornered the market on miserable, all was gay by comparison.

I met a beautiful, young, upper-class English girl named Fiona. Fiona was very shy. I asked her where the music was. She took me to a private club around the corner from my flat. The club was in a basement. Steps led past a coatroom, and then to a small table where we were greeted by the maitre d'. The room was low-ceilinged, with pink lighting, and jammed with young Englishmen wearing coats and ties and talking at the top of their voices. In one corner was the bar. When the music started people yelled louder. As the evening wore on, everybody was getting progressively drunker, and grappling with one another in sweaty confusion. In the wee hours, people poured out into the streets. Everybody was drunk and laughing, and seemed to be having a good time. But this was more like my parents' cocktail parties. Try as I might, I still couldn't find the music.

———◆———

"You ask him," I said to my sister.

"Why me?" she asked.

We were standing at the door of a trendy clothes shop on Earls Court Road, a slightly run down section of west London with a highly transient population. Rock and roll came blaring out of the loudspeakers. (Trendy clothes shops were one of the few places where you stood a good chance of hearing Jimi Hendrix or Cream.)

"Go on," I said. We were watching a red-haired salesman, about our age. He was wearing a jacket covered in a floral design and bright-red bell-bottomed trousers.

Linda walked over and spoke quietly to him. I stayed at the front of the shop. Linda came back. "He says he can score some hash. But we've gotta come back later."

Above left and below: Scenes from Hyde Park, London, 1967.

Above: Linda. "You ask him,"
I told her.

His name was Robin. He came from somewhere in the middle of England.

"How did you know to ask me?" he asks us.

We looked surprised. Didn't everybody smoke dope?

"Not a chance, mate," says Robin, as he starts to demonstrate the peculiar ritual of rolling the London hash joint. Three cigarette papers are extracted from a packet; two are laid down parallel to each other, licked, and gummed, giving them twice the area of a single paper. Then the third paper is gummed at right angles to the first two, adding length. A tobacco cigarette is ripped along one edge, and the tobacco taken between thumb and forefinger and dropped into the waiting cigarette papers.

Robin takes from his pocket a small brown block of hashish. He lights a match and holds it against the edge of the hash until a faint wisp of smoke rises. Robin leans over quickly and inhales the smoke. The heated hash is crumbled on top of the tobacco, and the process repeated until a small trail of hashish particles dots the tobacco.

The unwieldy combination of tobacco, hashish, and papers is gingerly picked up and rolled into cigarette form, one end of it drooping emptily.

Robin fumbles in his pockets for the cardboard edge of a cigarette package. A three-quarter-inch square piece is ripped off and, in turn, rolled into a tight cylinder around a wooden matchstick. This is carefully inserted into the drooping end of the joint and uncurled until it is solid against the paper, forming a filter. The joint is taken between thumb and forefinger, and the tobacco/hashish end corkscrewed into a little fillip, sealing the end.

Robin holds the joint up for inspection, a minor work of art. Smiles creep across our faces.

As we smoke, Robin tells us of London clubs, of the Marquee in Soho, the Roundhouse in North London. Robin seems intrigued by this brother-and-sister act that just appeared in a clothes shop in London seeking hash. I ask him if he knows of any new groups I should hear. He says the Who.

"Listen to the drummer," he says.

The next day I buy the album. The drummer seems to hit a hundred and thirty-two beats to the bar. The lead singer sings, "I can see for miles and miles . . ." over the high, driving notes of the lead guitar. "Miles and miles and miles and miles and miles and miles . . ." Right!

◆

Jimi Hendrix, a black American musician who journeyed to London, and re-emerged, psychedelically re-invented, at the Monterey Pop Festival, is playing the Royal Festival Hall, which sits on the south bank of the Thames in a modern cultural complex. It seems a strange place for acid rock, brightly lit, the stage hidden by a turquoise curtain. There is no place to dance, just rows of tiered seating, more suitable to a performance of Haydn's Symphony no. 6 in D.

Jimi Hendrix has a Relationship with his guitar. He plays it with his tongue. He puts it in his groin and thrusts it back and forth at the audience. He faces it toward the amplifier, and it screeches and howls, as if in protest. When the guitar is bad, he douses it with lighter fluid and burns it. He does all this while playing fast and mean. Behind him drive the drummer and bass player.

But the trio somehow seem impossibly small on the stage. They cannot triumph over the bright lights and the nature of the room. With no place to dance, even to move, everyone remains seated. In a space designed for the careful, subdued scrutiny of a lecture, Hendrix fills it with the howl of his amplifiers.

Filing out into the London night, the black Thames drifting quietly in front of us, Linda and I talk about how great Hendrix was. In America, where everything musical was seething like water boiling in a cauldron, Hendrix's show would have had people rolling in the aisles, but here in Britain his music just seems a mere speck in the eye of the Empire.

Above: Scenes from London. The houses off Fulham Road. The Queen's guard in Hyde Park.

———— ◆ ————

Slowly, a strange thing began to dawn on me: you never heard the Beatles, the Rolling Stones, Jimi Hendrix, or anybody on English radio. Instead, there was endless insipid and saccharine "pop" music (in its worst sense) played by a series of smarmy deejays. To an American, England was the mecca of the new music, and it appeared that England had no time for its own groups. How could this be? Where was the music?

———— ◆ ————

Linda and I have just driven to St. John's Wood and picked up the mail from America. She says, "There's something here from the Selective Service."

Just the phrase sets my heart pounding. "Oh, God. What does it say?"

"I don't know. There's a little card here. What does eye-vee-eff mean?"

"Eye-vee-eff?" I don't know. I-V? Roman numerals? Four F. That's it! Permanently unfit for military service!

I slam on the brakes and the car screeches to the curb. I grab Linda and hug her. "Four F," I shout. "Far out. Far fucking out." Passers-by stare at us strangely.

Now I will never go to Vietnam. I feel as if my life has been given back to me.

———— ◆ ————

The summer passes. The great elms of London's Hyde Park provide shelter for picnics. Linda and I travel to France and Switzerland. But, come fall, cold weather arrives and Linda decides to return to America. She does not seem to share my penchant for the gray brick, the black and white romanticism of *A Taste of Honey*. Besides, she's a girl and has never personally had to endure the terrors of the draft, the feeling that at any moment her life might be requisitioned. She didn't leave America as if her brain was on fire, the southern drawl of Lyndon Johnson fanning the flames. The memory of it all is still too fresh for me. I feel as if there is no going back.

———— ◆ ————

With Linda gone, it seems strangely quiet. It is January 1968. I rent what the English call a bedsitter, one room on the ground floor with a tiny refrigerator and a hot plate. The window looks out over a small square. Each day I attempt to write.

I take day-long walks through London, from Kensington past the Tower Bridge and back again; to Regent's Park and back again; across Hyde Park, 630 acres in the middle of London, where avenues of trees reveal perfect eighteenth-century vistas. I walk through Hampstead Heath, 790 acres in the north of London where Pickwick (of *The Pickwick Papers*) repaired for his day in the country. I visit the Houses of Parliament, sit in the park next to them, and envision the hundreds of years of English history. I can't get enough of London, but I also feel the need for some sort of employment.

Because I'm in England on a tourist visa, all work is prohibited. I am not even allowed to offer myself as a volunteer, though this is what I finally decide to do. I hear of a hospital in St. John's Wood that cares for autistic children, and I go for an interview. Sitting behind a low desk is Molly, a giant figure of a woman, with graying hair. Surrounding Molly are children in varying degrees of remove from what the rest of us call reality. They pretend not to notice Molly, standing with their backs turned and refusing to look at her. But if Molly were to move to another side of the room, they would soon make their way to her and slowly gather around her again.

Broadly, it is Molly's belief that autism is caused by a traumatic separation from the mother during the symbiotic period of the child's life, when he has no distinct sense of himself separate from the mother. When the mother abruptly disappears, the child retreats at the intense emotional shock. Molly tells me that the case history of each child in her program shows such a separation. Some of the symptoms are a withdrawal from all normal human intercourse, manifested by eyes out of focus, refusing contact, spasmodic movement, hands held in front of the face and wiggled there for hours on end, inability to speak, and acute anxiety.

Molly attempts to have each child, regardless of age (in the school the children range from three to eleven) regress back to the nursing stage, and then be re-reared. As a result, nearly grown children can be seen sitting in the laps of their surrogate mothers, as they attempt to get the children to cuddle, or to accept a bottle.

Some of the older children have progressed beyond this. At this stage Molly believes that a man can be as useful as a woman. I am given a child called Christopher who is developed enough that he will, sometimes, speak, though he doesn't speak to me for days, preferring to turn his back to me and wave his hand in front of his face for hours, lost in his fingertips, occasionally blubbering.

But Christopher and I have a little secret, though he of course can't openly share it. That is that I was once in a hospital myself, and I'm not always so sure that this reality business is all that hot either. I make no attempt to "cure" Christopher; we just hang out together.

Below: At the Marlborough Day Hospital, an "auntie" holds one of the children in her lap.

Slowly he comes around. First cursing, but finally sitting down and painting, Christopher grows so that he smiles when I meet him in the morning. Christopher and I enjoy each other. Christopher plays his reality games, refusing to recognize people if he's in a bad mood. Occasionally he lets fly a string of obscenities, which always causes the ladies in the room to suck in their breath, much to Christopher's barely concealed delight. Each day I hope that Christopher may come a little bit further, accomplish a little more, so that, maybe, he won't have to be institutionalized all his life.

One day I tell Christopher that he can do his lesson now and play later, or play now and do his lesson later. A look of despair crosses his face. He stamps his foot. He glares. His choice is repeated: now or later? Christopher spins and hurls himself

Left: Christopher.

against the wall, head buried in his hands. "Caught between the devil and the deep blue sea," he moans.

The mornings in the hospital spill into the afternoons, and the weeks in London turn into months. Occasionally friends from the United States show up, telling horror stories of the war, or adventure stories of drugs. Many are on their way to Morocco or Katmandu, having believed their visions, following the drug trails, pursuing gurus. (The Beatles by now have made known their alliance with the Maharishi. Almost simultaneously, Brian Epstein dies. The Beatles announce they are doing another movie, *Magical Mystery Tour*.)

A friend arrives on her way to India. In Turkey she will be arrested for attempting to mail hashish back to the United States. She will spend a year in a Turkish prison awaiting trial before she finally becomes so desperate she escapes, staying underground until she can get back to central California.

———◆———

On my way to pick up my car from service I am sitting on the top of a double-decker bus going around Trafalgar Square when I look down to see John Lennon's Rolls-Royce. I know it is his because Lennon had his all-white Rolls entirely hand-painted in the intricate, swirling patterns of psychedelia. As the car moves in and out of traffic, it is something to behold, the ultimate car of richness achieved, the car of bank presidents and prime ministers, painted like a flagship for all the freaks. Go, John. Nothing can stop us now.

———◆———

On the night of the broadcast of *Magical Mystery Tour* I am visiting the estate of a wealthy English family. The show is due to begin in five minutes, and the parents have us all still seated at the table with no apparent intention of finishing their port, or brandy, or whatever it is they're drinking. Once again I am unsettled by how little regard the English have for the Beatles. If need be, I intend to get up and leave the table. Whatever *Magical Mystery Tour* will be, it is certainly the latest word from the Beatles, and as such I have no intention of missing it.

Finally, though, the father of the household gives us permission to leave. I rush to the television and sit transfixed as *Magical Mystery Tour* unreels before me. At the end I know that what I have seen is not good, though I don't know why. The Beatles had long ago lost the privilege of fallibility.

———◆———

Back in London, a close friend of mine from Berkeley shows up on my doorstep. He had been traveling in Europe with his girlfriend on money collected from an insurance claim. They had quarreled, and she had returned to the United States. My friend had come to London, for to return to America would mean that he would be drafted immediately. His eyes have that hollow, somewhat distant look, as he pictures his future, all his choices ending in violence. Since he must confront this, he intends to take his physical in London rather than in New York or Berkeley, where the draft boards are now presented on a daily basis with tactics of draft evasion concocted by some of the best minds of our fevered generation. Perhaps here in London the board will be more lax, more easily dissuaded from inducting him. Of course, it is just a hunch, a crap shoot with his life on the line.

As the day of the physical approaches, my friend starts to stay up all night, night after night. The circles under his eyes grow darker. On the morning of his physical he shows me how, the night before, he has covered his body with scratch marks like some eleventh-hour junkie. His stare has an intensity that means to say to any man who would classify him as fit for induction that he intends that same man to stand next to him in that rice field and walk in front of him through that jungle.

My friend guessed right. The psychologist from Kansas at the U.S. Air Force Base near London is sufficiently daunted by the specter that he gives my friend a temporary deferment that ends up lasting through the war and until conscription is finally abandoned.

Recovery is not an instant process, however, and my friend returns to New York not knowing his future, hallucinating for weeks after the interview, the pressure riding with him across America, another young man stretched like a drum, ready to break. The pressure stays on him until he finds himself in a Zen retreat in the Ventana Wilderness, a year later, where he finally lets it go.

But before he leaves London, he introduces me to Jonathan Cott, and it is Jonathan who asks me, some time later, if I would like to photograph Mick Jagger. "Sure," I say.

———◆———

The Rolling Stones' office, at 46a Maddox Street, occupied the attic floor of a fairly old building and was one nook opening into another cranny. To get to it you took a coffin-sized elevator capable of holding two and a half people, fully loaded, if those two and a half were very thin and very friendly. Presiding over the Stones' office, from a high-backed Victorian wheelchair, was Jo Bergman, a diminutive American woman with a halo of black curly hair, whose feet, from her position on top of her chair, did not quite reach the floor. Jo sat surrounded by telephones, with a clipboard and notepad on her lap on which were written lengthy lists in minute handwriting, each list topped with a single, underlined name: <u>Mick</u>, <u>Keith</u>, <u>Brian</u>.

As Jon and I walked in, Jo was on the phone. She waved for us to sit on the couch. In a moment, she hung up, and issued forth a small shriek. "I can't *stand* it anymore. I think I'm finally going to go *crazy*." (Almost twenty years later, a conversation with Jo Bergman, by then vice-president in charge of film and video for Warner Brothers Records, starts in exactly the same way.) Then she smiles. Jon introduces us.

Below: Jo Bergman and her staff. Clockwise from left: Alan Dunn (peeking), Shirley Arnold, Fiona Fraser, Jo (seated), and an unknown woman.

Pages 68 and 69: Mick Jagger.

Jon and Jo discuss plans for the interview, which is going to be conducted some days hence. Jon and an American woman, Sue Cox, who works with Jo, will do the interviewing. Jo listens attentively, swaps stories with Jon, asks a few questions about me. She could not be nicer. As I come to learn over time, Jo runs the Stones' office as calmly as circumstances will allow, trying to maintain a sense of order, efficiency, and humanity in a situation fraught with people intent upon getting to Mick or Keith or Brian, trying to sort out the professionals from the fans and at the same time satisfy the needs of the group, arrange a flight for Mick, a car for Keith, answer the cable from Brian, who is in Marrakesh, saying that he is sending something back with William Burroughs's nephew and could Jo make sure that it is looked after?

The Stones have just finished a new record, *Beggar's Banquet*. Their last release, *Their Satanic Majesties Request,* came at the peak of acid mania: on the cover the Stones are pictured wearing capes and surrounded by castles and crescent moons on a cover reproduced as if in three dimensions. "Far out," we all said at the time.

I am not yet familiar with the process of making and marketing a record: write it, record it, mix it, photo session, album cover artwork, print interviews, radio interviews, television interviews, the tour. The record promotes the tour, which promotes the record. If you want to talk to one of the boys, wait until their record is coming out. *Beggar's Banquet* is about to be released. Mick is granting interviews.

So when the day for the interview rolls around I get out my cameras, test the shutters, clean the lenses, and go with Jon to the Stones' office. Mick is not yet there. I have no real idea what to expect. I know the Rolling Stones only through their music, the pictures of them from their album covers, and their reputation in the press. All of which is a bit daunting. They are portrayed to be everything the Beatles are not: the dark underbelly of the long-haired revolution. Where the Beatles are jolly moptops, the Rolling Stones are scruffy malcontents. Where the Beatles sang songs of love, the Rolling Stones sang "Have you seen your mother, baby, standing in the shadows?"

There is a famous story of the drunken lot of them careening into a gas station, demanding gas, and then pissing all over the pumps. Who knew whether this was true? It could have been, and that was enough. The Rolling Stones were dirty and nasty and that was the story.

So when Mick enters the room, I am expecting something that might growl if irritated. Instead, my first impression is one of the general neatness of the man, how his trousers are well tailored and crisply pressed. His attitude is that of a sophisticated man who knows both his strengths and his weaknesses. If, like countless others, I had somehow imagined that the Rolling Stones (Mick and Keith in particular) were kept in a sturdy cage, fed a diet of uncooked and slightly rancid meat, and only let out to perform, then I had simply believed their image machine. The Stones lived in the international city of London, were widely traveled and successful in their business.

In person Mick Jagger, once a student at the London School of Economics, is a lot closer to Noel Coward than to Sonny Barger, then the president of the Hell's Angels.

Mick says hello to Jo. Then we adjourn to another room and Jon and Sue start the interview. Jon's questions presume what he (and I and a lot of other Americans) seem to feel — the Stones are not just musicians but important writers as well.

Jon: "For some reason people don't think about the fact that you and Keith are great writers and your lyrics, like 'Get Off of My Cloud,' which are really good . . ."

Mick: "Oh! They're not, they're crap."

(Yeah? Well, they seemed pretty good to me as I bopped along the California highways in my VW bus. And many was the time that my friends and I would shout them in unison as loud as we could, so I knew I wasn't alone.)

Jon pursues, "*Satanic Majesties* is probably the most controversial LP you've had. . . . It seems to be a personal statement rather than a collection of songs. What were your original ideas about putting it together?"

Mick demurs, "None at all. Absolutely no idea behind it. . . . It took a whole year to make, not because it's so fantastically complex, but because we were so strung out."

At every turn Mick deflects any inflation of the music beyond its simplest level.

Mick says, "Pop concerts are just gatherings of people who want to have a good time, and I don't really think they have a higher meaning. . . . The Rolling Stones on stage just isn't the Boston Pops. . . . It's a load of noise. On record it can be quite musical, but when you get to the stage it's no virtuoso performance. It's a rock and roll act, a very good one, and nothing more."

In the face of the then highly accepted attention to pop lyrics, where they are pro forma printed and included with every record, Mick says, "I don't think lyrics are that important. . . . This is serious. . . . I read an article by Fats Domino. He said, 'You should never sing the lyrics out very clearly.'"

I move around as quietly as possible, taking photographs. We are in a small room; the window is behind me, covered with a thin layer of lace. There is not a great deal of light, but with the film pushed to 1000 ASA, it is adequate. I shoot three rolls of film, thirty-six pictures to the roll.

After the interview is over, I rush the film to the lab, anxious. I ask for enlarged contacts. All of this is exciting, reminding me of *Blow-Up*. This fluke of a photo session suddenly has revitalized my fantasy of swinging London, with me as an active participant. Imagine, Ethan photographing Mick Jagger. Have mercy!

The next day at noon the film is ready, and I'm at the lab early. "How are they?" I ask.

"Good," says Nick Blatchley, a friend who works at the lab and who knows how pepped up I am.

I take the contacts and go to a nearby restaurant that has tables outside. I sit down, take out the contacts, and study them. Again the feeling sweeps over me: here I am sitting in London on a sunny day, swinging photographer in a swinging town.

But as I study the photos, they do not seem as strong as I would like and shortly I have convinced myself that they are no good at all. The waitress has been peering over my shoulder.

"Did you take those?" she asks.

"Yes," I say. "I don't think they're so good."

"Mind if I have a look?" she asks. I hand them to her. "You're right," she says as she hands them back.

So now, in despair, I go back to the lab. "Nick," I say, "they're no good."

"What are you talking about," he says. "They're fine. Don't worry, they'll print up terrifically. Come here."

Nick takes me back into the darkrooms. There in the dull, red light, under the guidance of Robert Horner, the chief printer, one of the photographs is enlarged and exposed. As it becomes visible in the developer, the picture is sharp and crisp. Several of them are strong portraits. The lace over the window has created a wonderful, soft light. By the end of the printing session I feel that maybe they're pretty good after all.

I take the photos to the Stones' office. Jo, Jon, and Sue pore over them with delight. Sue says, "We had David Bailey in here the other day, and these are better than his." (Sue's judgment, not mine.) Heady stuff.

Jo, Sue, Jonathan, and I all grow to be friends. We have, after all, quite a lot in common. We are all Americans abroad, and, like all young Americans in one way or another, we are relating to, affected by, circling around the music. Jo has been doing this for years: she worked for the early NEMS Enterprises, Brian Epstein and the Beatles. She lived and worked in Paris in public relations with Marianne Faithfull, among others, as her client. (Marianne Faithfull was at the time one of the best-known English singers. Also, as Mick Jagger's girlfriend, she was one of the famous faces of swinging London. She would later attempt suicide while Jagger was filming *Ned Kelly,* and would consume hard drugs with a ferocity that became legendary.) In 1967 Jo went to Los Angeles (where she met Sue) and worked in radio until she got a call from Mick asking her to return to London to run the Rolling Stones' office.

The photos I took that day are good and appreciated, and so when Stanley Booth, an American writer from Memphis, Tennessee, arrives to do a piece on the Rolling Stones for *Eye* magazine, Jo suggests that I do the pictures. Stanley brings to London a dry, cynical southern humor. "I want to find out what's so *bad* about these boys. They say they's *bad,* but have they ever been to Louisiana?"

Left: Mick from the first Rolling Stone interview.

Above top: Ethan and Bill Wyman. Photo by Stephen Wyman.

Above: Bill Wyman.

Below right: Shirley, Charlie, and Serafina Watts, Sussex, 1968.

Stanley and I are soon on our way to meet bad Bill Wyman, bass player for the Stones.

Much to our surprise, it turns out that bad Bill Wyman lives in what can only be described as a perfectly comfortable middle-class home. Bill is married to Astrid, a Swedish woman with high cheekbones and long dark-blond hair, and has a son, Stephen, by a previous marriage. Bad Bill Wyman, it turns out, couldn't be nicer.

He speaks to us quietly, answering Stanley's questions. He seems as bemused by us as we are by him. The man who will stand on stage as if rooted there, who has stared out impassively as audiences throw themselves at the stage and are turned back, smiles easily at our jokes. He discusses with me his interest in photography. He brings out his cameras and lenses to show me. By the end of the day, Stephen is snapping pictures of the three of us together. Nowhere in this home is there any allusion to the madness I know to be churning in the minds of hundreds of thousands of Americans as they drift to the music of "2000 Light Years from Home."

—◆—

In 1968 Charlie Watts, drummer for the Rolling Stones, lives on a farm in Sussex, surrounded by antiques: player-pianos, early gramophones, and four-poster wooden beds. Charlie lives with his wife, Shirley, a graduate of the Royal Academy of Arts, and their daughter Serafina. A man of few words, Charlie seems often to be wondering what all the fuss is about. This can be fairly offputting if you felt, as I did, that the Rolling Stones were important to our time.

"You guys are the greatest."

"No we're not." (How can you contradict that? He's the drummer.)

Outside Charlie's door are the gently sloping hills of Sussex. Charlie Watts leads a measured, sensible life in the quiet countryside of England, surrounded by horses, goats, and things of beauty.

Keith Richards arranges to meet us at the Stones' office. In legend, Keith has been painted with the same brush as Mick: a rock and roll outlaw whose personal supply of contraband substances (the legend went) would be sufficient to defoliate large forests. And, indeed, when he walks in, Keith looks a lot more likely to be the stuff of his legend than Mr. Jagger. Keith walks with a swagger. He smokes incessantly, smoke curling around his head. He wears a ragged black cape, jeans, and a T-shirt. His hand does not quite close on mine when we're introduced, though he looks at me, speaking quietly, and says, "How ya doing, man?"

Once again, Stanley asks his questions, and later Keith and I climb onto the roof, London spread below us, and I take photos of this man reputed to be as dissolute as they come.

But this, of course, is pure speculation. I am much too timid myself to speak beyond the dullest pleasantries. As this leaves nothing for Keith to respond to, he mostly grunts in assent. Later we move to a flat near the office. Stanley asks questions, and Keith responds. It is clear even then that the one thing liable to spark a response from Keith Richards is some question related to solid American blues music. Stanley, coming as he does from the American South, spewing stories of swamp gas and Negroes, booze and bottlenecks, seems to do just fine. It's when Keith is smiling in reaction that I get a glimpse of his teeth.

Keith could be famous for his teeth alone. As opposed to the American fifties rock star stereotype where the very first thing you did after becoming a star (or before, in hopes of becoming a star) was to get your teeth straightened and whitened, America loving nothing better than a gleaming row of pearlies for its youth, Keith has instead the tooth line of a barracuda, sawlike and uneven. Constant cigarette smoking has stained them a spotty brown. I get the feeling that Keith enjoys his image, sending the timid spinning out of his path.

Still, I like it when people smile, or I did then, in my early photography. I could not have been more innocent in my appreciation. I might even have been so bold as to think that a smiling picture was a good picture. Anything that might provoke a smile would certainly have caused me to click the shutter. I enjoyed that and thought it revelatory to see these bad boys smiling. From what I had seen before, the idea that a Rolling Stone might smile was heresy. Though Keith's fearsome reputation might be mostly based on a profound impatience for nonsense — other than his own — such simple impatience didn't necessarily qualify him for the entrenched messianic power that was, along with Jagger, attributed to him.

For myself, I still had within me this notion of peace and light. I wasn't trying to promote that, but if these fellows were smiling and being pleasant right in front of me (I wasn't directing anything here), I would certainly take the picture. Such was my instinct. I would soon learn, however, that a smiling Rolling Stone flew in the face of the accepted image. A scowling and sultry Mick — this was good. A Keith

Richards apparently nodding out for the last time — this, too, was good. The desire is for undigested meat so people, like carrion eaters, can rise up on their hind legs and howl at the horror of it all.

Sad, bad Brian Jones would soon be their supper.

———◆———

I can't remember why, now, but I went down to see Brian alone. Perhaps Stanley had already interviewed him. But one day I found myself driving through the green hills of Sussex to visit Brian in his new house. With some fanfare, Brian had just bought the country home of A. A. Milne, the creator of Christopher Robin and Winnie-the-Pooh. It seemed somehow perfect that this blond-haired rock and roller should have inherited the house of Pooh. For Brian, with his blond pageboy haircut, looked like a fully grown Christopher Robin.

I followed the directions down classic, winding country lanes until a sharp turn on my right led me through some trees. The house sat in a small depression, asleep in the morning summer sun, surrounded by grass, and then surrounded by English gardens, a picture from a hundred years ago. The house was low-ceilinged, and I stooped to get in. Inside Brian was alone. He greeted me squinting, almost as if still asleep. We talked quietly of his house, his new pride.

Up close, apart from his golden Christopher Robin hairdo, Brian looked surprisingly old. He had bags below his eyes, and his face was somewhat swollen. He said he'd been up all night, some party. Brian talked excitedly, though in a quiet voice. He started to tell me one story, about his house, but then switched to another, a little spacey. There was a charm to it, like you might have expected from Kerouac's Neal Cassady.

Above: Brian Jones displaying "certain telltale signs."

Right: Brian with gun, outside his home in Sussex, 1968.

I didn't know then, not yet having learned to judge, by looking for certain telltale signs, that Brian's face was a road map of his various self-indulgences. With Brian, perhaps more than any rock and roller, it was as if he had chosen to wear the mantle of the crown prince of stonedness. And to do this he would remain constantly high. Few would have disputed his claim, even in California, where people were now setting daily records of higher and higher, just trying to catch up. Indisputably, Brian had been there first: it was his face, after all, squinting back at you from the cover of *Big Hits (High Tide and Green Grass);* his face curled into a wicked leer peering out of the mist on the cover of *Between the Buttons,* just announcing by that leer that he was so high it was a miracle the camera could catch him.

It was Brian who decided to travel to the Monterey Pop Festival, though he would not perform there, as if the ambassador from the English court. Pictures of him at the festival show him wearing a cape, its edges lined with fur, a collection of pendants and Moroccan jewelry around his neck. Here, too, he has that look on his face, smiling, as if from a long way away, the Cheshire cat from *Alice in Wonderland.*

But back at Brian's house in England, it's time to take pictures. At first I photograph in the house, Brian sitting still. But Brian seems slightly uncomfortable, just sitting there. He says he'll be right back. He leaves and returns wearing a shirt made out of an American flag. Immediately he begins to act for the camera, sneering at it. He walks outside to the statue of Christopher Robin that sits in the middle of the garden; he grabs it by the neck, strangling it. He gets a gun (not a Clint Eastwood, Dirty Harry magnum shitkicker, but a pellet gun used by the landed gentry to kill rodents). The gun he lifts in the air, butt end aimed at the camera, threatening. Then he lies down and takes aim directly at me.

If a bit confused about how the fellow who was just speaking in such hushed and reverent tones about his house, and Milne, and Winnie-the-Pooh could now be seen attacking everything around him, I still thought this was great. Here was a Rolling Stone doing Rolling Stone things! The images were stoned and rebellious with a slight edge of violence. This was the stuff.

And so I take pictures for an hour or so, pleased as can be. At the end I say good-bye and tell Brian how happy I am. When I get back to town I phone Jo and tell her.

"He's doing what?" she asks. "Oh, God. Hold on a minute." And Jo phones over to the Stones' press manager, Les Perrin. (Les is old school, Fleet Street, public relations, and has been around forever. He is highly respected by all. His job for the Rolling Stones, in contrast to the hundreds of clamoring starlets aching to get their names into the papers, is, more often than not, to try and keep the Stones' names *out* of the papers after one scrape or another.)

"You can't use those, Ethan," Jo says. "We have enough trouble trying to get that boy a visa."

———————◆———————

So, all of a sudden, I was a rock photographer. It didn't take long, after the first session with Mick, for me to have enlargements made of that session, and to take those around to other offices in London, and to continue to freelance for *Rolling Stone*.

At first, I simply attempted to find out where something was happening, and then I would show up, camera in hand. I went to receptions. I went to concerts. I became a rock and roll paparazzi, although without the true grit of all paparazzi, who wouldn't hesitate to explode a flash in the face of the most reclusive star at the precise moment that he (or she) was doing the one thing he wished the rest of the world didn't know. By my view, we were all supposed to be on the same side here. I was much too discreet.

———————◆———————

Granada Television arranged to film Jim Morrison of the Doors at the Roundhouse in North London.

Jo Durden-Smith was the producer of *World in Action,* a television show that frequently dealt with politics in popular culture. Oxford educated, with degrees in the classics (Latin, Greek, and ancient history), Jo was highly articulate, politically astute, with a perception, shared by many of us, of an identification between the political left and popular music. (Jo had flown to California and filmed Johnny Cash's performance at San Quentin.) Jim Morrison, who was now famous as the lead singer of the Doors, and who had a reputation as an angry young man, and who, some said, was the "American Mick Jagger," seemed the perfect subject for a Granada show. For, as with most American rock groups by this time, the Doors' music was laced with political and social assumptions.

Jo went to meet them at the airport. The English music press had been full of the arrival of Morrison who, in turn, seemed to feel he was the center of the universe. Immediately reports arrived that all was not as it should be. Morrison was surly. He had apparently no intention of cooperating with anyone. I heard all this from the sidelines. By the time of the filming at the Roundhouse, the producer and the pop star were hardly speaking to each other.

As the show began, Morrison came out dressed in his normal costume of black
leather trousers and jacket and white shirt. He seemed somewhat puffy-faced and
petulant. He pouted. The pout seemed to be Morrison's look. Combined with his
high cheekbones and long hair, it was the high-fashion look of a photographer's
model.

He walked slowly, a very studied slowly, to the microphone. He grasped it in
both hands and leaned his weight upon it, looking down. When he sang, he put his
lips directly to the mike and mouthed the lyric in such a way that it seemed that if he
wasn't careful he might inadvertently swallow the mike. He hardly moved. When he
was not singing, he hung his head down, drooping. He seemed to be playing to an

The Kinks

Jefferson Airplane

Marty Balin

Eric Clapton with psychedelic mini

Traffic

Stevie Winwood

Martha Flint

Dave Mason

Frank Zappa

McGuinness Flint

The Moody Blues

Janis Joplin

Cream

Eric Clapton

Jack Bruce

Ginger Baker

Benny Goodman

Leopold Stokowski

incredible tension that simply was not there. As the song reached a crescendo, he threw his head back and yelled, "WE WANT THE WORLD AND WE WANT IT [pause] NOW!" — the clear, intended rallying point of the set, the moment where he had come to expect audiences to cheer wildly in reaction to the incendiary rhetoric. But London was not New York or anywhere in America, and here the audience reacted mildly.

Morrison looked as if he might go home. "It's too bright in here," Morrison said, squinting into the lights. "I want those lights off," and he pointed out at the lamps, which were, of course, necessary for the filming. The lights stayed on. The music stopped.

"Turn off the lights," Morrison says again. The lights continue to burn.

"Turn 'em off, or I'm not singing." More silence. The lights stay on.

The audience starts to boo slowly. It's difficult to tell whether the audience is booing Morrison or booing the lights or booing the whole thing in general. But, finally, Jo is forced to kill the lights as Morrison simply refuses to sing. A short time later, Jo turns the lights back up.

Mick Jagger went to see this "American Mick Jagger." When asked what he thought of him, Mick is quoted as saying, "Boring."

In 1971, Jim Morrison is found dead in a bathtub in Paris. In 1983, *Rolling Stone* magazine features Jim Morrison on its cover. The headline reads, "He's Hot. He's Sexy. He's Dead," a finely honed cynicism, a headline for our time.

———◆———

Four days a week, I still go to the hospital in St. John's Wood and see Christopher. But Christopher is growing older, and somewhere in the long, gray hallways of medical bureaucracy, it is written that when a child turns eleven years old (Christopher is ten and a half), he can no longer go to the Marlborough Day Hospital. Soon Christopher will have to leave for some other institution where he will be permanently boarded.

And so, in the chill of the London winter, Christopher and I go institution shopping.

As we turned into the driveway we saw the house. It was made of solid gray stone and sat surrounded by dark trees that blocked all light. The stooped and gnarled woman who met us at the door squinted at us, and peered at Christopher like a hawk looks at a mouse, the little boy who meant money from the state. The house had stone floors, bare walls. There was no heat. The living room was empty except for one scarred wooden table that sat askew in the middle of the room, chairs scattered around it. We walked down dark hallways that led to gray bedrooms filled with rows of cots, blankets thrown over them. Every so often a child would appear and look at us, startled. Christopher was agog, staring at everything. It could have been a day at the zoo.

Above: Christopher.

Behind the house there was a weed-infested field.

"Want to take a walk?" I say.

Christopher walks ahead of me. Suddenly he screams, a deep-throated yell of pain. I look up. Christopher has discovered nettles.

I say, "It's all right, Christopher, it's all right."

But Christopher's whole life has been the stone city streets. Suddenly he is surrounded by hostile, green, "'orrible" stuff. Like some Disney forest from *Fantasia,* like some bad acid vision, the very ground on which he walks is alive and malevolent. Christopher holds on to me, shaking.

He wants to go back to the house. With dreadful intensity, he takes big, cautious steps, his knees coming to his chest, his feet placed down gingerly as if the field were mined.

To Molly I say the place is impossible, so soon Christopher and I are off to visit a modern brick monolith. This is much better. The rooms are warm; the beds have sheets. The vast majority of inmates are mongoloids. As they approach us with swollen heads and uncomprehending eyes, Christopher shrinks. But they are only curious, like horses, and cannot help themselves. And they are friendly. It is Christopher's persona to retreat to never-never land when scared, but there is some rapport between these madmen since they can in no way comprehend that Christopher is strange, and perhaps Christopher can in some way sense they mean him no harm. It is one of my last memories of Christopher, seeing him surrounded by these gentle mongoloids: torn between running away and enjoying the attention.

I tell Molly of the day, and that I hope Christopher can go there. Molly says soon he will have to go somewhere. I tell Christopher good-bye and he acts as if he understands. Got along without me before he met me. ⚓

10

LONDON, 1968.

"It's a circus," Jo says. And, this once, it is the literal truth. "The Rolling Stones' Rock and Roll Circus," to be precise.

"The Rolling Stones' Rock and Roll Circus" is to be a privately produced (by the Stones) entertainment spectacular for television. The first I hear of it is at a night meeting when Mick, Brian, and Keith meet with the director, Michael Lindsay-Hogg.

Michael is a baby-faced American, though a long-time resident of London, and when I meet him he is puffing slowly on the proverbial large cigar, though his young face is so innocent it belies the image. When Michael speaks, which is very quickly, one idea follows another, and there is a constant playful look in his eyes as if this is the best of times in the best of all possible worlds. If during the meeting Mick frowns or Keith groans, Michael can be seen to smile and then immediately abandon the idea as if he, too, had never heard anything quite as awful in his life. "Oh, yeah. Well what about this? . . ." Michael wants Ava Gardner for ringmaster. No? Then what about Brigitte Bardot? Plans are made for Michael to meet with Bardot in Paris. But Michael won't fly. Reservations are made on the train. Phone call after phone call. The meeting with Bardot is canceled. Show business.

Michael is known to the Stones as one of the original directors of *Ready, Steady, Go,* a well-respected live pop music television show from the early sixties on which groups like the young Rolling Stones appeared. Since the Stones have gotten to be too big to do such appearances, and since they now have an international market to satisfy, Michael has become the director of a series of promotional shorts for the Stones, the latest of which is "Jumpin' Jack Flash."

The idea of a rock and roll circus has everyone pretty excited. Here are the acts: Jethro Tull, Marianne Faithfull, the Who, Taj Mahal, and — spoken with a low voice and some awe, provoking the most enthusiasm — a "supergroup" that will perform just for this show with Mitch Mitchell (of the Jimi Hendrix Experience) on drums, Eric Clapton on lead guitar, Keith Richards on bass, and John Lennon, rhythm guitar and vocals.

There will be jugglers and knife throwers, elephants and tigers. There will be Danielle Luna, a better-than-six-foot black fashion model, a famous London face. There will be midgets and giants, a freaky music extravaganza. To top it all off there will be, of course, your hosts: the Rolling Stones.

Below: Mick Jagger, Brian Jones, Keith Richards. Late-night production meetings.

Below (bottom): John, Yoko, and clown at "The Rolling Stones' Rock and Roll Circus," 1968.

Right: The "supergroup" on stage. L. to r.: Eric Clapton, John Lennon, Mitch Mitchell, Keith Richards.

Rehearsals are held on the mezzanine floor of the Londonderry Hotel, a piece of American-influenced hotel design on Park Lane. The room has bright overhead lighting, acres of designer carpet. The sense of expectancy is tangible. Taj Mahal and his band are smuggled into the country. Their presence is not to be mentioned, for they will work here without the necessary permits. As Taj enters, Keith leaps to his feet and walks with great strides across the room to embrace him.

Taj Mahal's band sets up to rehearse. They play a slow, loping blues: "Take a giant step outside your mind." (Never had any generation been so exhorted to leave their minds behind. Though our mothers and fathers may have been told to leave their worries on the doorstep, we would abandon our entire frontal lobes.) Taj's band seems almost bewildered by the collection of English rock and roll heavyweights.

Jagger is there, as well as Pete Townshend and the Who. So is Mitch Mitchell. Jimmy Miller, the producer of *Beggar's Banquet,* sits watching and listening. Continuous cups of tea are brought in by little English ladies not certain of what they are hearing or seeing.

Production offices are set up around the city. A traveling circus is hired. In North London a sound stage is found, and the construction of a circus tent commences. It is decided that the audience will be dressed in variously colored ponchos and floppy hats.

When the appointed day rolls around, I pack my cameras, buy all my film, and drive to North London. It is eight in the morning, and all around the stage are the union hands, the assistants and grips, all performing their tasks many hours before the stars arrive. In the center of the stage is a two-story circus set, surrounded by semicircular rows of seats. Jo Bergman is wandering around with her clipboard; Jimmy Miller is speaking with Glyn Johns, sound engineer, who directs the placement of mikes. Tony Richmond, cameraman, oversees as the lights are trucked in and hauled up to the ceiling, pointed, spotted, and focused.

In the early afternoon, it comes time to rehearse the circus players. The floor manager speaks into his megaphone. "All right, let's see the circus."

Within ten minutes it is clear that whoever did the actual hiring, they neglected to get the A-team of the circus set. As the members traipse tiredly through their entrance a sorrier group of people would be hard to imagine. Without their costumes, the men wear T-shirts and suspenders and have not yet thought to shave. Whatever shapeliness the women once may have had is by now lost in the ten-thousandth plate of sausages, eggs, and chips. It is as if the entire circus had been woken in the middle of the night and sent scurrying underground during a German air raid and had only just emerged.

A fire-eater comes out and in desultory fashion lights and eats a flame or two. He does not appear to be awake yet.

Jo and I are standing on the sidelines making huge, unbelieving eyes at each other.

Above (top to bottom): Taj Mahal at rehearsal. Mick Jagger and Pete Townshend at rehearsal. Tony Richmond setting lights, Mick Jagger, Bill Wyman.

We are there to be excited, there to have these entertainers thrill us, take us back to our youth.

The floor manager again: "All right, let's have the knife throwers."

A man and a woman emerge. They do not look as if they like each other very much. Someone drags out a six-by-nine-foot piece of untreated, rough plywood, raises it upright, and stands behind it, just managing to hold it steady. The woman, looking none too pleased, goes to stand in front of it. A group of shiny, three-foot-long throwing knives is brought to the man. He stands maybe twenty feet from the woman. He takes each knife and balances it in his hand, swinging slowly back and forth. He drops a knife, which clatters to the cement floor. He bends to pick it up.

The woman assumes the pose, standing rigid in the center of the board, her arms held parallel to the floor, like Christ awaiting crucifixion.

The man leans forward slightly, bends from the waist, and rocks back and forth, gaining momentum. He takes careful aim and throws the first knife. It spins in the air, traveling quite slowly, and misses the board completely, crashing down on the concrete and sliding off into the recesses of the set.

"Sorry," the man calls. Again he leans forward, again takes aim and throws. The knife arcs a slow loop and this time it hits the board, though a good two and a half feet from the woman. It sticks only lightly and then falls out, crashing to the floor. It is clear the man has no aim at all; the knife easily could have drifted two feet in another, any other, direction. Still, he throws on.

Another knife loops in the air and hits the board, this one somewhere near her knee. Then another, above her head and to the left. Jo and I have turned our backs, now looking over our shoulders, as if at some horror movie. Two more knives are thrown, both hitting the board haphazardly, without direction. It seems a miracle worthy of the Catholic church that the woman has been spared.

"Okay," the man says, as someone brings him a glistening chrome axe the size firemen use to break through doors. He leans back and lets fly, and the axe spins, handle over head. It's so heavy that when it strikes the plywood background, still supported only by a man standing behind it, it causes the background to veer slightly, and the axe ricochets and falls to the ground.

"Okay. That's enough," calls the floor manager, in an act of infinite mercy.

The circus marches on. The elephants are brought out, followed by an assistant with his broom and bucket. A tiger (I am to shoot a photo of Mick and the tiger for a poster) can be seen caged in a corner of the studio. A trapeze artist does a twirl or two, does not fall and die, and it comes time to think of rock and roll, as the stars are now beginning to arrive.

Participation is the order of the day. Everyone wears some costume — a hat, a jacket, sometimes the whole works. Mick, in deference to the fact that it is the Rolling Stones' rock and roll circus, is the ringmaster. Keith is a pirate. Bill Wyman, a clown,

complete with red bulbous nose. Brian is at one moment a sorcerer, and then simply the Androgynous Man. John and Yoko wear black cloth hats; Yoko's is pointed like a dunce's. Together they look like Halloween trick-or-treaters. The Who are dressed like their alter egos: London street kids with big shitkicking shoes. Keith Moon giggles madly, threatening, as he always does, to suddenly spin out of control.

The doors are opened and a swarm of photographers from the English and foreign press soon fill the stage. Veterans all, they arrive with cameras and flash units hanging from their necks. It is clear that they have witnessed endless photo calls for princes and prime ministers, starlets and circuses, as they wait to take their shots.

The curtains open and the circus and cast are assembled. Bulbs flash, the questions are hurled forth.

"Mick, look this way, will you?"

"Brian, over here."

"John, where's Cynthia?" (Soon to be the question to take over the British press, at least when it comes to dealing with John Lennon. The British are not to take kindly to this American/Japanese artist who seems to have captured John's affections. Cynthia Lennon, John's then wife, was a classic example of the British man's dream: blond, beautiful, and waiting at home. So when John takes up with Yoko, it is seen as a slap in the face of the British ideal. As if that wasn't bad enough, Yoko was foreign, older than John, and still married.)

The costumed rock and rollers form a wide arc, surrounded on one side by the fat man, on another by the dwarf, in front by the photographers. The audience is admitted, the taping begins, and Jethro Tull, a fledgling act on Island Records, gets up on stage. Ian Anderson, the lead singer, wears a ragged old coat that looks as if it might have been recovered from the Salvation Army. His hair sprouts from his head in shaggy misdirection. He looks like some manic goblin you might discover under a mushroom. When he performs, he attacks the microphone, plays his flute, raises one leg in the air, and spins, while one eye, brow raised, sparkles madly.

Taj Mahal is next and he plays the same loping song as in rehearsal. But the audience is impatient. They await the Big Boys, and so next come the Who.

Pete, Roger, John, and Keith have done it before, and this you can tell. Their filming goes quickly and efficiently. Roger twirls the mike over his head in ever-increasing circles until it is swinging fifteen, twenty feet, at the end of its tether (out over the camera and crew), and then he jerks it back, bringing it to his mouth just in time for the next lyric. Pete rocks back and forth from one leg to another, guitar slung at his waist, waiting for the guitar break, as he plants his legs in an inverted V and his arm sweeps into a huge circle, swiftly arcing, hitting the guitar again and again, until he grabs it and goes running across stage, leaping in the air, his knees to his chest, and spins and spins around. John Entwistle stands perfectly still, though the fingers of both hands are forming and picking notes to keep up with Keith, the

mad, fastest drummer of rock, who seems to wish to play six notes to every other drummers' one, not to be outdone by the antics of Pete, throwing his drumstick in the air, watching it swirl away, grabbing it as it falls, never missing a beat. As the song ends, jets of water spew forth from his drum kit, spattering Keith and anyone near. Roger prancing, Pete spinning, John standing, Keith flailing: the Who.

Whenever filming is about to begin (since the audience, which is seated around the performing area, could be in shot), the floor manager goes to the audience and says, "Now, I want to see a lot of activity, a lot of enthusiasm! Come on!" And he stands in front of them like a cheerleader, his arms in the air, until he has worked them up to a fevered pitch. The audience loves it, swaying and yelping. Michael Lindsay-Hogg yells, "Cut." The audience, having a good time, keeps on swaying. The floor manager turns to them, as if they were cattle, and orders them impatiently to quit screaming.

I am never sure how the audience was chosen. They are mostly kids. I've been told that somehow or other tickets were given away free. I'm not certain the audience even knew, when they arrived, what they were going to see. So, it must have come as something of a surprise to them when Eric Clapton, Mitch Mitchell, Keith Richards, and John Lennon assemble on stage and break into "Yer Blues."

Mick Jagger is a phenomenal stage performer, along with the rest of the band presenting as riveting a rock and roll show as you can see anywhere. He dances, teases, and provokes. He seems constantly to move, so that though he is directly in front of you, you can still never quite catch him, never be quite certain of what has just passed. His performance evokes some of the fascination of watching an illusionist. But when John Lennon breaks into "Yer Blues," he stands rooted behind the microphone, only slightly bobbing at the knees, and singing thin-lipped. He delivers a performance of such simplicity and conviction that it is truly breathtaking.

Clockwise from above left: The Who. Young Julian Lennon and clown. Mick and tiger. John Lennon.

His voice is raw, his guitar playing, with Clapton's and Richards's, immensely driving. When John sings, "I even hate my rock 'n' roll," the presence of the pain that made him write the line is clear in his voice. John Lennon finally seems to have been a man who would never mask his pain. He ceased to believe the myth of himself, thanked Yoko for removing him from Beatledom, and would seemingly endlessly reiterate: It's just me, man. And I go through a lot of pain.

———◆———

"Clear the set, now. Everybody off the floor, and I mean *everybody* except Mick and the photographer." The floor manager is at it again.

This is my big cue. They are about to parade out the tiger. For a good fifteen minutes prior to the tiger's release, the trainer and the floor manager have been working to pump everybody into a state of hysteria about the potential danger of what is about to occur. The headline flashes through my head: "MICK JAGGER MAULED. PHOTOGRAPHER EATEN." I am probably not alone in my thoughts, though I imagine Jagger's to be simply: "MICK JAGGER MAULED."

As the tiger is led out, I am waiting anxiously, and Mick is waiting anxiously, and the rest of the assembled cast, far enough back not to worry, watch. I hold perfectly still, hardly breathing, as instructed. For some reason, I have chosen to shoot this with a wide-angle lens, so that in order to get the image size I want, I have to creep to within a few feet of the tiger's mouth.

"Slowly, now, slowly," goes the trainer. Isn't this how an animal is stalked? I wonder. You'd think that might make him nervous. Not this tiger, though. He seems to be on Serious Animal Downers. His eyes droop shut. Mick creeps up cautiously behind. Now we have him surrounded. Great. I crouch low, shooting upward, not three feet from his head. First, there is the tiger's head, then Mick Jagger, ringmaster.

"Hey, tiger," I say. The eyes drift open. "Okay, great. Hold that." And the film clicks through the motor-driven Hasselblad. I shoot only one roll, still nervous that this beast is going to suddenly awaken and fulfill his trainer's prophecy. And I am directly in front of him. Jagger is behind him and poised to disappear at speed.

"You got it?" asks the floor manager.

"Guess so," I say, as they lead the tiger away.

◆

As the clock has passed midnight, and then one o'clock, and then two, and the Stones have still not performed, the stress of the past few weeks of production and rehearsals starts to catch up with people. The floor manager, no doubt having long ago calculated the amount he stands to make in golden time and decided even that wasn't worth all this, grows increasingly grouchy. The audience has been pepped up and let down so many times that they are beginning to get punch drunk. And, for the first time in my short rock and roll life, I am tired and pissed off as well. All of us are drooping as the Stones come on.

The stage is set. The Stones assume their positions, cameras are readied, and the first take is called. Like an aging gunfighter who intends to vindicate a lifetime's experience, the floor manager flies at the audience, arms flailing, exhorting them to heights of hysteria. Nothing. The Who, notable troopers that they are, go out into the crowd to help. Still nothing.

"Come on," the floor manager yells, as if his professional life were on the line. I am so tired that all I register is a certain irritation at the antics of the manager. As the Stones perform, they seem good to me. They play "Jumpin' Jack Flash," "You Can't Always Get What You Want." Dawn arrives as the last numbers are being taped. A lot of weary people drift from the circus set in a corner of North London as the infamous and never-to-be-broadcast (though this is not known then) "Rolling Stones' Rock and Roll Circus" comes to an end.

◆

In the middle of filming, someone points out Ken Kesey, standing on the sidelines. Next to Kesey stand Rock Scully, somehow associated with the Grateful Dead, and a few others, a small band of notables from the Haight; this crowd had come to England to see if it was really what it was reputed to be. From the shadows they watch the filming of the circus. The next day, while visiting Apple, Kesey — he of innumerable Acid Tests, who proclaimed loudly and fervently, "Further! Further!," the Kesey who tried to unravel the truth within the truth within the truth, like the

Above: Brian Jones and Rocky the percussionist.

Left: Mick. "Please allow me to introduce myself."

layers of a rose — is quoted as saying about the circus, "It was all played to the ghost. The audience was a prop. It wasn't so important what was actually happening, but what appeared to be happening."★ Dear Mr. Fantasy.

—◆—

Not many days later, I get a call from John Lennon. He and Yoko are going to be at his house in Weybridge. Did I want to come down and take some photos?

John's house is in the middle of what is referred to as the stockbroker belt that

★From "The Rolling Stones' Circus," by David Dalton, in *Rolling Stones,* edited by David Dalton. New York: Amsco Music Publishing Company, 1972.

borders London on the south. It seems, in reaction to their early success, that the Stones and the Beatles (they probably had no time to think twice about this as they climbed the early rungs of the success ladder), aped the expected purchases of the well-to-do. John was quick to react against it. He refers to this house as a "mock-Tudor shithouse," and moves out within a year.

When I arrived, the front door was open; John and Yoko were upstairs. No one else seemed to be around. The house seemed mostly unfinished, as if no one really lived there. Next to the kitchen was a small room with an upright piano at one end, various guitars, and mementos from *Sgt. Pepper* scattered about. This room seemed the most used.

Above: John serenading Yoko.

Yoko came in, said good morning, and offered me some tea. John was still upstairs and would be down shortly. While we were waiting Yoko asked, "You want to see something, Ethan?"

Yoko reached over and picked up a package addressed to her "c/o John Lennon."

"You look at this. It's terrible."

I opened the package and moved aside the white tissue paper. Beneath it lay a small doll, like a Smurf doll, but it was difficult to tell since it had been so mutilated. Its features were smeared with charcoal, and a black-haired wig had been glued to the head in an effort to make the doll resemble some grotesque version of Yoko. Through the entire body and head of the doll large pins had been stuck. A note, written in an almost illegible scrawl, read, "You leave John alone."

In the quiet of the kitchen of this empty house, Yoko seemed strangely helpless in the face of such animosity. It went unspoken, though it was clear, that this was just a small token of the mushrooming resentment against Yoko, and it made me feel sorry for her. If whoever had sent that doll was motivated enough to do that, what might others have in store?

John came down. We went outside, and I started to take pictures, though somewhat aimlessly, as, really, I had been summoned and didn't know quite what to expect. John seemed to sense this, and he and Yoko disappeared to return shortly, wearing identical black capes. As if John (or John and Yoko) were doing my job for me, the capes created a simple, graphic look. As we now went about taking photos, each one took on a more striking quality. Yoko seemed more preoccupied than John, John more enthusiastic than Yoko. John, the Beatle who had been besieged by photographers for years now, seemed willing to try anything. He took a guitar and serenaded Yoko. He knelt in front of her as if she were some maiden from the time of Arthur, and John was the knight. John was in love, this was obvious. And his antics pierced through whatever preoccupation or reserve surrounded Yoko, and she would be charmed. It was impossible not to be. ⚓

11

LONDON, 1968.

"Could you hold the line, please? I have Neil Aspinall for you." Neil Aspinall is the managing director of Apple Corp., Ltd., the Beatles' newly formed company whose purpose will be to take control of all Beatle product. "Nothing you can do that can't be done," after all.

At the press conference held to announce the new company, John Lennon had said, "[It'll be] a business concerning records, film, and electronics, and, as a sideline, whatever it's called — manufacturing, or whatever. We want to set up a system whereby people who just want to make a film about anything don't have to go on their knees in somebody's office — probably yours."

The change in John Lennon was striking. No longer was every encounter with the press a deft delivery of charming and witty one-liners, bubbly entertainment at any cost. Times had changed. The Beatles' manager, Brian Epstein, had died from an overdose of pills. Their much-publicized relationship with the Maharishi had foundered. They had been through a great deal, and it showed. The Beatles were forced to fall back upon themselves.

Above: Neil Aspinall.

When Apple was announced, the Beatles released an ad that said, in bold type, "This Man Now Owns a Rolls-Royce." The gentleman pictured in the advertisement (it said) had submitted an idea (that other companies might have found too bizarre, it implied) to Apple Corp., and Apple had magically turned this idea into the profit that became a Rolls-Royce.

In the Age of Promise, the Beatles sang, "Baby, you're a rich man." Now the Beatles were extending a hand, promising everyone a chance to turn their dreams into reality, into money, making everyone truly rich, as if by magic. And who were the ultimate magicians? Why, the Beatles, of course.

In response, the lunatic fringe would come out of the woodwork as if suddenly endowed with supernatural strength and descend upon Apple and the Beatles until John would rush away screaming, "Don't give me no more brother, brother," George would be singing the "Sue me, sue you blues," and Paul, on the advice of counsel, would have "no comment."

Still it seemed at the time a grand idea. It had to be. It was a Beatle idea.

Now, several months later, Neil Aspinall is on the line. "Hi, Ethan," says Neil, speaking with the same Liverpudlian accent as the Beatles'. "I hear you've been photographing John. I'd like to look at the pictures. Why don't you come down to the office?"

Neil had been with the Beatles from the beginning, first as road manager, and now as managing director of their company. He is their oldest and most trusted associate. If ever there was such a thing as a "fifth Beatle," Neil Aspinall was undoubtedly it. ★

Neil's office overlooked Savile Row, and it was carpeted wall-to-wall with the bright green carpet that covered all the Apple offices and was in its way as much a trademark of Apple as the Apple logo itself.

At first Neil seemed gruff, as if he had heard it all before and knew that it was only a matter of time until whoever was in front of him would introduce, however subtly, their scheme, their con, their desire to meet the Beatles. But once Neil judged that you were not of criminal bent, he would open up and become friendly and down-to-earth.

I had brought to Neil's office not only the photographs of John and Yoko but also the photographs of Mick from the *Rolling Stone* interview, and the photographs of everybody from the "Rock and Roll Circus."

"So you've been working for those guys" (meaning the Stones), said Neil, poring over the contacts. They each wanted to know what the others were up to. Mick and John would snipe at each other for years. Mick from the first *Rolling Stone* interview: "They [the Beatles] were really hustlers then . . . 'Hey Mick, we've got this great song.'"

John was, characteristically, a bit more blunt: "You know, I can knock the Beatles, but don't let Mick Jagger knock them. Because I would just like to list what we did and what the Stones did two months after . . . He imitates us . . . You know, *Satanic Majesties* is *Pepper*. 'We Love You,' man . . . that's 'All You Need Is Love.' I resent the implication that the Stones are revolutionaries and that the Beatles weren't."‡

Neil marked some of the photographs of John, and I said I'd have them printed and get them to him. I knew that the Beatles were just beginning filming at Twickenham Studios, and I wanted to go.

"That's not possible, Ethan," Neil said. "We have people going down there all the time. David Bailey is down there today."

"Okay, Neil, thanks," I said, and (ignoring him) got into my car and drove down to where the Beatles were filming.

All the people on the film were the same people who had been at the "Rock and Roll Circus": Michael Lindsay-Hogg was directing, Tony Richmond was lighting/cameraman, and Glyn Johns was doing the sound. I walked in and said hello to every-

★See *The Love You Make: An Insider's Story of the Beatles,* by Peter Brown and Steven Gaines. New York: McGraw-Hill, 1983.

‡From *Lennon Remembers: The Rolling Stone Interviews,* by Jann Wenner. San Francisco: Straight Arrow Books, 1971.

body. If it came up, I asked, could they put in a good word for me? I'd love to do the pictures.

———◆———

When the photographs of John that Neil had requested were printed, I called and arranged to go see him.

Neil flicked through the photographs. "By the way," he said, "we've decided to let you go down for a day."

"I won't go for just a day," I said. (I will *never* know how that slipped out.)

"What?" said Neil.

"I need at least three days," I said. "One day could be terrible. Everything could go wrong."

Neil looked at me. "Okay," he said.

Right: Paul McCartney, John Lennon, and Yoko Ono in the studios at Twickenham.

Early the next morning I arrived at Twickenham. The Beatles were scheduled to be filming on the largest sound stage there, and it was daunting. To enter I had to pass through thick, heavy doors designed to keep all sound out, and which gave the impression that I was entering a vault. Above the door was a light and a sign that read, "DO NOT ENTER WHILE RED LIGHT IS ON." As with a vault, it's easy to feel that if you take a misstep an alarm will sound and a whole day's work will be ruined as all heads turn to look at you.

I pushed the door open very slowly, peeking through the crack. Inside, at what seemed a great distance away, was a raised platform on which sat Ringo's drums, surrounded by the amplifiers for John, Paul, and George. Lights were focused to highlight the platform; the rest of the stage drifted into darkness, seemingly endlessly. Around the stage were the cameras, and surrounding the cameras were the crew, cleaning lenses, loading film. Cables ran everywhere.

I slipped quietly through the door, closing it behind me, and stepped into the shadows to watch. Tony Richmond could be seen standing in center stage, his eyes cast toward the ceiling, issuing instructions to the invisible men on the catwalks above. Each day Tony planned to add a separate pool of color on the huge circular backdrop behind the stage.

There were no sets, no stage design beyond the Beatles' equipment, nothing particularly cinematic. There was no specific script for this movie. At the moment there was no title for it. There was only, somewhat, an idea for it, and the idea was that it would be a look at the Beatles making their new record.

Paul is first to arrive, wearing an overcoat and saying he took the bus (which somehow seemed unlikely). He walks over to someone who is reading an article about the Beatles from an English music paper. Paul reads over his shoulder. As John enters, Paul starts to read the article out loud, mimicking the writer.

Below left: Paul arriving at work. L. to r.: Tony Richmond, Ringo Starr, Linda Eastman, and Paul McCartney.

Below: Ringo and Paul.

Right: John arrives. "How long will they last?" reads Beatle Paul.

"Beatle John Lennon," reads Paul, "said today . . ."

John upgrades his entrance to that of the Hollywood star: throwing his head back, his arm straight at his side, hand parallel to the ground, mincing across the floor. Paul reads aloud: "How long will they last?" Everyone laughs.

The Beatles go to work. They play endless tunes, theirs and others. The presence of early American rock and roll is everywhere: "Stand By Me," "Blue Suede Shoes," "Johnny B. Goode," "Sweet Little Sixteen," "All Shook Up," "Don't Be Cruel," "Lucille," "Good Golly Miss Molly."

They consume cup after cup of tea. Piles of Styrofoam cups grow at people's feet.

I load my cameras and start to move around the stage, always shooting from the shadows.

Meanwhile, Michael Lindsay-Hogg sits in his director's chair on the edge of the stage. As the film is currently formless, Michael is pushing for an *event* to film, the big concert, some spectacular moment. Michael has to contend with four Beatles each with his own idea.

Paul seems to do the most talking, endlessly exhorting the rest of them to pull together.

Paul: "It's like when you're growing up and then your daddy goes away at a certain point in your life, and then you stand on your own feet. . . . It's discipline we need. . . . I think we need a bit more if we're going to get on with it."

George: "Well, if that's what doing it is, I don't want to do anything."

It soon becomes apparent that whoever was responsible for the film's shooting schedule didn't give much thought to the musicians' desires. Having to arrive at early hours and attempt to play music in a massive, cold sound stage has everyone edgy. Still, the film cameras never stop rolling, and, for three days, I take pictures.

When I pick up the pictures at the lab, I'm excited. (Of course, anything of the Beatles looks good to me.) Tony's pools of color show behind Paul's head, behind Ringo and his drums. One evening, I gather all my slides together and take them to Apple.

When I arrived to show my slides, Derek Taylor's press office was, as usual, swarming with people moving around with drinks in hand. Nobody would ever accuse the Apple press office of being stingy.

"Drink, Ethan?" said Derek. Derek Taylor was chief press officer for Apple and the Beatles. A slender man with a mustache, he moved with grace. He spoke very quickly, and had a professional charm that belied the fact that he also seemed to care.

I asked for a Scotch and Coke. That's what everyone seemed to drink at Apple, so that's what I had.

"Well, Ethan, you can see that there is no hope for you here," said Derek, indicating all the clusters of people. "Let's go down to Peter Brown's office."

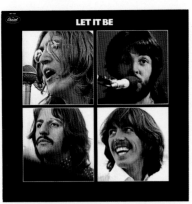

Above: The Let It Be *cover.*

Left (top to bottom): From the catwalks above the Twickenham stage. John Lennon. Glyn Johns and Paul McCartney. Paul.

Pages 104–107: The Beatles at Twickenham and Apple.

[103]

By comparison, Peter Brown's office was like a church. It was large with subdued lighting, quiet, and empty, with a huge portrait of John and Paul dominating one wall. (Peter Brown had been with Brian Epstein, as his personal assistant, from the very beginning. John Lennon was later to make him famous through the line "Peter Brown called to say you can make it okay / You can get married in Gibraltar, near Spain," from "The Ballad of John and Yoko.")

Derek went back upstairs as I unpacked the projector and all my slides, and set things up so that the projected images would fill one entire wall. I clicked through the first few. They looked good to me, so I turned off the machine and waited.

Derek opened the door and stuck his head in. "Listen, Ethan, I think John's in the building. Why don't you wait a minute?"

Peter Brown came in. He seemed a meticulous man, well dressed, and absolutely intent upon staying above the fray.

"Hello?" he said, not sure of who I was. I introduced myself and explained what I was doing there.

"Oh, good. Well, Paul will be coming in shortly. I'm sure he'd like to see them."

John and Paul? I hadn't expected that. Then Neil Aspinall comes in, accompanied by George, who is with an American singer and piano player, Billy Preston.

"What's going on, Ethan?" asks Neil. I explain. "Great," says Neil.

"Hi, Ethan," says George.

Paul comes in and enters into conversation with Peter Brown. The door opens and Derek walks in with John and Yoko. The room is filling up.

"Well, I heard it was all happening here," says Ringo, who is accompanied by Mal Evans, a large, friendly man, still the Beatles' "road manager," and known to Beatle fans the world over as the man in *Help!* who periodically emerges from the water and asks, "White cliffs of Dover?"

"You want to show us your pictures now, Ethan?" says Derek.

Image after image of the Beatles on the sound stage at Twickenham is projected, images where they are tiny in the space, images where John's (or Paul's, George's, Ringo's) face fills the wall. The show probably takes about twenty minutes. At the end, the lights are turned up.

"Those are nice," says someone.

"We oughtta do a book," says someone else, "and put it with the album." (With the album!? I think to myself.)

"Yeah. They're nice. Good work, Ethan."

And so it is decided that I will continue to work with them and that a book from the work will be made and that book will be released with the next Beatles album.

That all four Beatles converged on that one office that evening was a coincidence I never saw repeated. In all the months that follow I never again see John, Paul, George, and Ringo together except in front of the cameras filming *Let It Be.*

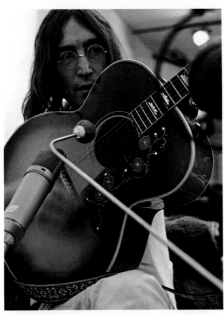

The cold, cavernous sound stage, the early mornings, the ever-present cameras, all prove to be too much. A quarrel between Paul and George breaks into the open.

"I'll play anything he [Paul] wants. I don't give a shit," lies George.

As Paul keeps after them all like a mother hen, it causes George to react: don't give me no more mother, mother.

George walks out and doesn't appear for several days. The quarrel makes the papers. Once again the English press whips itself into a frenzy. Did they come to blows? Are the Beatles breaking up? Who *is* that Japanese woman? Can this *really* be the end? While the Beatles go their separate ways, I go and visit my friends at the Rolling Stones' office.

[108]

There the battle rages over the album cover for *Beggar's Banquet*. Tom Wilkes in Los Angeles has produced the entire cover (titles, credits, everything) on a bathroom wall, and not the bathroom wall of your local hospital but the bathroom wall of some small border town where to sit on the seat is a triumph of personal courage. The walls are dirty yellow, grubby with graffiti. (Fortunately, Tom produced this package before "scratch 'n' sniff" was invented.)

The cover is foul, disgusting, humorous — the perfect package for the Rolling Stones. Decca, the Stones' record company, has refused to release it. It is in poor taste, they say, missing the point completely.

This is a battle the Stones are to lose. Whatever clout they can muster is ineffective. Decca refuses to budge. Soon the business of show asserts itself: the record must be released.

In bits and pieces word leaks out that "The Rolling Stones' Rock and Roll Circus" is not all that successful. In particular Mick is said not to be pleased with the Stones' performance. There is talk of a reshoot.

There is also talk (whispered, furtive) that Brian's drug habits have finally reached a stage where they impair his ability to function. Sometimes he fails even to show up. When he does, his performances can be erratic. Once the original motivator behind the Rolling Stones, Brian can no longer be counted on.

This is one kind of problem when it comes to the taping of a television show; however inconvenient, it can be shot again. It is more problematic when it comes to planning a lengthy tour to promote your record. And, in the end, the entire existence of the Rolling Stones rests on the success of their records.

I mostly hear about this later. At the time any mention of such a problem would have been much too sensitive to have filtered down to me. Still, there is no tour to promote *Beggar's Banquet*.

After the difficulties at Twickenham, the Beatles have decided to move the filming to the basement studio at Apple. In contrast to the Twickenham studio, with its reverberating acoustics (the province of filmmakers, not musicians), Apple is home. It is smaller, more intimate, carpeted.

Michael still has the same problem, though: "There's lots of good footage, but there's no story yet. There's no payoff yet."

He still wants to get the boys up to do something, deliver the grand performance in the grand locale. But the Beatles just will not move.

"It's either Tunisia or Tahiti or Tripoli," says Michael, urging them on.

Ringo: "What about Gibraltar?"

George (stonily): "You know it's just impractical to get all these people and equipment there."

Then Paul says, "Okay, yes, I'm sure we could set it up. . . . I'll tell you what, I'll come in with you as long as you get a couple of boats, like the QE2, and give away the tickets here. . . . Right! We get a nice time and a bit of sun."

Then John: "I just find a good feeling about singing in the sun, you know, and singing as the sun goes down and the moon comes up. It would be like on the roof in India, but we would be fully equipped, you know, just the sun."

Michael: "If you say yes and if we get it together, then will you go?"

John: "If we say yes to that, then don't bother about it. Let's leave it in the air and just think about it. . . . We can say yes now and suddenly decide no tomorrow. It's not going to make any odds. Let's just think about it."

"I'll be watching telly," says Ringo.

To which George remarks, "I think the idea of the boat is completely insane. It's very expensive and insane."

Personally, I'd hoped that Michael would get his way, for certainly he was correct: the camera liked to *look* at things. But there was to be no sunrise over the Sahara with Arabs and camels.

Paul again: "It hardly needs scenery. Really, it all should be about Ringo and his drum kit. . . . You can glide down from the roof to a one-shot of Ringo's face, being careful not to miss anything . . . like Warhol's things. Even a Tunisian amphitheater can be boring. I don't dig underestimating what's here."

Michael's hopes were just not to be. Perhaps in reaction to the fact that production had collapsed at Twickenham, and people feared a repeat, now it was grab-it-while-you-can. It came to pass that the farthest the Beatles would travel to do the show was upstairs to the roof of Apple.

On January 30, 1969, the Beatles performed together in public for the last time. It wasn't very public, really. They couldn't be seen from the street below, perched, as they were, on top of their own roof. People from adjoining buildings climbed onto their roofs and watched what was happening. In true British fashion, they seemed bemused. Savile Row was better known for its tailors.

The Beatles played "Get Back," "Don't Let Me Down," "One After 909," "I've Got a Feeling," and "All I Want Is You," all songs they had been rehearsing since Twickenham. On Savile Row a crowd started to gather, their necks craned upward, trying to catch a glimpse.

"Fabulous," says one girl. "Fantastic," says her friend.

"Bit of an imposition," says a merchant, "to interrupt all the businesses in the area."

An old fellow says: "Lovely crowd. Good quality. They sing well."

"Nice to have something for free in this country," says a minister.

Someone else calls the police.

I scrambled madly about the rooftop, changing angles, for if I was focused on Paul I would, of course, be missing John (and George and Ringo) and vice versa. It was a typically high-overcast, gray London day. In terms of photographic light, it was quite dull.

On the street below, the police arrive and are filmed as they consult with each other. Are they really supposed to arrest the Beatles? (By now the apparent sweetheart relationship between the Beatles and the British police has worn out. John has been busted in his flat and George is soon to be.)

But this time when the police get to the roof of Apple where the Beatles play overlooking the center of London, they take a wiser course: they do nothing. In a short time, the Beatles finish. John, ever debunking, walks to the mike. "On behalf of the group," he says, "I hope we passed the audition."

Above: the crowd gathered on Savile Row.

Left (l. to r.): Paul, Ringo, and John on the roof.

Above right: Brian Jones kicking the statue of Christopher Robin outside his house.

On July 3, 1969 — halfway through the last year of the decade that still promised to change the world — Brian Jones was found dead in the swimming pool at his home in Sussex. The coroner's report ruled it death by misadventure. That drugs were not somehow involved was inconceivable. It was just too easy to imagine the crown prince of stonedness, too drunk, too pilled, too fucked up, too many times.

But it was also an image that wouldn't come into focus, Brian drifting like an embryo in the pool at the back of the house where the statue of Christopher Robin could see it all, and, if there were any justice, somehow should have protected him.

Brian Jones's fans and friends and the people who worked with him cried. Brian was gone, and it was the first time in the age of nothing-you-can-do-that-can't-be-done that a face from the picture was irretrievably removed, so that no matter how you turned the picture to look at it, there was an empty space that could never be filled.

The law had been after Brian (as they had been after Mick and Keith). He had been arrested in May 1966 for possession of drugs shortly after the first raid on Keith's country home, Redlands. In October 1967, Brian was sentenced to nine months in prison. They released him pending an appeal. In May, he was arrested again for possessing cannabis. Twice during this time he was hospitalized for strain.

That these arrests bordered on persecution was supported by a London *Times* editorial relating to Mick Jagger's arrest. The *Times* says, "Has Mr. Jagger received the same treatment as he would have received if he were not a famous figure?" And they conclude that there is, at the very least, a "suspicion" that "Mr. Jagger received a more severe sentence than would have been thought proper for any purely anonymous young man."

Not long before his death, Brian quit the Rolling Stones. He could not have been happy to see the way things had turned out. The big problem for the Rolling Stones was, of course, that Brian could not tour because of his drug arrests. But all the people I know who knew the Rolling Stones since their early days say that Brian was the original mover, the one who motivated the group. Now Mick was emerging. It must have been uncomfortable.

It would take a long time for the fabric of hope and belief and commitment that came with music to unravel. It would be some time before the dissolution would be evident enough even to be acknowledged. Brian's death should have warned everybody, but it was seen as an aberration rather than a portent.

———◆———

I got a call that the new Rolling Stone was Mick Taylor and that they needed photographs for the press. Mick arrived at the rented studio and stayed as long as I kept shooting. That seemed to be the extent of his intended participation. Try as I might, I could evoke no apparent emotion, no reaction, no expression from him. It made me frantic. Ah, I thought, I'll smoke a joint, here, loosen things up. That's when I misplaced my camera. A Hasselblad with a motor-driven back is a sizable camera indeed. It must be twelve inches long (with a 150mm lens on it), and weigh at least seven pounds. But somehow I couldn't find it in this small studio out of which, I knew, I had not stepped. Mick Taylor waited patiently in front of the seamless paper, viewing all of this as if he had decided to stay at home and merely sent his likeness out to be photographed. The camera was eventually found (painfully long cannabis minutes later), having somehow slipped below the cushion of a massive, overstuffed chair. Now the long, blond wavy hair of Mick Taylor suddenly reminded me of Lady Clairol. Not much was accomplished that night. A photograph of a perfectly distant Mick Taylor was shortly released to the press.

———◆———

Now with Mick Taylor to perform with them the Stones announced a free concert to be given in London's Hyde Park. Granada Television would film. They asked me to do the photographs, and I arrived early at the home of John Shepherd, a slim and mustached Englishman who had spent a good deal of the last few years in Vietnam. (I could never understand why you would get near a place like Vietnam if you didn't have to, but John was one of those who seemed to like the aura attached to such assignments.) Mick Jagger was to meet us there.

John interviewed Mick while he sat in a high-backed wicker chair. Mick seemed fairly subdued. John's wife, Sonja, offered Mick some brownies, but he refused. Not Ethan, though. He ate two.

We left John's house and drove to the Londonderry Hotel, where the Stones had rented several suites that overlooked Hyde Park. There they changed before the concert. It was a beautiful day, and from the hotel windows you could see the crowds of people filtering into the park, the traffic swirling along Park Lane. It resembled the now-famous concerts in San Francisco's Golden Gate Park.

Above: Mick Taylor, the new Rolling Stone.

Right: One quarter of the crowd at the Rolling Stones' concert in Hyde Park.

[114]

It was when I became slightly fixated on the sunlight and the flow of traffic that I noticed that certain extension of time so characteristic of the cannabis plant, and it dawned on me that, of course, Sonja had spiked the brownies.

When the time comes to leave, the Stones exit the hotel and climb into the back of an armored van that is to deliver them to the stage. Once inside the van they are protected and invisible. We follow them in a car. As we drive into the park, the number of people starts to increase, slowly at first, and then more rapidly until the car starts to plow through them like a boat through water and (in my increasing stonedness) they seem to part like a school of fish in front of a diver. As the crowd gets denser and denser, people look around and, seeing this armored van followed by a carful of press, say, "Are the Stones in there? I'll bet the Stones are in there." And the crowd starts to push toward it. But by this time, the van has found its way through the fence surrounding backstage and safely deposited the Stones.

Now the noise and confusion of a rock and roll concert (my first at such close proximity to the stage) is apparent. Towers of speakers. Fences. People milling around, an expectant intensity in the air.

I peek around the corner of the stage. Where yesterday there had been the expanse of Hyde Park, now there are nothing but people filling in the natural amphitheater as far as you can see. Two hundred fifty thousand have come to see the Rolling Stones on this beautiful summer day. I start to move around and take pictures of the crowd. As if in carbon copy of the San Francisco concerts, a group of Hell's Angels are parked near the stage. As I walk over to them, they can be seen to be very young teenagers. One of them removes a long-haired wig, revealing his short haircut underneath. I find this so bizarre that I ask him to repeat it for the camera, which he gladly does.

On stage Sam Cutler, a cockney (who will later be hired by the Stones to assist on the '69 U.S. tour), walks to the microphone. His eyes are covered by sunglasses; a bandanna is around his head. "And now," he says, "the group you've all been waiting for — *the Rolling Stones!*"

Mick, Keith, Charlie, Bill, and the new one, Mick Taylor, come out on stage. Brian's death is on everyone's mind. Mick pauses and asks for silence. He quotes Shelley: "Peace, peace! he is not dead, he doth not sleep — He hath awakened from the dream of life." So, Mick, no doubt unwittingly, reinforces the reluctance on all our parts to coldly realize that Brian was now a dead person, a stiff. The one thing we didn't want to admit, and didn't.

Then a swarm of white butterflies is released. They have been kept in small cardboard boxes that they seem disinclined to leave, so that they have to be shaken out by various handlers; and they then, for the most part, settle on what is nearest — the stage, the amplifiers, the curtains — somehow not living up to the expected image of a cloud of white butterflies. Nevertheless, it is still a moving gesture.

I am taken to the side of the stage and hoisted up one of the towers. It is jammed with other journalists, the film crew, and assorted friends. There is no room to move at all. From where I am I cannot get a decent angle from which to photograph, and the constant shoving and squeezing makes me claustrophobic.

On stage Mick is dancing and singing, wearing a white costume with an almost medieval skirt. (The next day the stories of the concert read as much like a fashion report as a rock and roll review.) Toward the end of the show, they break into "Sympathy for the Devil." Rocky, the percussionist, beats the tall bongos as Mick yelps into the mike, "Please allow me to introduce myself. I'm a man of wealth and taste. . . ."

From the edges of the stage emerge dancing black men, their bodies covered in paint, wearing grass shirts and carrying spears, moving their arms in a motion like a tarantula taking steps. In the warm and very benign sunlight, in London's very civilized Hyde Park, the effect to me is hilarious even in my stoned and paranoid state. They seem like the caricatured bush Negroes of "Doctor Livingstone, I presume?" — an Englishman's vision of what darkest Africa was like when most of it was still an English protectorate.

To an American, these onstage black "savages" and the English Hell's Angels appear somewhat like Saturday morning cartoon villains. They are manifestly *not* dangerous. An American knows that in the wrong situation, both can be life-threatening. The English always think the American is either paranoid or prejudiced, since the threat is not perceived by them. Paul McCartney, for example, once decided to visit Harlem when he was in New York. "Hi. Do you know me? I wrote 'Yesterday'?" I read that, in no uncertain terms, he was immediately requested to leave.

"I stuck around St. Petersburg when I saw it was a time for a change," sings Mick. "I rode a tank, held a general's rank, when the blitzkrieg raged and the bodies stank," he continues, associating himself with the Devil, dancing across the stage.

Though these songs are dark portraits, they are not autobiographies. But 1969 is the time of the singer-songwriter. People have come to expect that they are speaking of themselves. Back in America, where one pill makes you larger and the other makes you small, people are not making any subtle distinctions.

———◆———

EMI refused to distribute John and Yoko's first album, *Two Virgins,* because the cover displayed a photograph of John and Yoko, nude, from the front. John called me because he associated me with *Rolling Stone,* and I sent the photo off to San Francisco. Jann Wenner promptly placed it on his cover.

When asked about how he would handle the reaction, John said, "Well, you know, sooner or later they're just gonna have to see it's just us, y'know, and lay off."

———◆———

It was to Derek Taylor's press office at Apple that, sooner or later, most of the madness made its way. Unlike all the others at Apple, Derek was required to maintain a

Above: One of the dancing black men who emerged during "Sympathy for the Devil."

Middle: Mick dancing.

Right: Derek Taylor, chief press officer for Apple Corp.

dialogue with the outside world, or at least with the press, which purported to represent the public at large. And though at times you could see through the weariness on Derek's face that he sometimes wished he were using his not inconsiderable skills to stay home and write a novel, Derek was still a believer. He hoped that the experiment of the Beatles, called Apple, would be a big success and that John's words would be vindicated and that people would not have to arrive on their knees. If that meant having to be patient with a lot of wide-eyed hopefuls until their schemes could be heard, then Derek would do his best. Practically, this meant that the press office was almost always a jumble of bodies, with Derek reigning from his large high-backed white wicker chair as he entertained one group of people (a columnist, or a manager, or Mary Hopkin's uncle) while others waited.

It got so I used to go into Apple almost every day, even after the filming at Twickenham had stopped. In the press office I met Richard DiLello, an American from Brooklyn whose hair sprouted in a massive circle around his head. Richard had stumbled upon his job as Derek's assistant much as I had upon mine. From his vantage point of a desk in the corner he watched as the schemers and dreamers laid out their plans in front of Derek. Richard's New Yorker's sense of remove was frequently amplified by that certain distance hashish can provide.★

In the press office all was ebb and flow. There was always a Scotch and Coke, or a hashish and tobacco bomber joint, usually rolled and smoked in the back room where films and tapes were stored. That's where Stocky lived.

Stocky was one of the many who had originally arrived at Apple with a book of poems and drawings and a heartful of hope. When Stocky was told there was no such animal as Apple Press, he still managed to talk his way in, and, once there, he hung out in the back room, bothering nobody, smoking quite a lot of dope. He would help out if asked, but he didn't seem overly anxious whether he did or not, was noticed or not. His most frequent position was on top of a row of file cabinets where he sat cross-legged. Then one day, having disappeared into the back room for a hit or two, I noticed that Stocky was gone. "He decided to go back to Boston" was the only explanation I received.

As could have been expected, Apple became the focal point of a lot of earnest people: some who wished to strike it rich, some who just wanted to be near it, some who wanted to judge it and see it fail. From San Francisco came many who thought they inhabited the same cosmic warp as the Beatles, individually and collectively. The common thread seemed to be the consumption of formidable quantities of LSD. When the inspirational acid dreams collided with the reality that Apple was, principally, a record company (albeit an experimental one), there were a lot of disappointed people, among them the Hell's Angels.

★Richard wrote a book, in many ways the best book about Apple, called *The Longest Cocktail Party: An Insider's View of the Beatles.* Chicago: Playboy Paperbacks, 1972.

An offhand invitation issued by George Harrison on a trip to San Francisco had resulted in the arrival at British customs of a couple of Hell's Angels, their old ladies, and their bikes. With amazing hospitality, Derek and the press office helped ease their entry, and shortly they arrived at Apple where they camped for two weeks, checking it out. True to form, they stormed and ranted if they weren't fed when they wanted to be, and generally kept people in a state of expectant anxiety as long as they were about. It was a situation that had to be ended.

Richard DiLello's book describes this scene: George Harrison walks into the room, says, "Hello, everyone," and asks, "Well, are you moving your stuff out of here tonight?"

The question provokes the obvious reaction: shocked silence and immediate hostility. Such a question directed at a Hell's Angel becomes an invitation to a knife fight.

A Hell's Angel known as Spider gets up and moves aside his old lady, who stands between him and George Harrison, and walks forward until he stands within inches of Harrison.

"Hey, man," says Spider. "I just wanna ask one question. Do you dig us or don't you?"

"Yin and yang, heads and tails, yes and no," replies George.

(Your outside is in. Your inside is out. I am he, as you are me, as we are all together. I say "hello" and you say "good-bye.") It is the perfect answer.

Spider says, "All right, man, I can dig it. We'll be outta here in ten minutes."

George turns and leaves. "Good-bye, everyone," he says.

"Gosh, he sure is beautiful," whispers one girl.

"Shut the fuck up, you asshole," says another.

◆

The concert on the roof ended the filming of *Let It Be*. I continued to work on the book with the designer, John Kosh, who had been suggested by Lennon. The day-to-day progress is marked by the London winter, cold, wet days blowing just outside the door.

I asked Jonathan Cott and David Dalton (still *another* American living in London, who had written a piece on the Rolling Stones' circus) to write the text. They would spend months going through the tapes, trying to decipher the unintelligibles.

At one time or another, I also photographed the rest of the Apple roster.

Mary Hopkin, the young discovery from Wales, was as sweet as she was reputed to be, though with a certain wariness. Probably no entertainer had been as repeatedly warned of the wicked, wicked ways of show biz as Mary was by her parents. Her song "Those Were the Days (My Friend)," produced by Paul McCartney, had sent her to the top of the British charts and made her famous across the Atlantic as well. She was one of Apple's first successes when most felt that everything Apple touched would turn to gold. We spent three days photographing around the southeastern re-

sort town of St. Ives. Around the time I was photographing Mary I was listening over and over to the strains of "Blue," by a new Canadian-American singer, Joni Mitchell. More powerful music from across the water.

Jackie Lomax waited expectantly for his star to rise along with Mary's. He had been in show business for some time, now; a Liverpudlian, he had been there when the Beatles were breaking. Now he had everything: one of the first to be signed on the Beatles' new label, an album produced by a Beatle (George), an intense public relations push. But it wasn't to happen. His first album just didn't catch on. Our work together was tinged with his determination that, at all costs, whatever he did now must be striking.

My work never satisfied him, and one day I saw him speaking with Justin (of Justin and Twiggy fame). Justin was Twiggy's manager and now was about to take on Jackie. They were holding in front of them a black and white photo of Jackie with his shirt off, his hair flowing, his eyes gazing into the distance. It was the end result of a process designed to glamorize, as it had countless models. Holding the print at a certain angle, I could see the marks of a knife that had been used to scrape away any minor blemishes on Jackie's skin so that he was left with a marblelike complexion. All in all, the photograph they held of Jackie was a very reasonable approximation of a young Greek god.

Actually I was quite impressed. That Justin had the manners of a petty criminal was a bit off-putting, but the image of Jackie was so cleverly created to drive young girls to distraction that you had to hope it would do the trick.

————◆————

The Rhada Krishna Temple was the name given to a group of chanting Hare Krishnas. George Harrison was producing them. Dressed in flowing orange robes, their heads clean-shaven, a stripe of paint over the bridge of the nose, they (or others like them) could often be seen on Oxford Street or Regent Street, small cymbals attached to their fingers, chanting endlessly the strains of "Hare Krishna," hoping for donations. I took them into a massive advertising studio in central London where they were surrounded by lights and stylists. They were pleasant but anxious. If the situation surrounding them became too tense, they would break into chanting, for all the world like primitives trying to dispel a demon. The chanting sounded good as it echoed through the huge space. They seemed prepared for an underlying hostility, but I liked them. Not surprisingly, it turned out most of them were American.

————◆————

Billy Preston just seemed happy to be there. Having showed up one day at the *Let It Be* sessions with George, he had played on the Beatles' album, and was now signed to Apple Records. Like Jackie, he, too, felt his star to be rising. Fortunately, he was right.

To be honest, I sort of felt *my* star was rising as well. After all, wasn't I now the photographer of the Beatles *and* the Stones? Wasn't my "record" (the Beatles' *Let It Be* book, the Rolling Stones' circus book) about to be released? It was sure to be a hit.

I went out and bought myself a fur coat. My hair was growing down my neck. I bought bright yellow pants and wide-lapel jackets, certain never to be run down at

Above left: Jackie Lomax.

Below: The author with bouffant hairdo in the Apple studio.

night. Surely my proximity to the stars made me somewhat lustrous as a result? If I was not a star, I was at least a moon, reflecting back the brilliance of those stars nearby. Of course, there were a lot of other moons floating about.

Everybody was a star at Apple, or thought they were. The receptionist would have been a star to the person who waited on the street outside. Of course there were stars and stars. Truly, a Beatle was a star. And Neil Aspinall, Peter Brown, Derek Taylor, Mal Evans — they were (somewhat lesser) stars, too, having been around so long. There were (even lesser) stars: Jack Oliver and Tony Bramwell. As they shared less in the light, they could be a little uptight, carefully nudging others aside lest there not be enough light to go around.

It is the constant tug of war that surrounds the rich, powerful, and famous. The principals are the flame and the hangers-on become a series of frantic moths circling about.

It took John Lennon to bring us back to our senses, many years later, singing, "Who in the world do you think you are, a superstar? Well, right you are. / But we all shine on, like the moon and the stars and the sun." All of us. Remember?

When Allen Klein's name was first mentioned in the back rooms of Apple, people reacted as if they'd just been told they had terminal cancer. Some said Klein was the cancer. Klein said the cancer was already there, and he was the surgeon.

Allen Klein had been photographed while holding a shotgun aimed directly at camera. He was an American businessman, but he spoke like a gangster. He was medium height with dark hair, and had a belly that hung over his belt like a southern cop. He had a reputation for being very tough. Additionally, he was the manager of the Rolling Stones. In pop Beatlespeak of the time, Allen Klein was to "Blue Meanie" what "Blue Meanie" was to "Girl Scout."

When Allen Klein took over as the Beatles' manager, he went from being notorious to famous. As a result, he was interviewed by *Playboy* magazine. He said the secret to his success was that when he got angry he would count to three before losing his temper.

I was more familiar than most at Apple with Allen Klein, since I also worked with the Rolling Stones. I knew that it could take a very long time to get paid by Allen Klein.

Klein was reputed to be "John's friend" because Klein was said to have convinced John (who *would* take a liking to people) that he, like John, was "working class," and like John an "orphan."

Paul McCartney was "Klein's enemy," perhaps because he really thought Klein was "working class," when he, McCartney, was "middle class" (the English class system). Or perhaps McCartney thought that Allen Klein really was criminal because McCartney's wife, Linda Eastman, came from a family of New York attorneys who purported to be certain that Allen Klein was a criminal. Whatever it was, Paul McCartney wanted nothing to do with Allen Klein, who wanted to represent the Beatles, even though Paul McCartney was of course one-quarter of the Beatles, and Allen Klein couldn't represent the Beatles without him.

Perhaps because the other three Beatles felt that Paul was trying to take over the group, because they sometimes felt that they were becoming Paul's sidemen and couldn't get their own songs on the album, the other Beatles said: "Hey, we all want to go with this, and we're three-quarters. Why don't you go along?"

The story was in the English papers every day: how Allen Klein wanted to take over the Beatles and make them solvent again by renegotiating their deals with EMI and Northern Songs. John Lennon said that the way things were going with Apple, they (the Beatles) would soon be broke.

This is the story I heard: Allen Klein came over to England determined to take over the management of the Beatles. He convinced John that he was the man. After John, George and Ringo followed.

Only Paul refused to sign. However many phone calls, however many meetings, Paul would not sign. Finally Klein gives up. He says he is going back to America. That night the Beatles gather in a recording studio. It seems inconceivable that McCartney is not greatly relieved that the pressure is finally off. Maybe now they can settle down, make some music, talk about things more calmly. At that moment,

Klein walks in. He sits down with Paul and, as the others look on, talks to him until dawn. Paul gives in, and Klein gets the Beatles. Perhaps this story is false. It is the story I heard, and it sounds true.★

◆

I ended up taking the single-sleeve photo for the Rolling Stones' "Honky Tonk Woman" because the original photographer kept casting these thin, elegant dolly birds for the ladies of the night when Mick wanted funk. Funk was among my capabilities.

Immediately, I started pounding the pavement in Soho, London's center for Italian restaurants and strip joints, but when I mentioned that I wanted a couple of strippers to photograph, I got continued variations of "Not on your life, mate."

It was hard to understand this modesty on the part of the ladies who pranced the stage clad only in garter belts, exhorting customers to throw money at them, but such seemed to be the case. I was finally told of two singers, not strippers, one black and one white, who worked in a club up in Camden Town. Coffee and Cream, they called themselves.

Camden Town is principally a residential working-class section of North London. The club where Coffee and Cream played was known mostly for its female impersonators. (It is a vagary of the British character that robust heterosexuals are heartily entertained by the sight of a grown man in full make-up, bumping and grinding across the stage. "Take it all off, ducky," they shout. Nudge, nudge. It is a vagary of the American character that such a spectacle used to be considered totally depraved. What was it that caused the American male adult to go into such a frenzy at the sight of long hair on men?)

Coffee and Cream were the straight act in this club. From the minute I saw them, I knew they were it. Cream was fat, double-chinned, with pasty skin. Her hair was ratted, peroxided blond, and her teeth were crooked and seldom brushed. Coffee wasn't half bad, either. I took Polaroids of them to Mick. He agreed.

Again I went back to the streets of Soho, searching for a club in which to shoot. "Cash in advance," they would say. "And not a word about it, eh mate?"

The Rolling Stones, in the tradition of their singles' covers, are all to be in costume. Mick's a sailor, Bill's a cop. Keith is a gangster passing money to the cop. Mick Taylor is the bartender with a charcoal mustache. And Charlie? Charlie's a gentleman drummer who lives in Sussex.

As usual, I'm nervous. Adjusting lights, I burn my fingers. Coffee and Cream walk through the door.

I soon realize that, coward that I am, I have failed to impart to them the true

★Peter Brown, in his book *The Love You Make* (New York: McGraw-Hill, 1983), insists McCartney never actually signed anything, despite the fact that he posed for photographs with the other Beatles and Allen Klein documenting the (now-alleged) signing.

reason they were chosen, and they have come sporting their very finest uptown clothes. After all, they are in show business, too, and this may be their big break.

Frantically I paw through the extra clothes they brought with them, trying to find something more suitable. "No, no. That's not quite it. What else have you got?" Trying to find something more outrageous, more grotesque.

The Stones arrive and Mick catches a quick glimpse of Coffee and Cream and folds over with laughter. They neither see nor hear this, and Mick quickly pulls himself together. He walks up to them and introduces himself, every bit the gentleman. Bill and Keith smile.

After the Stones have changed and the lights are set, I start to photograph. Mick walks gingerly up to Cream and, with great politesse, puts his arm around her. It is the high point of Cream's life, and she glows. Next to her sits Coffee, demure, as if she were in a church. I click away as Bill and Keith exchange money and pour each other drinks. The young Mick Taylor takes a towel and wipes the bar.

Though this is supposed to be Grunge City, the girls are having the time of their lives, it is too late to totally re-outfit them, and the photographer doesn't want to spoil their day.

In the end it plays, if only because the idea was so outrageous to begin with.

"I met a gin-soaked barroom queen in Memphis," goes the lyric. "I thought I'd take her upstairs for a ride . . ."

◆

Above left: An outtake from the "Honky Tonk Woman" session.

Below: The sleeve.

Pages 126–127: The Beatles from the last session at John's house. The breakup followed shortly.

About this time I had a strange feeling: I started to miss America. This came as somewhat of a surprise, for when I left America "never" would have been my guess as to when I'd return. In my early days in England, I had even thought about becoming a British citizen.

All my reasons for wanting to visit America again were emotional, of course. I still loved London, its parks and eccentricities. I loved the smell of the coffee shop up the block when it roasted coffee every Thursday morning. I loved pubs and English beer. I loved the English summer with its green hills, blue skies, and clouds. I liked the spring and fall, when the weather would change fifteen times a day, from overcast to brilliant sun breaking through clouds that would race across the sky, to hail, to sun, and back to overcast. Even the winter didn't bother me all that much.

The English had been good to me, but, in 1969, there were an awful lot of Americans in London, and I found that it was really the Americans who became my friends. It was terrific to go to an Englishman's home and eat overcooked roast beef and Yorkshire pud, Brussels sprouts and suet; it was just that in the end, it was like eating Japanese food every day, somehow foreign. And though the English were unfailingly polite and friendly, you had only to hear them speak about the Italians to understand that for them as well, all foreigners would be forever foreign ("You're a Yank, ain't ya?"). To an Englishman, a Yank and an Italian were more alike than not.

◆

Neil Aspinall had called, the Beatles needed another photo session, and I immediately started ambitious plans for the shoot. I recalled the many sessions with the Beatles that had become famous, and how I felt about them when I first saw them: the *Sgt. Pepper* photos, the Richard Avedon sessions. Every time you saw a new photograph of the Beatles, it would be as if a new era had been entered.

I intended to do a simple portrait, but also I wanted to get a background of clouds painted and photograph the Beatles floating in front of it. I looked into painters, the hiring of trampolines. I worked overtime to try to select the right images and the right ideas for the session. The studio I had booked, one of the largest in London, was buzzing in anticipation when Neil called and canceled. The session would be moved to John's house.

Since the photos of John and Yoko in the black capes taken at John's "mock-Tudor shithouse," John had moved. Now he and Yoko were bouncing around in a large white house, almost empty of furniture. In one room there was just the white piano where John would write "Imagine."

I got there before Paul, George, and Ringo, so I strolled around the grounds. In the back near the main house was a carriage house and outside it were stone statues, replicas of Sgt. Pepper and his Victorian friends.

Shortly the rest of the Beatles arrive, and we start to walk around together. I am not the only person with a camera. Neil has decided that a photographer from the

Daily Mirror will accompany us, as well as Mal Evans, also taking pictures. The Beatles, who don't seem much interested in this event anyway, don't have one person to focus on, and it is difficult to organize them for a shot.

John now looks like a cross between Fidel Castro and a Mexican bandito, wearing a full beard, dressed all in black, with a flat-brimmed Spanish hat and a wide leather belt around his waist.

Walking along with John, I compliment him on his new house. "Nice move," I say, innocuously.

"Yeah. Checkmate," says John with a wit that could cut you in half.

All the Beatles have changed since I last saw them. During *Let It Be* Paul had the full beard. Now Paul is clean-shaven, and John, George, and Ringo are bearded.

We all walked around the grounds together, the five of them (counting Yoko), Mal, the *Daily Mirror* photographer, and my assistant and me. There was no energy and no direction from anyone. Here they are standing in a field looking bored, here they are standing under a tree looking bored. Finally, I had them stand in front of the carriage house with the Sgt. Pepper statues, looking bored.

Who knew if they knew then they were about to break up? Only they knew what kind of bad blood was spilt during the Allen Klein negotiations. And, really, why did John insist on having Yoko with him all the time? If John brought Yoko, then would Paul bring Linda?

"Are you and Linda going to be another John and Yoko?" Paul asks himself in the liner notes on his first solo album. "No. We'll be Paul and Linda," he answers.

I knew I was shortly going to leave for America, and who knew what would happen then. I whispered to Mal, maybe he would take a photograph of the Beatles and me. Mal said okay, but then I lost heart. Everybody seemed to be having such a boring time anyway.

When the session was finished (the four of them in front of the carriage house ended up on their *Hey Jude — Greatest Hits* album), I said good-bye to everybody.

"Have a good time in America, Ethan."

"Thanks for everything, mate."

"Yeah. See ya."

Right: John's lyric sheet from the Twickenham stage for "Don't Let Me Down."

Below: Hey Jude, *the album cover that came from the last session.*

Overleaf: The last time I saw the Beatles working together, in the basement studio of Apple at the end of filming Let It Be.

When it was announced that the Beatles were breaking up, it caused a great sadness to a great many people. As only music can (*especially* our age of music), the Beatles' songs had marked the times through which we had passed. The Beatles had written and performed so many songs that there was always one that would remind you of something, help you out, or give you hope. Upon hearing of the breakup of the Beatles, the BBC disc jockey played "We Can Work It Out." That's what he wanted to accept. George was singing "Here Comes the Sun" on their last record, but *All Things Must Pass* became the title of his first solo album.

Now everyone had to get used to the idea that there were to be no more Beatles. As individuals they say over and over again that there are no more Beatles. ("I don't believe in Beatles," sings John, "I just believe in me.") And over and over again, people will refuse to accept it. In 1984, four years after John Lennon is shot and killed, the rest of them (George, Paul, Ringo, and now Yoko) gather in London to discuss the dissolution of Apple. An English reporter asks, "Are the Beatles going to get together again?" ⚓

CHAPTER

12

CALIFORNIA, 1969.

The blue sky stretched overhead, cloud free as far as you could see. Below, the gray freeway — even *that* seemed empty after England — stretched out for what seemed like forever: the combination made it seem like being inside some huge empty vault.

Day after day the sky was blue. It seemed eerie at first. Four days after arriving back, I traveled to Big Sur. I woke up the following morning to see dense fog that had rolled in off the ocean, covering the hills, obscuring everything. People put on jackets, pulling them closed against the chill. A friend arrives in a jeep, excited, saying, "Come with me." Five of us pile in, and we drive down the coast, small glimpses of the ocean appearing below us. The jeep turns off the road onto a dirt track and starts to head up into the hills, through the redwoods, past cabins with gardens, clotheslines. Handwoven God's eyes hang on the porches. The cabins are occupied by long-hairs who have chosen to live in the back woods, to grow their own food (and dope). The jeep climbs past them, driving farther up the mountain.

As we gain elevation, the fog starts to thin, the redwoods are below us, and the vegetation changes — becomes California oak, madrone, poison oak, and brown, dry grass. The jeep climbs over a ridge, out into brilliant sunshine. Below, the coastline is covered with an endless layer of fog. "Here, take this," says my friend and hands me a piece of broken glass. He takes out a candle and lights it. "Hold the glass over the flame, like this." He tilts the candle, causing it to smoke, and the glass darkens with the smudge.

"Now look at the sun."

The smoked glass becomes an even darker, improvised sunglass.

"There's a solar eclipse in an hour," he says, smiling.

On top of the hill, it is utterly quiet. Periodically hawks swoop out from the trees and arc below us, drifting down toward the fog. In an hour, we are all peering through smoked glass, our necks craned, as the moon passes slowly in front of the sun. When the eclipse becomes total, it is suddenly darker and cooler, but then warms again quickly after the moon passes by. California Dreaming. There really is nothing like it.

———◆———

In San Francisco on the radio they're playing "Honky Tonk Woman," with the distinctive cowbell beginning, the drum intro, with the guitar coming in chunk, chunk-chunk, low down and dirty, and I feel proud that I was involved. When I first hear

Below: Keith Richards in Stephen Stills's house. The beginning of the U.S. tour, Los Angeles, 1969.

this I am waiting for my mother to come out of a Western Union office where she has just wired money to one of her children.

◆

Back in America, 1969. When the year began, the American troop strength in Vietnam was reaching its peak: 550,000 men. Thirty thousand Americans had been killed and more than 20,000 others would be. In the previous year, Martin Luther King, Jr., and Bobby Kennedy had both been assassinated. The Chicago Democratic National Convention had seen rioting in the streets, complete with police clubbings and gassings. The turmoil no doubt helped Richard Nixon become the next president of the United States.

Music and politics, once joined in a common cause, were diverging. Politics had become confrontational. If you were committed to it, sooner or later you would find yourself on the street. And the street was getting uglier and uglier. Music didn't require confrontation. If you were in tune with what music meant, you took it easy, stayed laid back. The politicos would insist that if you were not part of the solution, you were part of the problem, but the zapped-out would suggest that that was doublespeak. If you were "good energy," then that, like karma, would translate itself into the common good. Besides, music was still the best time around.

It spawned the festival at Woodstock, where the up-and-coming, down-and-out, long-haired, freaky, and high, all showed up and for four days camped outside and listened to the music. Except for the Big Three (Dylan, the Stones, the Beatles), everyone who was anyone in music went to Woodstock. And if Dylan was not there, he was amply represented by the Band, whose lyrics and delivery displayed the same worldly hipness as Dylan.

The Who were there, along with Crosby, Stills and Nash, Joan Baez, Jimi Hendrix, Joni Mitchell, John Sebastian, Sly Stone, Country Joe and the Fish. But mostly, of course, *we* were there, newly visible. "Wow, look at you," went one performer after another. "You're beautiful. *We're* beautiful."

Someone then coined the phrase "Woodstock Nation" for all these scrubless hairies, and a helicopter shot shows the "nation" at its first convention, spread out over the fields, impervious to the rain and mud. Periodic announcements from the stage would deliver reports of lost children, warn people of "bad acid," the housekeeping chores of the nation. The *New York Times,* reacting to the mud and mire, would ask, "What kind of culture is it that can produce so colossal a mess?" We called it "getting it together." We were proud.

"Hey, it happened, didn't it? Nobody got hurt, did they?"

"That's a half a million people, man. No fucking police or anything."

"It was a good time. All right, man?"

People still believed that music was going to change the world.

Woodstock became the fifth largest grossing music film (through 1980 the figure was $16,200,000) and it still sells, played back via videocassette in living rooms across the country: four days with the freaks on parade.

At the close of the festival, we saw a subdued Jimi Hendrix, intensely concentrating, perform a solo rendition of "The Star-Spangled Banner" on electric guitar, single notes arcing into feedback, howling, crackling with the noise of all that amplified electricity. The old anthem newly played for the half a million gathered, and for all the filmgoers thereafter. Jimi Hendrix, a black, psychedelic star for the Woodstock Nation, will die from a drug overdose the following year, 1970.

———— ◆ ————

Drugs. With America tearing itself apart, split down the middle about everything, everybody pointing a finger at everybody else, there was no way anyone in the counterculture was about to admit that drugs were a problem. Drugs were what first turned a lot of people on. The nightmare consequences of marijuana as conjured up by such unforgettable phrases as "killer weed" and (a 1930s movie) *Reefer Madness* became part of our disdain for all drug-related information that had been passed down to us. The red-eyed, zapped-out grass smoker became an affectionate member of R. Crumb's cartoon populace. (Flies buzzing around their heads, all the women with mammoth breasts and jutting buttocks, all lusting after each other all the time. And Mr. Natural, white-bearded guru for the kids, on the make himself. "What's it mean, Mr. Natural?" "Don' mean sheit.") Or a strip from London's *OZ* magazine: a longhair walking down the street, a bubble emanating from his head. The bubble is full of swirls and crescent moons, lizards and stars. The long-hair spots a cop across the street, and suddenly the bubble retracts into his head, like toothpaste back into a tube, until the cop passes, and then once again, his eyes popping out, the long-hair's manic visions sprawl as a smile creeps across his face.

Or, even later, Zonker Harris from "Doonesbury": gentle Zonker who likes to talk to his plants and play submarine captain submerged under the surface of Walden Pond. Zonker who is not at all ambitious, just wants some peace and quiet, and a reasonable life in the country.

Of course, there were drugs and then there were drugs. The palette of available drugs had been considerably expanded since the early days of a little marijuana and some LSD. Now there was speed that would keep you awake all night, keep you talking, talking. And there was angel dust — what a name — which turned out to be something derived from animal tranquilizers. There was heroin, too. With heroin came the syringes that would also be used to inject Methedrine.

A drive down Haight Street was not what it used to be. From the explosion of wide-eyed kids, a certain desperate edge had crept in. Now people would watch you very closely as you walked along, looking to see if you wanted to score, or if you were a narc. And there was unquestionably the vibe, as people would say then, that whatever lay behind all this, it no longer had anyone's best interests in mind.

Still, hard drugs were a rarity. That they were there at all was probably because no one believed (like marijuana, like — not too much — LSD) they could really hurt us. We were "sunlight," we were "golden," sang Joni Mitchell about Woodstock.

◆

I went to see *Easy Rider*. Two freaks (Dennis Hopper, Peter Fonda) decide to go to New Orleans for the Mardi Gras on their motorcycles. They meet Jack Nicholson along the way. They take some acid before they go to the Mardi Gras, but not much happens. At the end of the movie, Dennis Hopper is riding his motorcycle by himself when he is passed by two southern good ol' boys (driving a pickup, shotguns on their rack) who yell out at him: "Get a haircut." Hopper gives them the finger.

In a long-shot that includes the motorcycle and the pickup, a gun barrel protrudes and then there's an explosion of flame as the shotgun blows away Hopper and his motorcycle, the explosion echoing through the theater as bits and pieces of the flaming motorcycle fall earthward and drop on the road. As the pickup drives away, the movie ends.

"What the *fuck* do they wanna do that for?" I ask. "Now *I* want to go out and blow up some motherfucker for blowing him up. What the fuck good does it do? It just makes people crazy, that's what it does. It just polarizes people. It's fucking insane." I holler this into the San Francisco night, and my friends look at me strangely. But now I look around me, wondering where the next crazy bastard with a shotgun is. Paranoid again.

In England I had learned to like waking up in the morning without having to wonder whether someone was going to take a shot at me as I walked down the street, or whether some friend was going to be drafted, or whether some other friend was going to o.d. America, 1969. Too goddamn intense.

Above left: Mick Taylor.

Right: Mick Jagger's suitcase photographed as a possible cover for the live album. It couldn't be used because I stuck the joint in the hat brim, insensitive to the Stones' visa problems. "Didn't you shoot any *without it?" asked Mick in a pained voice.*

Overleaf: Mick on stage, Oakland, California, 1969.

In November 1969 the Rolling Stones arrive in America to begin their first U.S. tour since 1966. In Los Angeles, they set up camp, rehearsing during the day, at night retiring to houses high in the hills. Nobody really knows what this tour is going to be like. A lot has changed since 1966 when the Stones were staring out at crew-cutted American boys with their Sandra Dee girlfriends. In true show business style, the Stones are opening out of town.

It's a two-hour drive through the high plains of Colorado east of the Rocky Mountains to get from the Denver airport to the college town of Fort Collins. The Stones are to play the gym, and as we all arrive for the sound check that afternoon, the few students who are hanging around stare at Mick and the others as if they were some alien life form. Mick is aware of the eyes upon him, and every so often he'll just do something, jiggle his ass, or smile. Something, some little piece of shtick, just to let them know he knows they're watching, or maybe just to brush up on his licks.

That night the hall is packed, the kids have waited through the opening acts, and Sam Cutler, who performed the same duty at Hyde Park, comes on stage and delivers the line he will deliver again and again for the rest of the tour: "Ladies and Gentlemen, let's welcome the GREATEST ROCK 'N' ROLL BAND IN THE WORLD!" The band races out and launches into the first number with every intention of being exactly that. The rush is intense, and the audience is immediately on its feet, arms waving. It certainly seems as if America is glad to have them back.

Back in L.A., the Dupont house perches on the very top of a hill overlooking the endless panorama of streets and houses that make up the L.A. basin. This is where I stay with Jo Bergman, Stanley Booth (who by now is embroiled in a fifteen-year odyssey of work on his history of the Stones, *Dance with the Devil*), Charlie Watts, and his wife, Shirley. The house, which is being rented for some enormous sum, is a pretty good example of upscale L.A. tacky. It is all view. The wall facing the vista is covered in mirrors so that it, too, reflects the view. The mirror is smoked glass with gilt veins so that the reflection is redefined as some interior designer's idea of Greek opulence. In the middle of this reflecting wall sits the gas-jet fireplace. The floors are wall-to-wall yellow shag carpet.

One night when I return late, everyone is either out or in bed. The main room is deserted. Reflected in the gilt mirror are the sparkling lights of L.A., miles below, and burning in the center of the fireplace are four naked gas flames, so that the spectacle of the bare gas jets and all the endlessly reflecting lights seems some shrine to American wastefulness, every Third Worlder's idea of the American Way.

The phones never stop ringing. The details of the tour are still being sorted out, promoters held in line. All of L.A. wants tickets. It is at this house that the cast and crew that will make up the tour assemble.

Sam Cutler has established himself as personal liaison for the "boys." He is ever intense, mindful of his new position. There is Ronnie Schneider, the business head of

Below and right: Mick on stage in Fort Collins, Colorado.

Below: Checking artwork for the Let It Bleed *cover. L. to r.: Al Steckler, Keith Richards, Mick Jagger.*

the tour (and Allen Klein's nephew, though struggling to break from Klein on this tour). In his New York manner he says completely gross things to everybody. "Ethan," he says, "that's some old lady you have. She swallows."

Ronnie is delighted with himself for this remark, and laughs uproariously. Ronnie's the kind of guy who carries binoculars with him when he travels, and while you're attempting to get an answer to a piece of business he'll be scanning the windows of the hotel across the way looking for women undressing.

Jo Bergman seems to have at least one telephone to her ear at all times, and somehow manages to be the even keel among the male megalomaniacs.

One day there's a knock on the door. Standing just outside is a short, stocky, olive-complexioned man wearing a double-breasted pin-striped suit and a wide tie. His hair is jet black, glistening, combed back above his ears. In his left hand, he holds a cigar. On his pinkie finger is a diamond ring. All in all, he seems an exact replica of one of the gangsters I used to watch on *The Untouchables*.

"Hi. My name's Pete Bennet. I just came by to see Mick and the boys," he says in a slightly raspy voice that fits the image as perfectly as his suit.

"Ah, could you hold on a minute?" I ask, backing away from the door, wide-eyed. I rush into the other room and ask anyone if they've ever heard of a guy called Pete Bennet.

"Pete," Ronnie shouts. "How ya doing?" *Everybody* knows Pete Bennet, it seems. He's one of Allen Klein's right-hand guys. When Mick and Keith arrive later, they smile at this American specter, but it's all friendly. "How ya doin', Mick? How's it goin'? Lissen, I'd like to get a picture, if you don't mind." Pete gets them to stand still, and I take the picture. Pete asks for the film, and says he'll take care of it. "Thanks," he says to me, shaking my hand. "What's your name?"

Not only does Pete know everybody, I'm told, he's got pictures of himself with them to prove it. The one most often mentioned is of him with President Nixon at the inauguration.

That night Pete is in the limousine with Jo, Stanley, and me as we aim toward the backstage entrance to the Fabulous Forum. Between us and the entrance there are lines of police barricades, and helmeted rows of L.A.'s finest, holding truncheons. Though we should have all the necessary clearances, the police are refusing to let us pass. The driver is frustrated and starts to lose his temper. The cop responds, pointing with his truncheon, "I said to move along, buddy."

Pete steps out of the limo. He asks to see the officer in charge. The cop takes one look at Pete and backs off. Shortly there is gathered a small circle of officers quietly conferring. In equally short time the barricades are moved, and we drive smoothly through, just like in the movies. "Thank you, gentlemen," says Pete.

Inside the Forum, the energy is intense. All activity stops as the Stones walk through. All eyes follow them. They disappear up the long concrete corridor, back

to the dressing rooms. There the privileged few who know somebody who knows somebody to get them backstage wait, clustered in bunches, drinks in hand. Their eyes dart about nervously; conversations are brief, unattended by speaker or listener, ready to be broken off at a moment's notice should one of the Stones walk in.

L.A. is the first big night. L.A. is 18,759 people stacked to the rafters. The Stones are ready. Preceded by security (Allen Klein is there, too, walking in front of them, a proprietary air about him), the Stones head toward the stage. Once again, as Sam makes his announcement, the air is split with a roar as the entire stadium leaps to its feet. I walk down in front, showing my pass. The large security force edges aside to let me through. Turning back toward the crowd I see all the faces looking up at Mick, following him as he dances around the stage, their eyes totally rapt. You can see in the crowd the music-business dignitaries. Though they assume a cooler attitude than the fans, their eyes are just as focused, not wanting to miss a thing.

The set starts big, but in the tradition of show business pacing, it slows to allow Keith a steel guitar spot ("No Expectations"). Mick sits next to him on a stool. Then the set kicks up again with "Midnight Rambler." It is another song from the dark side, a song of undefined menace, describing a character somewhere between a cat burglar and an assassin.

Left (top to bottom): Two friends of the band. Bill Wyman, Keith Richards, and Bill's wife, Astrid, backstage.

Above right: At the Fabulous Forum (l. to r.): Glyn Johns, Booker White, unknown, Keith Richards, Charlie Watts, Mick Jagger, Mick Taylor, Cathy, and Gram Parsons (back to camera).

[141]

> *If you ever catch the Midnight Rambler*
> *I'll steal your mistress from under your nose.*
> *Well, go easy with your cold fandango*
> *I'll stick my knife right down your throat . . .*

It is a good song to get the crowd going as Mick plays out his evil persona. He takes off his studded belt and whipping it over his shoulder, falls to his knees, slamming

the stage. The band plays a single, percussive thump. The stage lights burn deep-red. Mick looks out at the audience. "Honey, it's no rock 'n' roll show." *Thump!* "I'm talking about the Midnight Gambler / The one you've never seen before."

The song starts to pick up. The band is like an old steam engine coming to life. Soon Mick is up and roaming the stage again, and the song ends in crescendo.

"Let me see you out there, L.A. You're beautiful," says Mick. This is the cue for Chip Monck to turn up the house lights in the stadium. (Stage and lighting designer, Chip has come to the Stones from Woodstock, his voice famous for the "bad acid" announcement.) Encouraged by the house lights, the kids from the back of the stadium, the true zapped-out Rolling Stones fans, rush to fill the aisles.

The Stones break into "Honky Tonk Woman." Then one rocker follows another. Now the crowd is roaring, surging through the security guards, who wisely let them pass, crushing against the stage, pinning me against it so that I have to raise my cameras above my head and slowly squeeze out.

On the stage above, Jagger and the Stones are safe, riding the energy of the crowd and the pulsing of "Street Fighting Man." The show is a gas, the crowd is absolutely gone, and the Rolling Stones are back in America and blowing it away.

Hail, hail, rock 'n' roll.

———◆———

Shortly, we're on a plane for Oakland and once again walking through columns of police to get to the backstage. Once again, it's a massive auditorium (Oakland Coliseum), and once again the Stones rush on to a tumultuous welcome. Mick plays with the crowd, dancing to the lip of the stage, tempting the hands that reach out to touch him, quickly drawing back.

Backstage tensions run high. Ronnie Schneider and Bill Graham have to be separated, going after each other with their fists. Since the beginning they have never gotten along. This in turn reflects upon the Stones, and Graham has been badmouthing the Stones and their organization for days now. On the dressing room wall, directly above the mounds of fruit and cold cuts, is a black and white photo of Graham giving the Stones the finger. Someone takes a felt-tip marker and draws a bubble out of Graham's mouth, filling it with the words "Here is where *my* head is at."

San Francisco is Bill Graham territory. San Francisco also lays claim to being the center of the hip universe, second only to London, and of the many who visit London, most return saying that San Francisco is second to none.

The hip cognoscenti of San Francisco wish to praise the Stones, but they want and expect the praise to be returned. The problem is, of course, that the mean ol' Rolling Stones have just been around too long and have neither the time nor the inclination to indulge in an orgy of mutual stroking. So the Stones become the new bad guys in town, which is a wonderful joke to the original bad rock 'n' roll band of all time.

Above: Bill Graham's welcoming poster with the Stones' response.

Left: Mick on stage.

By Oakland two more people have joined us. One is Michael Lydon, a freelance writer. The other is John James.

Michael arrives wearing blue jeans and a rumpled shirt; sandy hair hangs past his shoulders. Michael lives in Mendocino. He seems to be a gentle man, one of the many affected by the sixties who try to live a relatively simple and honorable life. Michael has written several pieces describing his experiences with prominent musicians. This story on the Rolling Stones will be his latest, and of course the Stones are the biggest, most legendary band he's yet to encounter.★ Michael seems glad to be there, easygoing, one of us.

Which is all that John James is not. James is a fat man with a pallid complexion. He looks as if he has a permanent aversion to sunlight and vegetables. He arrives after the show in Los Angeles, purporting to be from the Dodge Motor Company, promising fleets of cars at every location the Stones will appear, and general assistance whenever needed. What he receives in return for this is never exactly clear. That such an arrangement might interest the Stones is undeniable. Mick's concern that expenses ever be kept to a minimum is well known. ("Mick said I could do whatever I wanted as long as it was cheap," Jo Bergman says, describing her marching orders from Mick when setting up their offices in London.)

Michael is later to write that John James's name had been shortened from "something long and Italian." Whatever the relationship, James would be with us for the duration of the tour, and, as he promised, Dodge cars would be provided at every location, only to be left, keys in them, at various and sundry spots across America, abandoned by cast and crew alike, easy come, easy go, the established protocol of a traveling rock and roll show.

◆

"Hey, you can't go in there with those," says the guard at CBS, pointing at my cameras. The Rolling Stones have just arrived to tape *The Ed Sullivan Show*.

"He either comes with us, or we're leaving," says Keith, not one to mince words.

With us is David Horowitz, the public relations man hired by the Stones. It would appear that whoever hired him or his firm did so on the basis of some show business word of mouth before show business included rock 'n' roll. David Horowitz is wearing a powder-blue jacket and polyester pants. He is an ever-pleasant man in his early forties but frequently nervous, not having the slightest idea how to deal with the band. His is the province of the television producer, "personalities," and people who know how to play the game. ("I wish I could do what you guys do," he says to me one day. "You just seem to do whatever you want.")

"Those are the rules," says the guard. "No cameras." He's an old guy, maybe in his fifties, and he stands at the entrance to the several acres of buildings that make up

Above: Mick and Keith in Carmel Valley, relaxing before the tour.

Right: On stage for The Ed Sullivan Show.

★Michael's stories of these musicians are collected and published under the title *Rock Folk*. New York: Dial Press, 1971.

[144]

the CBS stages in L.A. The almost famous and the very famous pass before him daily. He's there to let you know he's not impressed.

"Right, then," says Keith, spinning on his heel and walking in the other direction.

David Horowitz's counterpart, who works for CBS, is a young guy, but he seems equally nervous.

"Hold on, could you?" he says, chasing after Keith. He calls back to the guard, "It's all right this time. I'll take care of it."

The rest of the Stones have stopped and turned to watch this minor fracas.

"But those are the rules," repeats the guard.

Keith has stopped.

"No, no. This is different. I'll take care of it. Don't you worry," says the CBS public relations man.

"Come on. Please," he says to Keith.

Keith shoots a look at the guard, and then walks past with long, striding steps. I gather my cameras and follow. David walks next to me, visibly shaken.

Inside the studio, the set is some television designer's idea of "far out." Tall crescent shapes rise from the stage floor to approximate an underground cavern. The stage behind is lit with orange gels.

Bleachers are set up in part of the studio for a small audience, but they are empty except for a few of the younger employees of CBS who have found out that the Rolling Stones are due to perform.

Around the stage are large television cameras set on wheels, huge cables protruding. In shadow standing behind the cameras are the operators, old union guys, wearing headsets. Hanging from the ceiling everywhere are television monitors.

Mick and the Stones are standing center stage. The floor manager holds his clipboard at the ready, and Ed Sullivan is brought out from backstage. He is heavily made

up and looks as if he's just gotten off the plane from New York, which he probably has. He walks up to Mick and shakes hands.

The floor manager approaches and says, "Mr. Sullivan, we'll just tape the introductions now and do the band later if that's all right."

Ed Sullivan nods and adjusts his tie in a nearby mirror. Below the camera directly in front of the band are the words of introduction chalked out on a board. Ed Sullivan indicates he is ready.

"All right and taping," says the floor manager, stepping back into the shadows.

With polished enthusiasm, Ed Sullivan faces the camera and begins one of his famous introductions. "And tonight, from England, we have with us the Rolling Stones!" He turns toward Mick, who has been waiting patiently. "Hello, Mike," says Ed Sullivan.

"Cut!" yells the floor manager. Sullivan looks surprised. "Mr. Sullivan, that's 'Mick,' not 'Mike.'"

Sullivan squints his eyes at the chalkboard. "Oh," he says.

Mick and the others wear ear-to-ear smiles.

"All right and take two."

"And tonight, the act you've all been waiting for. Will you welcome back the Rolling Stones!" Sullivan lifts his arms in the air, urging on the nonexistent audience. "Welcome, Mick. What number will you be playing next?"

"Cut!"

Sullivan looks over toward the floor manager.

"Mr. Sullivan, we're not sure what order we'll be using the songs in, so please don't ask him to say what he's playing next."

Ed Sullivan nods. The Rolling Stones wait.

"All right and take three . . ."

". . . the Rolling Stones! Hello, Mick. It's good to have you on the show again. What number . . . Oh, sorry," says Sullivan.

*Above: Ian Stewart having fun
standing in for Bill Wyman at
The Ed Sullivan Show.*

*Below left: "That's Mick, not
Mike, Mr. Sullivan."*

"Cut," says the floor manager. Mick is bending over with laughter.

The next time Sullivan gets it right. He says good-bye to Mick and the Stones and leaves. The taping progresses. The songs are to playback, but Mick is going to record a live vocal (meaning when the show is aired, the sound of the instruments will be from the record, but Mick's singing will actually be from the taping of the show). The Rolling Stones perform three songs and shortly we're back out in the California sun, heading into the hills.

A week later, when the show airs, Mick and the others are gathered to watch themselves. Gales of laughter greet Sullivan's introduction. But as he says "Will you welcome back the Rolling Stones!," holding his arms in the air, waves of high-pitched female screams suddenly come from the set. Screams? There was no audience. But the producers of the show would have you believe that all of CBS was besieged by adolescent girls, closeted since the early sixties, the British Invasion all over again.

The screams persist, rising in volume through the songs, conjuring up images of young girls whipping themselves into a frenzy. As he watches, Mick seems depressed.

"That's too bad," he says. "I really tried to do a good job singing those songs."

———◆———

Little Richard paces the stage of the Whisky à-Go-Go on the Sunset Strip. Mick and Keith watch from the shadows. Little Richard bulges against the confines of his gold lamé suit. A gold cape is draped across his shoulders. The heavy pancake make-up on his face is starting to run from the sweat he's building up. His eyebrows are carefully plucked; his mustache is pencil thin. He's working the crowd, lecturing to an all-white audience.

"All I hear today is about the Beatles. Beatles. Beatles. Beatles. Or about the Rolling Stones. The Rolling Stones. Why, shit!" yells Richard, talking very fast. "Why, I taught them EVERYTHING THEY KNOW. SHIT!" A high-pitched yelp escapes his lips. He is high camp. "Look at me. Have you *ever* seen anything so beautiful?" Above his coffee-colored face his hair is pomaded and sprayed into a stiff pompadour. "Shit," he says. "Shee-yit!"

He sits down at the piano, a stream of words cascading from his mouth. "SPLISH-SPLASH-I-WAS-TAKIN'-A-BATH-LONG-ABOUT-A-SATURDAY-NIGHT . . ."

He pounds the piano. Pure, early American rock and roll. Little Richard comes from Main Street, Macon, Georgia. As he would be the first to tell you, it's a long way from Macon to the Sunset Strip.

"LUCILLE! PLEASE COME BACK WHERE YOU BELONG. LUCILLE! PLEASE COME BACK WHERE YOU BELONG . . ."

"AM I BEAUTIFUL?" he yells to the audience, carving out a place for himself, a black rock-and-rolling Liberace.

Then, later, he yells, "Okay, they tole me you was out there." He drops his voice.

"Tonight," he tells the crowd, "we have with us Mick Jagger and Keith Richards from the great Rolling Stones." Then he yells, "AN' I TAUGHT 'EM EVERY-THING THEY KNOW! GO ON NOW. ADMIT IT. *SHIT!*"

Heads turn, trying to find Mick and Keith, but they are well back in the shadows. Silence.

"I know you're out there, Keith Richards! Hey, Keith! Mick!" Silence.

"HEY, C'MON BOYS. THIS HERE IS LITTLE RICHARD. TELL 'EM I TAUGHT YOU EVERYTHIN! GO ON . . ." Pacing the stage, "AIN'T I *JUST BEAUTIFUL?* SHIT!"

Keith says, "You're beautiful," loud enough for Richard to hear.

"You bet I'm beautiful. Shit!" says Little Richard, proud as can be.

Now the audience has found them. Heads turn. People start whispering to each other. It's almost palpable, the feeling that people are immediately concocting a rea-son, any reason, to come to the table and speak to them. It would soon no longer be Little Richard's show. As he pounds into another song, Mick and Keith get up to leave. They're the megastars, bigger legends than this black guy who had his first hits back in the fifties when Elvis came out, and who's still singing his rock 'n' roll.

———◆———

For three weeks the Rolling Stones take their show on the American road. Each night audiences leave their seats to come rushing to the lip of the stage, arms outstretched. Though this is constant, as is the line-up of songs, each show takes on an individual character, tainted by the times and the city the Stones are in.

The Chicago show is played near the old slaughterhouses and its mood is dark, inner-city, incipiently violent. A man without legs, dressed in a ragged army jacket and T-shirt, hair hanging to his shoulders, is carried over the head of the crowd and placed on the right edge of the stage, where he stays through the show, his eyes glued to the prancing Mick.

In Mississippi the dressing room walls are covered with framed posters of football players and cheerleaders. The audience that stares back at the Stones contains no men with long hair. The girls wear pleated skirts; their hair is stiff with hair spray. The public address system interrupts the show to announce that the night's curfew will be extended past eleven P.M. in honor of the Stones' appearance. Part of that evening I spend in the dressing room talking to the armed Mississippi guard, testing my prej-udices from the very early sixties and the days of protest marches against segregation, wondering how he feels about these long-haired foreigners whose opening act is black (Chuck Berry). It's all the same to him, he says, in a tone that somehow makes me glad I'm not there alone.

Once we're out in middle America we're really a small group of strangers in a strange land, more together than apart. In 1969 the Stones mostly take commercial airlines. As we walk through the airports, people invariably stop and stare, not nec-

Right: Mick and unknown American. On the road, 1969.

Below, top: Keith backstage in Mississippi gymnasium, with photos of sports figures on the wall.

Below, bottom: An audience.

essarily because they recognize the Rolling Stones. It is enough that such a strange-looking group exists at all, and, of course, they were followed everywhere by their photographer, a dead giveaway that they must be somebody.

Some people didn't care who it was. I was approached once by a middle-aged woman while I was standing in the lobby dripping with cameras, waiting for the Stones to come down from their rooms prior to some show.

"Could I have your autograph, please?" she asked.

"You don't want my autograph," I said. "I'm just the photographer."

"Oh, no," she said. "I know. You're One of Them."

"No, I'm not," I said. "Really."

She looked at me closely. Maybe it was the hair. She handed me a pad.

"It's for my little girl. She'll be so happy."

Not really, I thought, taking her pad.

◆

Sitting out on the uneven surface of the runway was a tail-dragging twin-engine DC something-or-other, the best — the only — airplane that a last-minute and intensive search was able to locate when someone (who knows?) had overslept and the normal commercial airlines couldn't manage to get the Stones to the next city on time. It was difficult at such times not to think of the fate of the Big Bopper and Buddy Holly. It was never questioned that new flights, new transportation, would be arranged and that the cast and crew would somehow arrive at whatever destination however many thousands of miles away, on time and ready to play. They always (or almost always) did, even when it meant separating into different groups (as it did this time), the crew keeping the original reservations, and the Stones, Ronnie, and I now traveling on this antique that turned out to have no pressurization and no heat, so we all huddled, wrapped in blankets and woolen hats, while the engines roared outside.

The Stones seem to take it all in stride; they are old hands. They play endless hands of cards, especially a bastardized form of poker, Bill Wyman's specialty, where seven cards are dealt to each player. Each player then makes two three-card hands and discards one card. The two hands are then placed face down and each hand is bet separately, with the minimum bet one dollar. In order to win, one player must win both hands; otherwise the pot stays. If you do not bet a round, you are out of the game until there's a winner of both hands. The net result is that everybody bets every round, hoping that the winning hands will split, which happens much more often than not. The pot then stays. It could grow to be a couple of hundred dollars.

One day Ronnie is spitting and spewing, complaining that he, somehow, should have won a hand. Keith interrupts.

"Cool it, Ronnie," he says, "we're just killing time. Nobody's playing to win."

Ronnie Schneider (Mr. Money) is shamed into silence, lest a few dollars appear too important. Like hell they're not, I think, holding my cards to my chest.

Above: Closing the show in Mississippi, where the college students in the audience were given special permission to stay out past the 11 P.M. curfew.

Left: Charlie on stage.

[151]

Even with diversions, even with the inevitable rush that comes every evening as Sam announces to the expectant crowd, "Would you welcome the *greatest rock 'n' roll band in the world*," and the Stones come running out into the audience's wall of sound only to echo it right back to them, even with all of that, being on the road becomes relentless, boring. As much as the shows somehow manage to retain their character, the ceaseless travel grinds everything into a bland sameness. At such times the individual regional qualities that I knew to exist in America disappeared. The food was uniformly frozen and tasteless. The rooms were apparently identical. (Years later an Englishman, one of the Who's road managers, would cast an appreciative light on this arrangement: "I love Holiday Inns. It doesn't matter which town I'm in, I can wake up in the middle of the night and always know where the bathroom is.") Walk

Left: Mick and Keith win a
hand from Mr. Money.

Below: Mick and B. B. King.

Right: Mick and Chuck Berry.

into the room and turn on the television. Every television announcer seems to be the same person telling the same story. Down the hall from the room are the ice machine, the Coke machine. Look out the window. American cars fill the parking lot. Especially in the broad Midwest, the landscape, without mountains, without hills, leaves the eye nothing to focus on. Every other day the time zone changes. What time is it? Does it matter? All hours lead up to showtime. After the rush of the show, back to the hotel. The locals who manage to find out where the Stones are staying make it to the lobby, huddle together, trying to find out what room Mick's in, Keith's in. If there is an open room, more often than not the atmosphere is strained by the anxiety of the newcomers. A girl bent on scoring Mick Jagger is about as interesting as a junkie without a fix; her attention span is very short.

The Rolling Stones drone through America, playing gymnasiums in small towns, coliseums in large ones. The movement of the tour is ever eastward, inexorably toward New York, the site of the last two shows. At Madison Square Garden, both shows are sold out.

Once they reach the East Coast, the Rolling Stones set up headquarters in the Plaza. As with Los Angeles on the West Coast, the Stones use New York as their base and sortie forth from there.

The Lear Jet that is to take them to the Baltimore show is too small to accommodate any but the band. The rest of us board a bus that gets stuck in New York traffic. We arrive just in time to watch a smoke bomb come arcing out of the audience and explode in a wide cement trench that (happily) lies between the Stones and the audience. The show halts momentarily, but quickly proceeds as the container is taken away. Throughout the tour security has been effective. Once in the hall the Stones go immediately backstage and stay there until the show. They are out of the auditorium before the audience. Nobody gets backstage except those who are wanted backstage. Even the remotest signs of trouble are dealt with far from the Stones. Those of us who travel with them, identified by our badges and, by now, familiarity, travel easily back and forth through the several layers of security (the outermost provided by the hall or by the promoter, the innermost by the Stones). As you get to the dressing rooms, everyone knows everybody, so that the inner sanctum is generally peaceful except for the ongoing business of the tour. It's an arrangement that seems to suit everyone just fine.

Above, top: Backstage, Keith napping before a show.

Above, bottom: The author with his Rolling Stones tour pass.

Right: Mick on stage in Miami.

———◆———

Whoever overslept this one, there seemed no real reason for concern. After all, the Stones had hired their own plane. So when the first flight plan was voided, a routine request for another was filed. It was only when that plan was denied that the possibility of a problem arose. It was an inadvertent misfortune that the Stones chose to fly to Miami on the same day President Nixon chose to lunch in New York. Since he was coming only for lunch, the airport was shut down until Nixon left several hours later.

Down in Miami or, more accurately, in a field some thirty or forty miles outside Miami, thousands of kids sat expectantly.

The Deep South had not welcomed this event. There would be no half a million unwashed hippies congregating in their back yard, à la Woodstock, not if the locals had anything to say about it. And, in a litany of reactions indicative of the time, the promoter of the Miami show was threatened variously with lawsuit, injunction, and canceled insurance, the legal intimidations. His other businesses in the area were boycotted. There were threats on the lives of his wife and children. So what began as a reasonable business venture escalated into the kind of confrontational politics for which the sixties were famous.

It was well past sundown by the time the Rolling Stones reached Miami. It was

past midnight before they arrived at the concert site and even later before they went on stage. Huddled in front of the stage, again in mud, the audience waited. It was cold, dark, and gloomy. Occasional fires could be seen burning throughout the crowd. When the Stones finally appeared on stage, the crowd leapt to its feet, arms upraised in salute, and a great roar of appreciation erupted as the band launched into "Jumpin' Jack Flash."

It's so cold that clouds of mist come from Mick's mouth as he sings. Because of the cold the guitars refuse to stay in tune. In spite of this the Stones play into the small hours of the morning, mindful of how long the crowd had waited for them. A thin pink line barely edges the horizon as the last chords from "Street Fighting Man" echo over the crowd. Waiting apart from the stage sits a massive helicopter, slate black against the early dawn. The band leaps into the cargo hold and I climb up the side of the ship into the cockpit with the pilot. It seems a disconcerting height for a helicopter. It is just barely becoming light as the big ship rises off the ground. You can see where the thousands were camped, and then the chopper pulls away, skimming over the Florida everglades. With the sound of the chopper blades, and the swamp spread out below, I think that Vietnam must be like this, half a world away.

◆

Back in New York the phones *never* stop ringing. New York is the Big Time, and in New York everybody is a Very Important Person. Supplying tickets to just Pete Bennet's selection of Very Close Personal Friends would have been confusion enough. New York is where the East Coast cognoscenti will check out the Rolling Stones.

At his suite at the Plaza, Mick invites me in. "Leonard Bernstein's coming up. Stay here, okay?" Leonard Bernstein comes rushing into the room, his black cape swirling behind him. He is effusive. Mick's English manners come to the fore. How nice to see him. He introduces me. "How nice to meet you," says Mr. Bernstein. Mick and Mr. Bernstein exchange mutual compliments, the small talk of the very famous. I stand at a discreet distance. Leonard Bernstein is anxious about the crowd. About what to expect from ten thousand rock and roll fans. Mick is immediately solicitous. Ethan would be glad to go with you and take you to your seat.

"Would he?" asks Mr. Bernstein.

"Of course," I say, flattered, really. Now, Mick says, he has to change. He hopes Leonard will enjoy the show.

Walking through the crowd, my Stones' pass taped to my chest, I escort Leonard Bernstein to his seat. He is very grateful. He gives me a big kiss.

◆

Madison Square Garden always appears slightly threatening, sitting squatly in the middle of not-the-most-hospitable section of the not-always-friendliest town in the world. The crowd that couldn't get into the show swirls about on the street, ignoring police barricades. Heads peer into the limos looking for the Stones. I feel a certain relief as we're waved past and swallowed up by the maze of tunnels.

In Madison Square Garden, the other rock stars come to have a look. Dylan is rumored to be there. Backstage Jimi Hendrix is talking with Charlie Watts. Janis Joplin is in the audience.

Glyn Johns has flown in from London to record the two shows for a live album (*Get Yer Ya-Yas Out!*). Miles of cable lead from the stage to the recording truck where he sits, adjusting dials, checking levels.

The Stones' security, so effective on the road, is pressed to its limits in New York. The pressure to get backstage is intense. New York has benefited from the publicity of the entire preceding tour. By the time the Stones arrive in New York, their presence seems everywhere. They are written about in the papers, spoken of on television. Hour after hour, the radio stations broadcast Stones songs. The heavy rock stations have their over-amped deejays frothing at the mouth. The Rolling Stones are in town! Get down! Get down! By the time the show rolls around, the Rolling Stones fan, following all this from the beginning, would be massaged into a state of acute hyperintensity. At the edge of the stage by the barricade where the uniformed security stand guard is where all that promotional energy that says "Come and get it. You've got to have it" meets "You can't go back there." The labyrinthine tales concocted by the earnest fan, tempered by the general street rap in New York, where truth is never an obstacle, are spilled before the impassive guards.

"I'm from Mr. Jagger's doctor. I have an emergency prescription . . ."

"It's a matter of absolute life and death . . ."

"These are urgent legal documents. The show cannot start without . . ."

"No. I have to deliver them personally."

"Listen, you, my father is the attorney general, and when he hears . . ."

Mostly, the pleas fall on deaf ears. The mood can turn ugly quickly, as the two pressures collide. "All you're gonna get of the Rolling Stones, buddy, is to look at 'em on the stage. Now back to your seat or you won't get that."

"Fucking pig."

"I'm warning you."

"Pigfucker!"

The Rolling Stones never see this. Back in the dressing rooms, they're tuning up. These are the closing shows. Then they'll fly to Muscle Shoals to do some recording.

Onstage Sam Cutler announces, speaking above the high-pitched squeals of amplifier feedback, "Everything seems to be ready. Are you ready? . . . We're sorry for the delay . . .

"Is everybody ready for the next band? . . . Are you ready, New York? The biggest band to visit New York in a long time . . .

"They've done the West Coast, they've done all sorts of other places in America, now they're in New York . . . Be cool. Have a fantastic time . . .

"Let's really hear it . . .

Above: Jimi Hendrix and Charlie Watts backstage at Madison Square Garden.

Overleaf: The Rolling Stones on stage in New York.

"Let's welcome the *greatest rock 'n' roll band in the world* . . . THE ROLLING STONES! THE ROLLING STONES!"

The crowd explodes. The Stones come racing on stage. "Jumpin' Jack Flash" blasts into Madison Square Garden, and the inevitable goose-flesh rush creeps up my spine one more time.

"Oh yeah!" says Mick as the song ends. "Thank you kindly. I think I bust a button on my trousers. Hope they don't fall down . . . You don't want my trousers to fall down, now, do you?"

"YESSSS!" yells the crowd.

The Stones run through their paces. They play early American rock 'n' roll ("Carol" by Chuck Berry). They play their arrangement of traditional blues ("Love in Vain" by Robert Johnson). But, as in other shows, they start to kick it up with "Midnight Rambler" and the Rolling Stones whip into life, the Original Bad Boys of Rock 'n' Roll.

"'Paint It Black,' you devil," shouts a girl from the audience, requesting an old Stones tune and awarding Mick his dark-demon accolade. The band begins and Mick answers, "Please allow me to introduce myself. I'm a man of wealth and taste . . ."

"Sympathy for the Devil" swells to fill Madison Square Garden.

"Pleased to meet you," sings Mick, "I hope you guessed my name. / But what is puzzling you is the nature of my game."

As well it might, as the lyric catalogues a list of the Devil's work (according to Jagger/Richards). Mick sings in the first person: "I was around when Jesus Christ had his moment of doubt and pain . . ."

But mixed in with this apparently absolute identification with the Devil is "I shouted out 'Who killed the Kennedys?' / When after all it was you and me." Nothing other than a liberal call for collective responsibility.

It all rushes past, slippery and indecipherable, pushed and carried by the "greatest rock 'n' roll band in the world," working hard to carry the audience away, the only indisputable purpose of a rock 'n' roll show, as the Stones would be the first to tell you.

Mick calls the house lights on, and Madison Square Garden is on its feet, like so many audiences before them, dancing and swaying to the music.

"We're gonna do one more and then we gotta go," yells Mick as "Honky Tonk Woman" fades.

The guitars of Keith Richards and Mick Taylor start the strong chording that sets up an oscillating rhythm almost like a submarine's Klaxon, and Mick sings, "Everywhere I hear the sound of marching, charging feet, boy / For the summer's here and the time is right for fighting in the street, boy."

Bill Wyman's bass plays strong, descending notes, Keith and Mick kick it back

Above: Mick thanking Charlie for a glass of water. The Rolling Stones like each other.

Below left: Keith Richards.

up again, and Charlie hits the cymbals, bass drum, snare, pounding to a climax. Keith is crouched, his knees bent, his right arm pumping. Mick Taylor picks single notes, twining through the solid wall of sound the band now pours out.

"Yeah," yells Mick. "Hey, said my name is called disturbance. I shout and scream, I'll kill the King. I'll rail at all his servants."

On the chorus, Keith rushes to the mike, joining in, singing, "Well what can a poor boy do? / 'Cept to sing for a rock 'n' roll band? / 'Cause in sleepy London town there's just no place for a / street fightin' man."

"No!" yells Mick. On the last note, Keith flings his arm into the air, Charlie plays the closing drum roll, and the Rolling Stones race off, jogging through the security, down the concrete halls, leaping into the open, waiting doors of the limousines, out of the hall before most of the audience realizes they've left.

All through America, 1969, the Stones have been leaving crowds yelling, pumped up by this wholly ambiguous anthem for our time, "Street Fighting Man." As Mick and Keith encourage everybody on to new heights of confrontation, they concurrently issue this disclaimer: "We're with you all the way, only where we live people don't behave like that." ("In sleepy London town there's just no place for a street fighting man." In fact, the only demonstration Mick Jagger ever attended was the one in London held in front of the American embassy, and it was very pacific.)

Both the Stones and the Beatles have tried to grapple with the same problem. They have seen American youth (their fans) protesting in the streets. There's been some desire to come out and support those against the war, those who want change. "You say you want a revolution / Well you know / We all wanna change the world," sings John for the Beatles, that lyric, too, impelled by the raspy power of the guitar behind it. But they can't quite seem to make the radical leap either: "If you go carrying pictures of Chairman Mao / You ain't gonna make it with anyone anyhow."

"But when you talk about destruction don't you know that you can count me out?" is the lyric on the single of "Revolution One" released in America. But the lyric on the album is "count me out, in," the old yin/yang again, hello/good-bye. As sympathetic as the English might be, they are just not as conversant with the violence in the streets and what it means to be there.

I follow closely behind the Stones, rushing for the same limousines. But when I get there, the limousines are full. Important New Yorkers — with their unerring instinct for finding the right party — have left the backstage early, parked themselves in the Stones' limos normally reserved for second-stringers like myself, and sit there, all dressed up and very determined not to be moved. The directive of security is to get the Stones out before the audience is out of the hall. People scramble for the available spaces, and the cars are waved out, doors pulled shut as the limos accelerate. It is the first backstage chaos since the beginning of the tour, and I'm standing there with cameras hanging off me until a voice says, "Here, come with us," and I climb into the back of another limo.

"Hi, man, I'm Janis," says Janis Joplin as her car drives through the exiting crowd and turns right, which — though I hardly know New York — I know not to be the direction of the hotel. I am seething with all the righteous anger of the working stiff pre-empted by a bunch of starfuckers.

"Ah, he ain't so hot," says Janis of Mick, slurring her words. One of Janis's entourage introduces herself and invites me up to their hotel. But I'm too uptight, not comfortable with the prospect of wandering through the infamous night streets of New York with several thousand dollars' worth of cameras draped around me. I take a taxi back to the Plaza.

"What the fuck's the story?" I yell at Ronnie and John James. "I'm supposed to be working here and some clowns come along and take my place in the car and I'm wandering the streets of New York! Can't you guys even keep it fucking organized, or what?" They watch me quietly, waiting for my ranting to stop.

Then John James gets up and in a very low voice, as if delivering unto me a pronouncement of inestimable importance, says, "I'm just gonna tell you one thing. Don't ever yell at me. It doesn't matter what has happened. You just don't ever yell at me."

Above: John Lennon.

Right: Melvin Belli's office in San Francisco, before Altamont.

Below: Ronnie Schneider and one half of John James.

Though I know this is meant as a threat, my anger insulates me from it. "Well just don't fuck up again," I say, being careful not to yell.

Ronnie comes by later. "Ethan," he says. "You should take it easy. You really shouldn't talk to him like that. Okay?" Still angry, I say nothing. "Anyway, I've come to tell you we're all going to California to play a show in San Francisco. Ask Jo about the tickets and all that."

"Oh, they're gonna do that?" I ask.

"Yeah. Bring your old lady," says Ronnie. "She's hot."

◆

Melvin Belli's office in downtown San Francisco is done in a style reminiscent of a turn-of-the century bordello except that where the full-length portrait of the scantily clad female would normally hang, there is a huge portrait of Belli, dominating everything. The room is in chaos. It is two days before the now-famous free concert to be given by the Rolling Stones, and a site for the concert has not yet been determined. The Maysles are there filming as Ronnie Schneider and John James watch Belli insist, in a booming, flamboyant voice, that he will shortly unravel the very complicated mess in which everyone seems to find themselves (and in very short order, too, as there is a private plane waiting to take him to his country home).

Also in this room (besides me and Jo Bergman and an unknown host of others) is an uncomfortable-looking man who seems at home with neither the three-piece lawyer set nor the rock and roll crowd. His name is Bill Cutler and he is wearing a light blue patterned jacket and polyester trousers. His hairline is receding and he sports a thin mustache. He looks like he might call Oakland home, and, indeed, he is the owner of Altamont Speedway, across the Bay from San Francisco in the direction of Sacramento. When the city of San Francisco withdrew its permission for a concert in Golden Gate Park, there was a mad scramble to relocate, and Mr. Cutler seems finally the man with the goods.

Meanwhile, all the tons of equipment of the Stones' '69 tour — the stage, the amplifiers, drums, mixing boards, lights, trusses, scaffolding, super-troupers, and miles of cable — all carted across America from Los Angeles to New York, are now back on the West Coast under the able supervision of Chip Monck, and being dismantled from the first San Francisco location and trucked out to the site at Altamont.

Altamont is expected to be as big as, hopefully better than, Woodstock. After all, Altamont is on the West Coast, close to San Francisco, the spiritual mother of the free festival, home of innumerable freaks, and the show will star the "greatest rock 'n' roll band of all time." Everyone expects some version of Woodstock West.

"Mr. Jagger, what is your opinion of the mass concerts such as Woodstock and the Isle of Wight?"

"Well, they all happened in the same year. I think next year they will be more — huge and better organized."

"Why are you giving a free concert in San Francisco?"

"Because there's a scene there and the climate's nice . . ."

And because they just wanted to, though they were unlikely to say that. Indeed, they'd say everything but. The sixties had been *so* incredible. The once scruffy, outcast, and completely extreme Rolling Stones were now mainstream heroes to an entire generation. It was not the Stones' image or inclination to say publicly that they dug what was happening, dug all these new kids being as outrageous as (more than) they had ever been. Such reverse adulation was left for the more direct Pete Townshend to sing (in *Tommy*): "Looking at you, I get the power. Following you, I get the beat."

But it was, at least the way I read it, definitely being done as a salute to the audience from the Rolling Stones, a thank you for all the records purchased, all the concert tickets bought, a celebration of the community that music had created. Jumpin' Jack Flash, *you're* a gas, gas, gas.

I was on the second helicopter flight out. I had watched Jagger, Ronnie Schneider, and Charlie Watts board the first flight, after Mick, while waiting to leave, had walked up to a girl who was standing motionless in the middle of the pier. She was wearing sunglasses and a miniskirt, and clutching a purse. Mick walks to her side and, pursing his lips, places a princely kiss upon her right cheek. The girl reacts not at all, standing frozen in place, eyes straight ahead. All the while, Albert and David Maysles, who had joined the tour in New York, keep filming until the chopper lands and takes Mick away.

It was back shortly to pick up me and the others. The bay dropped away below as the helicopter crossed above Berkeley and then headed over the hills, brown and dry after the California summer. As we approached the site, an endless line of cars could be seen strung out below, pulled to the side of the road and left abandoned. Then I made out the outline of the raceway, a small speck of a stage, with the speaker towers and scaffolding for the lights jutting out of the crowd, which was huge, stretching out all around the stage, filling the small valley formed by the hills. People had been arriving for two days — from the moment the final location had been announced — bringing sleeping bags, lighting fires, camping out, waiting for the Stones. It was soon clear that the location was unfortunate. The dry hills, now trodden upon by hundreds of thousands of people, were an immediate dustbowl. There was not a tree in sight, not even a bush. The idyllic vision of the concert in Golden Gate Park (acres of grass, swaying eucalyptus, and the endless blooming of landscaped gardens) quickly dimmed. But if Altamont appeared somewhat inhospitable, what the hell: after all, at Woodstock they had sat in the rain for days.

When I stepped out of the helicopter, though, the first words spoken were: "Did you hear what happened to Mick?"

"No, what?"

"Some kid came rushing up to him. Punched him in the face."

"What? Why?"

"No one knows. He was shouting, 'I hate you, I hate you' — something like that."

Behind the stage chaos compounded itself. Chain-link fence had been thrown up to isolate the area from the rest of the crowd. There was a small trailer where Mick and the Stones now waited. In front of that was a tentlike shelter near some stairs leading to the stage. There were a lot of Hell's Angels.

As I walked to the trailer I saw Mick come out. He seemed all right, but subdued. I decided not to wait around. I walked out from behind the stage and started to circle the crowd that was encamped in front. I went looking for the new families, somebody giving birth, some re-enactment of the events of the Woodstock Nation that I had experienced only through the media.

The numbers were certainly present. As I walked around, people would occasionally smile at me, a red-eyed half-squint, and raise their hands in a "V" sign. Here and there through the crowd tie-dyed banners waved in the heat. Isolated figures could be seen swaying to the music of the opening acts, their eyes closed, their arms moving through the air as if they were swimming. The peace symbol — the airplane shape enclosed in a circle — stood planted on top of a pole stuck in the earth like the insignia of a Roman legion. Thousands of long-hairs had brought their children, now three and four and five years old, young freaks, and they knew it. Frisbees spun through the air. At the edge of the crowd stood a long line of green outhouses. Beyond them along the speedway stood numerous automobile wrecks, carcasses from demolition derbies held there, icons of another generation's idea of a good time.

I didn't see any babies being born, and I didn't feel any particular sense of community. People were just passing time, getting high, waiting for the Rolling Stones.

Back behind the stage the mood didn't seem to have improved. Mick came out of the trailer wearing the red and black cape with its El Greco folds that he had worn at the outdoor concert in Miami. He and Charlie went down to the improvised tent where, amid Hell's Angels, they drank a beer and seemed to try to relax. I heard there was some trouble when Jefferson Airplane performed, but I saw nothing.

With the night fallen, the Stones went on. As I had done every night for the previous month, I prepared to go out with them. As I walked toward the stage I was blocked by two Hell's Angels. Was I okay? they wanted to know. Told that I was, they signaled to a couple of other Hell's Angels who walked on either side of me as we moved toward the stage. The closer we got, the more congested it became, until at the ramp leading to the stage they just picked me up between them and carried me, depositing me on the edge of the stage as if I were an inanimate object. There I saw Stu — Ian Stewart — for all intents and purposes the sixth Rolling Stone. He had been with them since the very beginning, had seen them through the frenzied female riots in Germany, through the drunken Scots' brawls in the slums of Glasgow. By 1969 Stu was both their road manager supreme and a fellow player, on stage every night at the piano to perform "Honky Tonk Woman" and "Little Queenie." Stu, a

Above: Altamont from the air.

Scot, has one of the more finely honed perspectives on the Rolling Stones. He has seen and been through it all with them, but without the cloak of personal stardom, since he was never an identifiable Rolling Stone. Nothing ever seemed to faze Stu, whose imperturbability was as developed as his cynicism.

But here on the stage at Altamont, Stu looks worried. He moves about grimly, trying to clear people away as they push to the very edge of the performing area itself, their eyes riveted on Jagger. The stage actually *sags* under the weight of the crowd, and when combined with the weight of the Stones and their equipment, it sways when the crowd shifts. It feels as if it might collapse, taking everybody with it.

Above left: Mick and Hell's Angels backstage at Altamont.

Pages 168–169: Mick on stage at Altamont. The stage was so overloaded it seemed as if it might collapse.

If it appears dense on stage it is much worse for the crowd in front. The truly maniacal Stones fans who arrived earliest have planted themselves at the lip of the stage and rooted, not wanting to move lest their place be lost, as the crowd behind them swelled. In the natural course of things as the crowd grew, the pressure toward the stage increased. By the time the Stones come on, the pressure of the several hundred thousand people behind them jams those in front to the lip of the stage. There is no room between them for anything to pass, anything at all.

For a very short time, I am on stage, but quickly I know I just don't want to be there. I'm just another person adding to the confusion, to the weight, another person to make Stu crazy. I walk to the back of the stage, escorted by Hell's Angels; then I'm hoisted to the top of a van that is parked behind the stage where Al Maysles is filming. I still don't get it. It just seems that the idea for the free concert isn't going as well as we expected. I keep thinking it's just the last gig, it'll be over soon. Just another rock 'n' roll show.

From where I am the lights that create back light for the Rolling Stones shine onto the upraised faces of people closest to the stage. As the light falls off, the faces fade, become indecipherable, part of the compressed mass of blackness stretching out endlessly in front of the stage. Suddenly, in the midst of that mass, where there is *no* space, absolutely no space at all, I see a circle of bodies open, crazily, like a sea urchin's mouth, quickly widening until there is an empty circle maybe thirty feet in diameter, and I stare aghast, knowing that the only way for that space to open is for people to swarm back over and on top of themselves and those behind them, manhandling each other out of the way. I feel as if I am witnessing a physical impossibility.

Then, in the center of the circle, hulking, vague forms, the backs of Hell's Angels, can be seen, their arms pumping up and down. The music stops.

It is hard to tell what is happening, and when it subsides the music begins again. The empty hole once again fills with people, becomes once more a solid ocean of humanity stretching to the horizon.

The music starts up again. Shortly, there is more violence and another crazy black hole opens and people scramble and arms pump. Occasionally people scream at the Angels until the Angels swarm over them, beating them to the ground. The music hesitates but keeps going as the Stones try to just get by it. Because at any Rolling Stones concert there is *always* some business going down in the front rows, and always the Stones play through it, play to the house, to all the other tens of thousands that can't see or don't care about what's going on in the front row. It was as if, at Altamont, the only law that held any sway was the show business law that the show must go on.

So the Stones kick it up again, but soon another fight breaks out. This time sawed-off pool cues can be seen, their butt ends brought crashing down on collapsed forms, and it is clear that the Angels, for whatever reason, are trashing the crowd, and I start to think, "Why the fuck doesn't Mick do something? Just stop it."

Mick goes to the microphone, and I think, "Good. Now this will all stop," and Mick says, "Hey, hey, people. Sisters — brothers and sisters — *brothers and sisters* — come *on* now . . . Let's just give ourselves — we'll give ourselves another half minute before we get our breath back. . . ." Then it's like everyone holds their breath, and things seem to calm a little. Shortly the music starts again. But immediately the fighting erupts again too, the Angels wading into the crowd, flailing away. Again the music stops and Mick asks, "I mean, like people, who's fighting and what for? . . . Why are we fighting? . . ."

Mick's not calling anybody down. Instead he seems to attempt to reason with the mindless violence — maybe murky but unmistakable — going on right in front of him. His reaction seems to me so timid, as though he's talking to (as I came to photograph) some idea of a peaceful community he's heard so much about, not to these bedraggled, stoned, inner-city refugees.

Mick says, "I can't see what's going on, who is doing what. It's just a scuffle. All I can ask you, San Francisco, is like the whole thing — this could be the most beautiful evening we've had this winter. We really, y'know, why, why — don't let's fuck it up. . . ."

I stand on top of the truck at the back of the stage, hardly taking photographs, feeling blown out and hopeless, just wanting it to stop. Wanting Mick to actually *do* something, though I don't know what, and then Keith says, direct Keith, "Either those cats cool it, or we don't play." And I think, "Right! Right, now it'll have to stop." Keith points to a guy and says, "That guy there . . . If he doesn't stop it . . ." Then things seem to calm for a little bit. But not for long. Another hole gapes open, people careen away, the show stops, and then slowly stumbles on again, until it is clearly hopeless.

There are no police, no law at Altamont. The Woodstock Nation is to look after itself. The Hell's Angels are the only security.

I can see the beatings from where I stand. They all take on a dreadful similarity. Still, it is not possible to see precisely what is happening or who is hitting whom. I look right at the melee that turns out to be the stabbing of Meredith Hunter as he is buried under a swarm of Hell's Angels, but by then it's just another brawl, another unholy hole opening up. I am too far back to hear anyone say anything about a gun, too far back to see that that particular set of pumping arms is holding knives. Then the music stops again.

Mick says, trying to keep it together, while the idea is being slaughtered in front of him, "If we *are* all one, let's fucking well *show* we're all one. Now there's one thing we need — Sam, we need an ambulance — we need a doctor by that scaffold there . . ."

There is need for a doctor because Meredith Hunter has been stabbed multiple times. He will die. Before he was killed he was seen holding a gun. The gun was later found to be empty.

The sound of "Midnight Rambler" drifts out over the audience.

The unceasing and apparently unstoppable violence causes a sense of unreality to take hold. Time slows down, crawls to a halt, as when on drugs, and I pity the poor bastards on LSD. Still, somehow, and I have no idea how, the show finally comes to an end. I hear the opening chords of "Street Fighting Man," signaling, as they had the whole tour, that the show is finishing. I climb down off the top of the van, and start walking back to where I think the helicopter should be. I walk quickly, wanting nothing more than to get *out* of there. I walk from the stage into complete blackness, as rapidly as I can, hurrying to get to the helicopter early. I bump against a chain-link fence in the dark and realize it is between me and the chopper. I walk along it. I wonder if I will be stopped but I see no one. I wonder if there was someone, whether they would let me pass, honor the usually sacrosanct passes I carry. I come to a gate but it is locked. I take off all my cameras and push them under the fence, get down on my stomach, and slither after them. Then I can see a few dim lights in front of me. I run toward them as fast as all my equipment permits. The music has stopped from the stage and that means the Stones will be rushing to get to the helicopter as well.

I am one of the last there, and the helicopter is jammed. But someone recognizes me and pulls me on board. There are no seats. I crawl onto the floor, lying across someone's legs. The helicopter tries to take off in the normal manner, straight up, but it can't. We are too many. It starts to taxi, gathering speed down the runway, until it finally lifts, with agonizing slowness, off into the night sky. Nobody speaks as the helicopter passes over the darkened hills. It lands with a bump, overloaded, taxiing to a stop.

I didn't know what had happened, didn't know then that someone had been stabbed to death. I just knew it had been out of control and very ugly, and I was glad to be out of there, glad that it was over. I went back to the conservative hotel on the top of Nob Hill in San Francisco, climbed into bed between clean sheets, and went to sleep.

The next day I talked to Mick and I can't remember what question I asked, but I remember his answer, which was "It could have been me." I first thought how amazing it was that he could have thought about himself when there was such mayhem and violence all around him, and then I remembered that here was a man who for years now had been playing riotous crowds, who had been dragged off stage before, who knew he could be hurt when he was up there. And, quite a while later, I saw the Maysles' film of Altamont, *Gimme Shelter,* and in it I saw a Hell's Angel whose eyes were quite literally bulging out of his head, whose hands clenched and unclenched themselves, who pulled at his hair, and who was clearly stoned, violent, and precipitately murderous, standing not eight feet from Mick Jagger, a cosmopolitan, rather slight Englishman and rock singer. Though they both paid homage to the Devil, only one of them was in show business.

A slow howl, like the dying breath of some dumb animal, erupted over the next days and months, arising from people writing and talking about Altamont. All of those who considered music and its revolution as worthwhile reacted as if they had been assaulted, as, of course, they had been.

Recriminations flew. People railed at Jagger, calling him Satan and Lucifer, assailing his image. The Stones were called callous and capitalist. Ralph Gleason, who was an editor for *Rolling Stone* magazine (and whose reputation had swelled with the music of the sixties, in no small part because of the influence of the Rolling Stones), termed Jagger "lofty, elitist, and absolutely amoral."

A woman who called herself Detroit Annie delivered a judgment from the street: "Mick and the boys, you see, have signed this pact with the Devil. First of all they get the Power — just enough to pull off a few pranks and fantasies — have some fun, you understand. But don't waste your sympathy on the devil. He ain't trustworthy . . ."*

The more political recalled the Chicago Democratic National Convention and People's Park (for Berkeley is just down the road), and they tally the cost of revolution. In this context the Hell's Angels are the "People's Pig."

As for the Hell's Angels, Sonny Barger says, "There were . . . people in there that . . . kicked a couple of bikes over and, uh, you know, broke a couple of mirrors. I don't know if you think we pay fifty bucks for them things or steal 'em or pay a lot for them or what? But most people that's got a good Harley chopper got a few grand invested in it."

Radio interviewer: "I can dig it."

Barger: "Ain't nobody gonna kick my motorcycle . . ."

Radio interviewer: "Right."

Still some others, from the early Haight-Ashbury days, who had hoped to somehow make credible in the twentieth century the old Indian respect for the land and the spirit that lived there, wrote: "It may be that some of the difficulties at the Altamont Rock Festival transpired because the organizers didn't take time to make the proper preparations. Such would be: Formally asking the local Earth-Spirit for permission to use his space; requesting indulgence of the grass, insect, and bird beings whose homes and bodies would be trampled on. . . . Such was done at all the Gatherings of the Tribes — the first Be-In in Golden Gate Park."‡

Certainly Altamont was the beginning of the end, stripping away all the conceits of togetherness heralded only four months earlier at Woodstock. The frightening thing at Altamont, and everyone noticed it, was how so much of the audience wasn't

*From "You Always Get What You Want," by Detroit Annie, in *Altamont,* edited and introduced by Jonathan Eisen. New York: Avon Books, 1970.

‡"Ecco-Notes from Earth Read-Out," in *Altamont,* edited and introduced by Jonathan Eisen. New York: Avon Books, 1970.

just high, they were *gone*. Their eyes were not entranced but vacant. There were reports of kids writhing in the mud, kids burning each other's faces with cigar ends, burnt out for real. Too gone to react or understand, we were all wimps in the face of the Angels.

———◆———

Mean Mick Jagger was sitting in the small rented airplane waiting to go to Miami. We sat there all day. Finally the pilot starts the engines, and one of them backfires. Jagger is halfway out the airplane door before he realizes what happened. ✧

Right: "Us" at Altamont.

[173]

CHAPTER

13

ENGLAND, 1971.

With Pete Townshend at the wheel, the six-liter Mercedes was traveling up the M1 north of London at over 130 miles per hour. Any car traveling at 130 mph is to a car traveling 60 mph as a car going 70 is to a car fully stopped. I watched from the rear seat as we overtook cars on the motorway as if they were parked.

Townshend was talking animatedly to John Wolff, the bald road manager for the Who, known familiarly as "Wiggy." "Not a hair on me anywhere, mate," he would explain. Pete, Wiggy, and I were headed north to Leeds to join the rest of the Who for a performance that night.

Wiggy and I had met a couple of weeks previously after Glyn Johns (who was producing *Who's Next,* their first studio album since *Tommy*) had called to say that the album was almost finished and, although there were several companies developing ideas, the Who still did not have an album cover. Glyn mentioned that one of the tunes dealt with getting away from it all, and that Pete had a Land Rover, and maybe something could be done with that, you know.

So the Land Rover was procured and Wiggy and I and occasionally Sy, another member of the Who's entourage (short for "Cyrano," and he looked it: a long nose bulbed at the end and hair that grew to his shoulders), would go driving around the English countryside, drinking and smoking dope. They would tell stories of being on the road with the Who, stories of madness and destruction and a lot of booze.

I got it into my head that the photograph should be set in something resembling a dry lake bed. It was a look common in American advertising of automobiles. As a dry lake bed was out of the question in England, we looked instead for an unobstructed, treeless hillside. It is a peculiarity of photographers to care about these things, opaque to others, and for days we searched, until it became a running joke when Wiggy saw me: the American who liked English beer who needed to find "an area of outstanding beauty without any trees."

But we got the photographs. When Pete saw them he justifiably wondered what a Land Rover perched on a quite unobstructed hillside in the English sunset with its headlamps gleaming had to do with the Who's latest record. The Who's only alternative, however, was a cover delivered the day before to the recording studio: a 24-by-12-inch montage of extremely fat naked women. It was rejected because Jimi Hendrix had already done something almost identical on one of his albums, only the women in that instance were not fat. It was decided that I would follow the Who to a weekend gig in the Midlands, and out of this, it was hoped, a cover would emerge.

As the Mercedes raced north, one of the cars in the slow lane would occasionally decide to use the passing lane and pull out, so that now it was as if we were closing on a parked car at 70 mph from the rear. Pete would look up from his conversation with Wiggy and apply the brakes. I watched the speedometer drop from 130 to below 100 to 60, so that it did feel as if we had come to a complete stop. The big Mercedes accomplished this so smoothly that I was repeatedly impressed, but in a captive fashion like some prisoner grudgingly forced to admire the solid construction of his cell. As soon as the other car pulled back into the slow lane, Pete would once again accelerate up to 130 and past. This happened repeatedly until, truly unable to stand it, I slumped down in the back seat and closed my eyes, leaving my fate entirely in the hands of Peter Townshend, whose reputation was built, at least in part, on the total destruction of his equipment when he performed.

This sudden whirlwind of destruction grew to be a trademark of the Who both onstage and off. As Townshend would destroy his guitars, raising them over his head and smashing them against the floor, into the amplifiers, the feedback howling, smoke rising for effect, so Keith Moon would destroy his drum kit, kicking it away from him, taking the kettledrum and raising it over his head, throwing it at the audience. Offstage Moon was known to have driven a Rolls-Royce into a swimming pool, and rumor had it that the lot of them had so ransacked a Manhattan hotel that they were thereafter banned from staying anywhere in the city.

That afternoon they entered the dining room of a middle-class hotel in Leeds like some outlaw gang in a Western: the bald Wiggy, the curly-haired Daltrey, and the ever-manic Moon. The customers turned to stare, pausing from their shrimp cocktails in Thousand Island dressing with thin pieces of buttered brown bread, to watch as the normally nondescript process of ordering lunch is turned into an encounter laced with threats of personal violence.

Wiggy to the waiter: "And if it's not just how I ordered it, then, hear me out now, I shall rip off your arm and beat you to death with it."

Upstairs, in Keith Moon's room, bottles of brandy were opened and consumed, the first stirrings of a rush to manic abandonment that seemed the daily fare of the Who's drummer. Moon was so legendarily crazy that I always felt it best to keep my distance. Still, he was ever the gentleman, smiling and bowing, weaving might be another word. "Ethan, my good man, a spot of brandy, then?"

———◆———

That night, after the gig, we still had no idea for a cover, but the Who flaunted destruction, so destroying a dressing room for a possible album cover seemed natural.

Lights were drawn from the stage, remounted, and used to light the dressing room. The hall had reluctantly agreed (there's really not much you can do to six cement surfaces). But it was as if, permission granted, the idea lost its appeal, and it

Below (top to bottom): The Who on a rehearsal stage. Pete Townshend. Roger Daltrey.

was a desultory destruction that resulted in a few chairs being broken up and the specter of Moonie bashing his fist through some bottles.

The next morning we were off, a caravan of Mercedes, Jaguars, and Rolls-Royces, one after the other, stopping briefly in the ruins of Leeds to photograph the Who leaning against blown-out brick buildings, a look characteristic of English groups since the Beatles. But it was not enough for a cover, neither that nor the dressing room, and I knew it.

The cars pulled on to the motorway and headed back to London. It was a typical English day: the sky would be clear, and then suddenly clouds would blow in, and the sky would darken and sheets of rain would lash the landscape.

Following the lead car (in which I sat), the caravan traveled at Pete's speed, that is to say at 130 miles per hour and above. As the car would run into a squall it was as if it had suddenly been thrown into a lake, so dense was the water when encountered at that speed. Visibility would drop to nothing, for even German engineering cannot create a windshield wiper to deal with that stress. Pete would slow down to 60 or so and wait for the squall to pass.

It's quiet in the car, the morning after the gig of the night before. I'm still wondering what we are going to do about a cover, and as with the journey north, a good deal of my attention is consumed wondering if I'll survive, when I look out the window and see huge cement blocks thrusting randomly out of acres of black ooze. A

[176]

totally surreal sight, it reminded me of the monolith — the slab — from Stanley Kubrick's *2001: A Space Odyssey*. But we were traveling so fast that the shapes vanished almost immediately. I turned my head quickly to catch a last glimpse.

At the next roundabout, Pete says, "Well, do you have any ideas?"

And I say, "Well, there were these shapes back a few miles, and . . ."

Townshend spins the wheel of the Mercedes, and the entire caravan follows, and again at 130 we careen back toward these shapes, screeching to a halt. The Who and entourage step out of their cars. (We are looking — I am later to discover — at a slag heap, a collection of almost solid industrial waste into which concrete pillars are thrust to keep the waste from shifting.)

I grab my cameras and we all walk out onto the dark reef of the slag. The sky is still gray as occasional drops of rain fall. At first I direct them to react to the slab as Kubrick's apes and astronauts react in *2001:* approaching cautiously, arms upraised, almost touching it. But this is too much a re-creation, and somebody, probably Pete, walks up to the slab and starts to piss on it. The others follow suit. Those unable to urinate on cue are aided by little film cans filled with rainwater.

In the early 1970s anyone familiar with the Who is also going to have seen Kubrick's slab, unclear in its meaning but mythic in proportions, somehow mystically related to death and rebirth. For their next cover, the Who piss on it. Such was the nature of album cover art at the beginning of the seventies.★

———◆———

Album covers. The Rolling Stones' (*Through the Past Darkly*) had been my first (the five of them, before Brian's death, with their faces pressed against a sheet of glass). I had suggested the idea to Al Steckler, from Allen Klein's office, who in turn suggested it to Mick. Much to my surprise, Mick agreed. Mick suggested we destroy the glass for the back cover. The assistants in George Nichols's studio — probably the most elegant still studio in London at the time — stood shocked as twenty sheets of eight-by-ten-foot glass were shattered in a flurry of bricks.

Album covers became part of the mythology that rock music created. The Stones, the Beatles, and Dylan had started it, the Stones most outrageously (dressing up as WACs with Wyman in a wheelchair). Perhaps the most famous was the Beatles' *Sgt. Pepper's Lonely Hearts Club Band.* It was the first gatefold (double sleeve).‡ This was done by Michael Cooper. At about the same time he also did the cover for the Stones' *Their Satanic Majesties Request.*

An album cover not only showed a group in its latest incarnation (and that's the word, they were changing so often), the covers also became an entertainment themselves, something to spend time with. The lyrics, with renewed importance, would generally be printed on the liner or the sleeve. (With the notable exception of the Stones'.) The players would be given credit, sometimes on a song-by-song basis. The list of credits — including design and photography — expanded until a record jacket seemed to contain as many credits as a film. (Management by . . . Manager's assistant . . . Album coordinator . . . Spiritual advisor . . . Rib joint . . . and on.)

So when the latest word in record form arrived, you'd put the record on and then sit and listen, turning the cover in your hand, examining it. The same obsessive attention that music was receiving could be shared with a cover, for there were the visual clues. And the same attention that would insist that the very last groove of a

---

★The gray sky is a little dull so it is replaced with the sunset from the Land Rover photograph.

‡After *Sgt. Pepper,* acts that had any stature would demand a double sleeve, a practice that was to last into the late seventies, when the recession hit the record business.

Above and right: The Rolling Stones' Through the Past Darkly *session.*

[179]

Beatle record, played backward, would reveal that "Paul is dead," would find mysterious figures encrypted in the bark of a tree on the cover of Dylan's *John Wesley Harding,* significance where none was intended.

So it seemed to me at the time that the album cover was the summit of musical photography. There the photograph became more than just a photograph, it became an icon, incorporated into the community, something directly allied with (maybe even an amplification of) the music.

To create an album cover, the process was generally the same. As the album neared completion the need for a cover would assert itself, and a phone call would be made to the chosen designer or photographer, followed by delivery of an acetate (a single cutting of the album on disc; this was before cassette players were universal). A set of lyrics would be included. Listening to the music, some allied concept would hopefully emerge. If not, a simple photo session would be arranged.

More and more now I spent time looking at things, going to museums, leafing through magazines, studying other photographers' work, trying to decipher how a photograph had been taken. A lot of the craft was still a mystery.

I asked Tony Richmond how to light. He had been lighting cameraman on both the Beatles' *Let It Be* and the Stones' circus — though his list of credits is more distinguished still, including Nicholas Roeg's *Walkabout* and *Don't Look Now.*

"By looking," he said, a statement both simple and difficult, since looking is the essential action, but there's a great deal of craft in interpreting what you see. It was emphatically not the answer I wanted, which would have been completely specific: well, you take a 500-watt lamp and place it at a 45-degree angle to, and six feet from, the subject's left.

Light became increasingly intriguing. Natural light. Artificial light. Soft light. Hard light. The color of light. The physics of light.

There was new equipment to examine, from the many available lenses of 35mm photography to the larger format of two and a quarter inches (Hasselblad). Then the still larger formats: four by five inches, eight by ten, half-plate, and whole-plate. These were cameras that had to be on a tripod, where the photographer disappears under a dark cloth, and views an image on a ground glass, upside-down and backward. I was learning the trade of what I had, quite by chance, become: a photographer, or more precisely, a "rock photographer," a very small cog in the large wheel of the business of show.

———◆———

There were few of us to begin with. Baron Wolman who — in San Francisco — did candid portraiture for *Rolling Stone.* In London Gered Mankowitz did the early Rolling Stones' covers. Also from San Francisco was Jim Marshall, hook-nosed, very intense, with a gripe against everybody. To Jim everyone not in the room was a cocksucker. Jim cared deeply about his photography, but his anger and paranoia always seemed to get in his way.

Bob Seidemann created images that haunted. He photographed the Grateful Dead standing amid the endlessly identical houses of South San Francisco, the whole image underexposed except for their faces, so they appeared like apocalyptic figures, arrived to wreak havoc. Bob did the montage of the adolescent girl holding a silver airplane for Blind Faith, and the Magritte re-creation for Jackson Browne's *Late for the Sky*.

In Los Angeles, Barry Feinstein worked with Tom Wilkes producing notable album covers. Later there would be Norman Seeff, from South Africa, once a doctor by trade. Norman's work, almost always black and white, consisted principally of slightly diffuse portraits of singers or groups in varying degrees of ecstatic abandon, as Carly Simon in *Playing Possum* on her knees in boots and tiny black negligee in front of the photographer's seamless paper.

In 1970, Annie Leibovitz became the staff photographer for *Rolling Stone*. Trained at the San Francisco Art Institute, Annie brought a highly scattered energy to her work. Always threatening to trip over her equipment and destroy it all, Annie completely disarmed her subjects. She would give them a direction, at first tentative, and then laugh, and go, "Great, great." Annie's early work, despite her disclaimers, indicated a talent that soon seemed to eclipse everyone's.

In 1973 *Rolling Stone* published *Shooting Stars,* a collection, edited by Annie, of photographs taken by those who worked entirely in music. Even as rock photography drew some attention to itself, it remained a very obscure profession, difficult to explain to the average person.

Still, there was a growing group of us who were making our living at photographing, designing, packaging rock 'n' roll.

LOS ANGELES, 1971.

Below: Peter Asher.

Peter Asher, once famous as head of Apple Records' Talent Division, where he signed James Taylor, and, prior to that, as "Peter" of Peter and Gordon ("Everyone's Gone to the Moon"), had gone — instead — to Los Angeles (which some say is stranger than the moon), taking James Taylor with him. Peter, who at first appears so shy that he may hesitate to ask you for the time, has somehow successfully managed to ask various record companies for the millions of dollars that become due to the artists he manages and produces (James Taylor, Linda Ronstadt). Also with Peter had gone Chris O'Dell, of "Apple Pisces Lady" fame (Leon Russell), from Tucson, Arizona ("Get Back"). Chris is friends with the Beatles and the Rolling Stones, a sweet and softspoken American lady immensely solicitous of everyone's well-being except, of course, her own. Chris drops to under a hundred pounds before she puts the brakes on.

James Taylor has prospered on his return to America in part because *Time* magazine places him on its cover, as the most visible exponent of what *Time* calls "The New Rock: Bittersweet and Low." *Sweet Baby James,* the album immediately preceding his new one, for which I am to do the cover, sold a bittersweet 1.6 million copies

(which gave Taylor the experience to later write, "I need a strong hit / from that money machine").

Chris calls me and I call Peter and a session is arranged. Taylor shows up at the small rented studio in Hollywood. He is tall with a deceptively commanding presence. He wears a wrinkled blue shirt and old herring-bone trousers held up by suspenders stitched with images of half-moons and cats.

A no-frills session. There are no art directors, no assistants, just the two of us.

I take a Polaroid and show it to him. This is a way of involving someone in the photo session (as the Polaroid is a close approximation of the image), so the sitter doesn't feel quite as removed from the process. Taylor looks and nods but doesn't react. I offer a few pleasantries, take another Polaroid, show it to him. Nothing beyond what appears to be a completely benign indifference.

Somewhere in the course of a reasonably successful photography session, the photographer is obligated to draw something from the sitter, to overcome the sitter's reticence or paranoia about how he looks, the personal baggage everyone carries that identifies with his face (and, in show business, sometimes just to penetrate the wall of ego that stares back with the warmth of marble). Generally this is a mutual effort, approached obliquely, based on the tacit assumption that, in the end, nobody really wants to look bad.

But with Taylor whatever I say meets with no response. Roll after roll of film passes through the camera, but his expression is unvarying, a look that would be bored if it could rise above indifference. Since this portends certain failure for the session if it keeps up, I finally ask in desperation, "Can you do anything? How about a smile?"

To ask for a smile is to admit failure.

A purely beatific smile spreads across James Taylor's face. "Could you do that again?" I ask. The smile returns, as if he kept it in a pocket behind the half-moons and cats.

SAN FRANCISCO, 1972.

In San Francisco, I photograph Boz Scaggs.

I met Boz in London where Glyn Johns was producing Boz's second album. Boz was tearing at his hair, a man almost through recording his record, most of the tracks completed, without a single lyric written.

I remember Boz, a great cook, standing over a stove in Pacific Heights, San Francisco, pouring wine into lobster sauce, stirring, tasting. Soon to become the very elegant Boz.

For Boz's album *My Time* I attempt to recreate a quality of portraiture common in the Renaissance. Such portraits were generally head and shoulders, always in a room with a window. Out the window would be a pastoral scene, but the spatial relationships were never quite right, as if the landscape was infinitely far away and

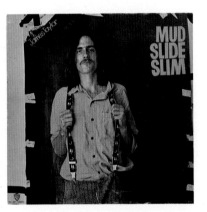

Left: James Taylor.

Above: The album cover.

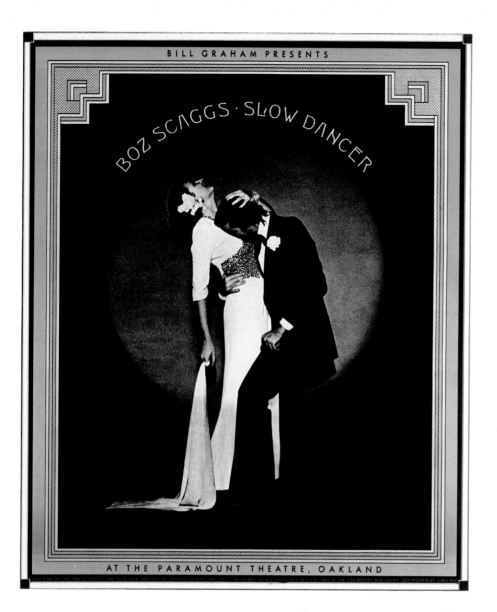

somehow had been cut and pasted into the window. Because I was fascinated, I tried to recreate this, building a two-wall set and commissioning a painting of a moonlit landscape for out the window, an appeal to the romantic.

Boz and I sit getting drunk in a bar. Boz talks about the pros and cons of being very famous, which Boz is not, yet. Boz is for it.

"Yeah, but you know," I say, "I was having lunch with these two people who were really close friends of Jagger's, and the question came up whether he really trusted anybody, anybody at all. And they didn't think he did. That's a pretty big price."

"Doesn't matter," Boz said.

Moshe Brakha and Ron Coro would create the image that would do best for Boz Scaggs, a perfectly tailored elegance, like a forties movie transformed into color. Two albums in a row would sell platinum (one million units). Boz would be managed by the notorious Irving Azoff (have you heard what's wrong with Napoleon? He had an Irv Azoff complex). Boz would achieve the fame to which he aspired. But, as with

Above left: Boz Scaggs. I was on the floor from an excess of gin.

Right: The photograph for Boz Scaggs's My Time cover. "An appeal to the romantic."

so many others, it would take its toll. Boz rode the manic wave, carrying a Dristan container to clear his nose in public places. Shortly he disappeared, re-emerging some years later to tell *San Francisco* magazine that his sons were what mattered and that the road show business sends you down is a dangerous one indeed.

LOS ANGELES. RITA COOLIDGE.

For years a backup singer, Rita was making her first record produced by the distinguished David Anderle, one of the few to whom Los Angeles really was home (he was born there) and who thereby didn't always appear to be lost at sea. Rita's folks were southern and Christian. Her sister, also a singer, married Booker T. of "Green Onions" fame, who would later give the world Willie Nelson singing "Stardust." They had a ranch in Malibu.

We went to the ranch to shoot. Rita wore a black cape and rode horses and walked around as I took pictures. As it does almost every year, Malibu had just had a brush fire. As Rita walked through the blackened branches, she looked like an Indian princess.

Later Rita would marry Kris Kristofferson. She would arrive briefly in a limousine to visit an old friend who was having a wedding reception. Rita was famous now, too, and it looked as if it had been hard.

THE CALIFORNIA DESERT. LEON RUSSELL.

Glyn Johns produced the record. To play on it, Glyn recruits the cream of English rock 'n' rollers: Bill Wyman, Charlie Watts, Eric Clapton. I say to Leon, making conversation, "You must have loved England."

"England loved me," said Leon, subjugating an entire country to his ego. ♪

Above: Rita Coolidge.

Left: Carlos Santana, who traveled with his own mini-shrine.

Right: Members of the Santana band, more carnal in their pursuits.

[186]

14

LOS ANGELES, 1972.

By 1972 the Rolling Stones had their own corporate logo (a lapping tongue protruding between unmistakable bright-red lips) that spun around in circles in the center of their records, was emblazoned on T-shirts and jackets, was made into little gold pins for the Inner Circle, and now drooped happily painted on the fuselage of the Electra jet chartered for their first American tour since 1969.

They have a new record out, *Exiles on Main Street,* a great title for the new Rolling Stones: the once-ragged band of London's cold-water flats are now English tax refugees living on France's Côte d'Azur. Stories of Bill Wyman lunching with Marc Chagall appear in the press. The gaunt outlaw of rock 'n' roll, Keith Richards, lives in high-ceilinged splendor. This portends a big change, for the Côte d'Azur is, after all, about fine wine, food, and the mythical light of the Impressionists, and hardly at all about rock 'n' roll.

In Los Angeles, Mick and Keith are once again domiciled high in the Hollywood Hills, way at the top of Sunset Plaza Drive, in a house belonging to Michael Butler, the producer of *Hair.* Like a lot of L.A. houses, it is imitation French château. The workers for the 1972 tour are stashed at the Beverly Rodeo Hotel on Rodeo Drive, Beverly Hills.

Except for its address, the Beverly Rodeo could be any of America's faceless hotels, an unimposing three-story structure sandwiched between shops. The lounge is done in deep-red leather and lit almost entirely with tiny-flamed candles in red jars so, coming in out of the bright L.A. sunshine, your eyes need several minutes to adjust. The Rolling Stones tour party (dubbed "S.T.P.," some said for "Stones Tour Party," others for the hallucinogen of the same initials; the usual ambiguity) takes up most of one floor. By the time I arrive, called down from northern California, most of the crew have been there for a week. The old hands (Chip Monck, Jo Bergman, Glyn Johns, Ian Stewart) are rapidly bringing themselves up to speed. The big change is the absence of Ronnie Schneider, or anyone from the Allen Klein organization. Ronnie has been replaced by Peter Rudge, whose suite at the Beverly Rodeo is the hub of all activity, where the phones are constantly ringing, and the doors slam shut in people's faces as Peter enters into one of the myriad negotiations prior to the start of the tour.

Peter Rudge, twenty-six, is an Oxford-educated Englishman whose entry into rock and roll was as manager for the Who on their American tours. Dealing with

Who madness is deemed education enough for Rolling Stone madness, and now Peter is submerged in the details of the new tour. His hair hangs over his collar, he wears an open-necked button-down shirt, a blue blazer, blue jeans, and loafers, the soon-to-be-common look of the rock manager. Peter is maniacally intense, having undertaken, for unknown compensation, to oversee the innumerable details of the largest Rolling Stones tour to date. Peter smokes incessantly, bringing the cigarette to his lips and taking quick, staccato puffs, then crunching the cigarette out. He is able, in the unimprovable phrase of Robert Greenfield, to say "completely offensive things to people that make them smile." It is a quality Peter employs a lot.

I am waiting in the hallway outside Peter's room for my salary negotiation to

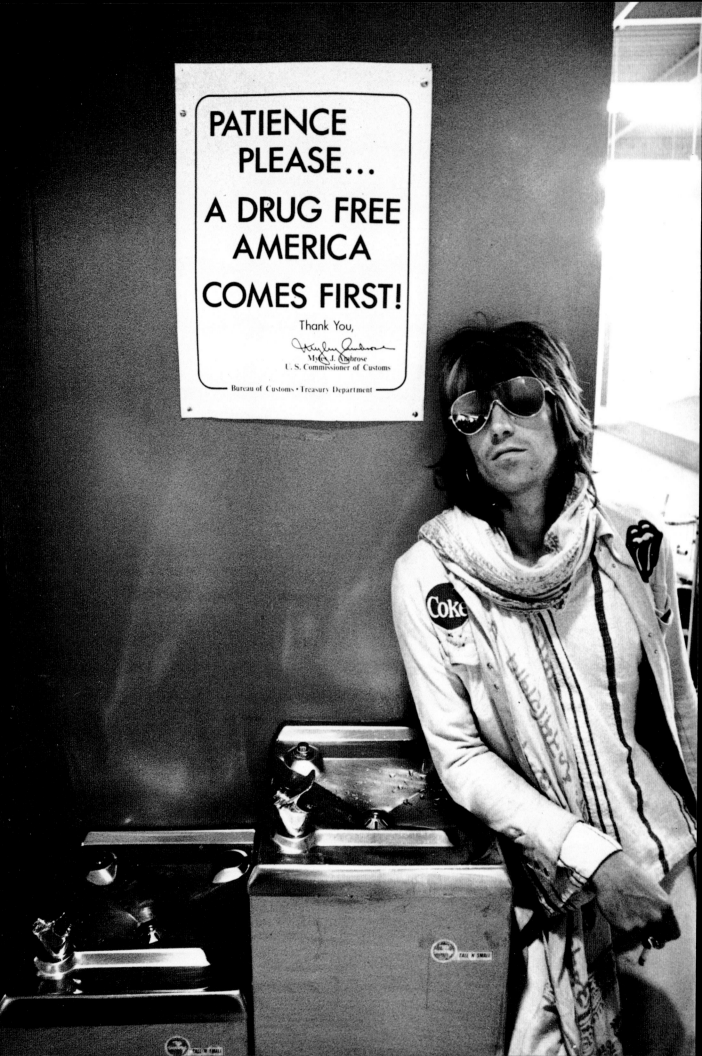

take place. My request will be small. After all, I am a very minor player in the scheme of this tour. I want only what I received on the 1969 tour reasonably adjusted (upward) to take into account the effect of inflation, a cost of living increase, as it were.

The door opens and Jim Price, accomplished trumpet and trombone player, who will — with the tempestuous Bobby Keyes — constitute the horn section for this tour, walks out shaking his head dejectedly. I have similar luck, and when I leave I am glad to have hung on to what I earned in 1969.

Whatever was wrong with the 1969 tour, which ended, after all, at Altamont, Peter was determined would never happen again. Charges leveled at the Stones for high ticket prices and unprofessional behavior were to be addressed. This tour was bigger, better, more prepared. The Rolling Stones now traveled with their own doctor, film crew, make-up man, bookkeeper, baggage handler, and several layers of security.

Already the tour was garnering more media attention than had the 1969 tour. This may have been in part due to the efforts of Bob Gibson and Gary Stromberg, whose public relations firm (Gibson & Stromberg) was to David Horowitz's (of the 1969 tour) what Perrier and a little toot in the back room is to a three-martini lunch.

Gibson and Stromberg had offices in a small building in the middle of Sunset Strip. The doors were always open, and there was a sign above the entrance that said, "Two Press Officers — No Waiting." Young and beautiful girls would wander in and out while Gibson and Stromberg were on the phone to *Time, Life, Esquire, Rolling Stone,* and *Saturday Review,* all of whom were planning major stories on the tour.

The Stones were now a bigger story than ever. "They are the last of the Sixties," says *Time* magazine (which also says they "need publicity about as much as the Second World War"). But something had happened since 1969, something to excite this much attention, and no doubt that something was Altamont. For at Altamont, it was clear to see from the film, it could have been Mick who was attacked, even killed. So now an act (Mick Jagger and the Rolling Stones) already acknowledged as sexual was further charged with the prospect of violence, creating that media delight: sex, violence, and, hey, rock 'n' roll. What could be better?

But Peter Rudge, harried and intent, was determined that the violence, never overtly mentioned, would never materialize. (And it never does. Though threats of violence are common and, much later in the tour, there is even a bombing, none of this ever intrudes upon the Stones. Peter even meets with the Hell's Angels to try to soothe their still angry feelings.) Wherever the Stones go, security is double- and triple-checked. Every member of the cast and crew is issued a red laminated-plastic identification badge with his or her photograph on it, the letters S.T.P. above, and Peter Rudge's signature below. Even the Stones wear these, posing patiently for Polaroids. (This goes for the supporting acts and their entourages as well. But when I approach Stevie Wonder's people about polaroiding Stevie, I am told to get out of their faces, Stevie is a Star. So I do. Later when they learn that Mick and Keith have been polaroided, they tell me they've reconsidered. Stevie would be glad. Show business.)

But, despite the months of planning, on the day of the first show in Vancouver, the Rolling Stones' tongue-emblazoned jet is stuck on the ground because the necessary flight plan apparently has not been filed. Everyone is in an uproar. Alan Dunn, who oversees these things, is talking with the pilot, trying to find a solution. The excitable Marshall Chess, president of Rolling Stone Records, totally engulfed by the momentum of the tour-about-to-happen, is shouting, "Where's a telephone? Get me Trudeau on the phone. Immediately." With an unquestioning belief in the sanctity of our rock 'n' roll mission, Marshall attempts to track down the prime minister of Canada to get special clearance for the Rolling Stones to enter Canadian airspace.

Marshall fails and instead the jet lands at an airport near the Canadian border. A string of limousines drives out onto the tarmac to greet it. Shortly, the Rolling Stones tour party is racing along empty Canadian freeways on its way to the opening show.

By 1972 there were a lot more photographers around. Annie Leibovitz is covering for *Rolling Stone,* Jim Marshall for *Life.* Ken Regan of *Camera 5* is covering for *Newsweek* and the wire services. I am covering for the Stones, but as an economy measure will be switched to the payroll of *Saturday Review* when Terry Southern shows up to write the article.

Terry Southern (of *Candy* fame) replaces William Burroughs (of *Naked Lunch* fame), who was originally scheduled to write the piece. Truman Capote (of *In Cold Blood* fame) comes to replace Robert Greenfield for *Rolling Stone.* Robert, whose work is consistently the best of the tour, leaves, screaming "Starfucker!" about Jann Wenner. Truman Capote is accompanied by Lee ("Princess") Radziwill (of Jackie Onassis fame) and Peter Beard, as his photographer (later of Cheryl Tiegs fame).

In addition, the tour travels with its own film crew, Robert Frank and Danny Seymour. (Robert is a Museum of Modern Art photographer whose book *The Americans* is a foreigner's perspective on America during the 1940s. His photographs, in montage, make up the album cover for *Exile on Main Street.* Robert now makes movies. Danny is his soundman/assistant, and looks the quintessential Greenwich Village–dwelling filmmaker, gaunt with long black hair sticking out from under a beret.) There seems to be universal liking and respect for Robert, who has more access to the Rolling Stones (for a cameraman) than I had ever seen before. And each and every city newspaper sends its cameras and reporters to catch the act.

The number of cameras, recorders, and writers now surrounding the Stones lends an almost campaignlike quality to the tour. In fact, the Stones are crisscrossing the United States during the 1972 presidential campaign. While Nixon sits in the White House giving interviews and acting presidential, George McGovern is hopping

Above (top to bottom): Mick, Keith, and the tongue-emblazoned jet. Limos meeting us for the trip into Canada. Robert Frank boarding. Keith and photographers (l. to r.: Keith, Bobby Keyes, unknown, Ken Regan, Jim Marshall, Ian Stewart).

Right: Mick Jagger and Lee Radziwill.

[192]

all over the country. Ken Regan, who supplies *Time* and *Newsweek,* among others, with a lot of their photography, flip-flops back and forth, spending one week with McGovern, the next with the Stones. The parallel does not go unremarked, but it is Robert Frank, with his journalist's flair for seeing what is around him, who notes the essential difference. He says, both perplexed and worried, "I have never seen anything like this. Everything is always pointed inward here. They travel everywhere, but they never look outside."

Traveling with the Stones, the expectation is that everything will come to you. In the morning the doctor arrives with the day's supply of vitamins. Transportation is always provided. Every person on the tour has been assigned numbers for their baggage, which will then be waiting in the assigned hotel rooms. With the access-providing S.T.P. badges, tour members roam through hallways closed to the public. While George McGovern is trying to establish "name recognition," the Rolling Stones are as famous as the Second World War.

As for the showmanship of it all, the Stones are as great as ever, strutting out in front of one sold-out amphitheater after another, bringing the crowds to their feet, leaving them yelling and dancing, following — in city after city — their opening accolade, "the greatest rock and roll band in the world."

And it is always a gas, even as the backstage starts to resemble a snippet from the "People" section of the newsweeklies, to go out in front of the stage, the huge audiences buzzing in anticipation, to hear the roar that greets the Stones as they come running forth, Jagger parading, the familiar tunes blasting from the amplifiers. Chip Monck's lights reflect from a huge mirror that gets transported from city to city, illuminating the band simultaneously from front and back, so that it's as if searchlights were beamed into the sky and reflected back to find the Stones. As in 1969, the crowds leave their seats and are jamming in the aisles, their eyes fixed on Jagger and the Stones, all of them wanting to be blown away, wanting the band to take hold of their

minds and bodies and deliver rock and roll oblivion, that elusive commodity of the sixties.

In the slowly stabilizing times of the seventies, people still yearn for a little rock 'n' roll oblivion. They turn to the Rolling Stones, who, as much as any mortals can, deliver. That's what they get paid for.

When Terry Southern joins the tour, he strides backstage, the very figure of debauch, his hair shaggy, his eyes red, stomach protruding, arms outstretched.

"Keith," he yells, grinning. Keith leaps up and, with that special affection he seems to hold for some, strides forward, and the two embrace.

"How ya doing, baby?" says Terry.

In New Orleans, the rock and roll blowout that Terry came to see (not so much to see as to be, really) catches up with him. A little too loose, while edging by one of Louisiana's finest on his way to the stage, Terry stumbles and an assortment of rolling papers, illegal pills, and poppers pour from his shirt pocket. Terry scrambles to pick them up and jam them into his pocket. This is deemed to be too much by the powers that be at S.T.P., who do not wish to deal with any drug arrests in the American South. Terry is told he's off the tour, and as I'm now working for *Saturday Review,* I'm told I will go as well.

The next morning in the humid sun of New Orleans, Terry Southern and Richard Alman, the writer for *Life,* sit on the roof of the white-pillared hotel and, the real world intruding, discuss alimony payments. Terry is subdued, his imminent exile from the tour impending. But he is forgiven (it is hard to bust a friend of Keith's for loose behavior). Still, the message is heard: get down to business or be gone.

◆

When Truman Capote showed up in Dallas (the town that sells postcards of the Texas School Book Depository with little *x*'s marking "The Window," "First Shot," "Sec-

Above, left, and right: The Rolling Stones on stage.

ond Shot"), his arrival was awaited with some apprehension. What did Capote have to do with rock and roll? What did Princess Lee Radziwill have to do with rock and roll? What did Peter Beard, who was preparing a book depicting the slaughtering of alligators in Africa, have to do with rock and roll? Mick may be androgynous, but compared to what? Truman Capote?

Capote had appeared not infrequently on Johnny Carson's *Tonight Show,* and his high-pitched voice was probably as famous as Jagger's lips. Capote had a notoriously wicked humor. Could he be trusted? What was Capote doing writing for *Rolling Stone*? What *did* all this have to do with rock and roll? It seemed to make everybody a little nervous. Rock and roll.

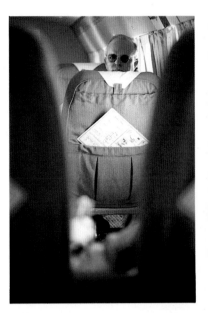

Clockwise from left: On board the Stones' plane. Truman Capote checking it out. Richard Alman (from Life) speaking with Charlie. Chris O'Dell and Keith. Bianca Jagger and Terry Southern.

Above: Keith Richards with
Terry Southern.

Below: Mick being made up.

As I'm signing the register at the Sheraton in Washington, D.C., Chip Monck walks up behind me and pops an amyl nitrate capsule under my nose. Instantly my heart begins to pound. Saying thank you to the desk clerk, I turn to walk down the hall, the ceiling expanding at the same rapid rate as my head. Chip Monck, laughing maniacally, disappears to coax a couple of stewardesses into the hotel. The hallway of the hotel takes on cathedral-like proportions. Having no idea how long this will last, I retreat to my room.

Shortly, I hear yelling going on down the hall. Chip Monck and the hotel manager are standing nose to nose.

"I know nothing of any lamp that has landed in your courtyard. I know only that there is no lamp in my room, and I would like one immediately, sir. I am a very busy man," booms Chip.

Later that night the single largest amount of cocaine I had ever witnessed was spread out on a large glass mirror and consumed with the ferocity of starving mosquitoes. Better than halfway through the tour, the road has everyone in its grip. The irresolvable conflict between how boring the road is and the nightly rush as you're surrounded by people dying to get off distorts all the rules. The tour members behave like visiting royalty, presuming diplomatic immunity, some magical distance from the rules governing normal human behavior.

The manager of the hotel brings Chip Monck another lamp.

"That's very kind. Thank you very much," says Chip in the exaggerated gentle-manly tones he uses when commanding others to do his bidding.

The Washington, D.C., concert takes place at the Robert F. Kennedy Memorial Stadium. The preoccupation with security, with protecting the principals, especially in the huge coliseums, is still very much on everyone's mind. This stage is built exceptionally high, creating a problem soon to be common in festival events. The fans down in front, those who waited the longest and cared the most, get pressured by those behind them until they are forced against the front of the stage, which is higher than them. From there they can see nothing. Crushed, overwhelmed, some faint and their bodies are passed overhead to be carried out by security. In Washington occasional smoke bombs come hurtling from the rafters. These are quickly doused by watchful stagehands.

Above: Keith on stage.

Left: Mick and Keith backstage.

"Honey, it's no rock 'n' roll show," sings Mick, prancing across the image of a Chinese dragon breathing fire, painted on the stage floor.

Washington, D.C., is the last show I will see of the '72 tour. Returning to California, I will read about Keith taking a swing at a photographer who refused to stop taking pictures, how the Stones will be jailed, and the mayor of Boston will effect their release so they can play the sold-out show at the Boston Garden. "I don't want to be responsible for any riots," says the mayor.

Mick Jagger will celebrate his twenty-ninth birthday at Madison Square Garden in front of twenty thousand people. Later, on the roof of the St. Regis, at the corner of Fifth Avenue and Fifty-fifth Street, a celebratory party is thrown, the guest list for which reads like the "Best of *People*": Andy Warhol, Truman Capote, Count Basie, Dick Cavett, George Plimpton, Muddy Waters, Lee Radziwill, Woody Allen, Bob Dylan, Zsa Zsa Gabor. The party marks the departure of Mick Jagger and the Rolling Stones from the annals of pop stardom to the peculiar realm of the international celebrity, like Liz and Dick (Mick and Bianca). What did all this have to do with rock and roll?

In the aftermath of the '72 tour and the blowout in Madison Square Garden, Jo Bergman, who has stood by the Rolling Stones since the days of the attic office in London, leaves. She fears she is on the verge of a nervous breakdown.

"In 1969 it was just us," she says. "Who was there? Mick, Keith, Bill, and Charlie. Mick Taylor. Astrid. You, me, and Stanley. Sam Cutler. Stu. Ronnie Schneider. Chip. Just thirteen people. By 1972 Keith was packing a gun, and the drug dealers were following us from town to town."

Jo retreats to the Isle of Man. She is reacting to what she has seen around her: rock and roll can kill you.

Terry Southern publishes his article. It is a rambling attempt to marvel at the far-outness of it all. He could have stayed home. Robert Greenfield goes home to write his book with care and concern.★ Truman Capote, who had everyone so worried, does not deign to write anything. "There was nothing to write about," says Truman, catty little fellow. "It was boring."

Show Business. In 1972, the Rolling Stones are big business getting bigger. By 1984 a Rolling Stones tour is a sponsored, packaged event that will include merchandising rights, sale of programs, a major theatrical motion picture release, a home-cassette sale, box-office receipts, and — just like the good old days — it will promote the latest record. The Rolling Stones ("the last of the Sixties") will earn a reported $1,397,000 each show, the devils.

"I know. It's only rock 'n' roll," sings Mick. "But I like it." ✤

Above: Pressure. Jo Bergman and Peter Rudge, later in the tour.

Below: Mick. "It's only rock 'n' roll."

★Greenfield's book, *STP: A Journey Through America with the Rolling Stones* (New York: Saturday Review Press/E. P. Dutton, 1974), remains the best and most comprehensive account of the '72 tour.

CHAPTER

15

NEW YORK CITY, 1972.

While Mick and the Stones are blowing them away in Madison Square Garden, John Lennon is living in the West Village, preoccupied with the considerable difficulties he is having with U.S. immigration. Though all objections to his staying in the United States centered around his arrest for possession of cannabis in London in 1968, there were those of us who suspected the reasons might be different. John's trouble with the U.S. Immigration and Naturalization Service seemed to start about the same time John decided that his life as a human being might encompass both the political and the entertainment worlds.

◆

Her [Yoko's] reason was peace. I'd been singing about love, which I guess was another word for peace.

— John Lennon★

LONDON, JULY 1969.

The party thrown to celebrate the release of "Give Peace a Chance" was held in the Chelsea Town Hall on the King's Road. The party was an Apple promotional event to break John and Yoko's new song to the press. The room was decorated with flowers; posters proclaiming "Peace" and "Love" hung on the walls. On the stage in front of the room was the "Plastic Ono Band," quite literally made of plastic: standing cylinders and cubes. The centerpiece of this sculpture was a collage of black and white photos of John Kennedy, Martin Luther King, Muhammad Ali, Marilyn Monroe, and many others.

Ringo was there, and Derek Taylor was there. Paul didn't make it, nor did John and Yoko, since they'd been in a car accident in Scotland the week before and just been released from hospital. Despite the obvious plea made by both the song and the posters, the party was not dissimilar, on the surface, from the one held at the top of London's Post Office Tower to kick off Mary Hopkin's single "Those Were the Days." Both had an open bar.

Over and over, the words "All we are saying is give peace a chance" echoed through the room. People stood randomly scattered, drinks in hand, as if at a giant cocktail party. To me, with my American fervor, there was something infinitely depressing about this message of hope received in this manner, and so, after drinking

Below and right: The opening for "Give Peace a Chance" at the Chelsea Town Hall.

★From *John Lennon: One Day at a Time,* by Anthony Fawcett. New York: Grove Press, 1976.

too many drinks myself, I walked through the hall, encouraging people to form themselves into a line (like the snake at an American high school dance). Before long we were wandering through the hall singing along with the record. Richard DiLello would write about the snake, "It coiled . . . back and forth, mindless and dazed by its own locomotion. . . . Mercifully the event called itself off by eight o'clock."

Indeed, the event seemed indigestible to most of the crowd, which consisted mostly of the English press, a cynical group at best, and the staff of Apple, loyal employees. Wasn't war and peace an American problem, over the sea and a long way away? What did the Beatles have to do with it (for the Beatles were still together then)? And John Lennon was a Beatle, some said the leader of the group. Wouldn't it be better if the Beatles just stayed out of the whole thing?

"Listen," said John, "when they ask next time, we're gonna say we don't like that war [Vietnam], and we think they should get right out."

"The continual awareness of what was going on made me feel ashamed. I burst out because . . . it was just too much for me." To *Rolling Stone* he says, "I thought it was about time we just fucking spoke about it [revolution], just like I thought it was about time we stopped not answering about the Vietnamese war."

"Give Peace a Chance" is released on July 7, 1969. In November of that year John returns his medal honoring him as a "Member of the (Order of the) British Empire" (M.B.E.) to "protest Britain's involvement in Biafra and support of America in Vietnam." He also says that he returns the M.B.E. to protest "Cold Turkey" (his latest record) "slipping down the charts." For those who thought Lennon's return of the M.B.E. was an affront to begin with, this piece of levity only enraged them further.

To Jann Wenner he says, about the M.B.E., "It's mostly hypocritical snobbery and part of the class system."

John and Yoko start a media blitz to promote peace. For John it is simply doing

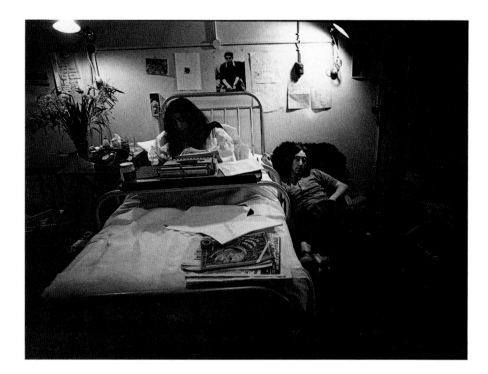

what had worked so well for the Beatles. They hold the Bed-In at the Amsterdam Hilton, inviting the press in to interview them. Film taken at the time shows them leaning back against a wall in their pajamas, obviously exhausted, speaking quietly to each other, while the room is filled with inquiring journalists. "Christ!" Lennon would later sing, "You know it ain't easy."

For their Christmas message they release a poster, "War Is Over (If You Want It)." The posters are plastered all around the world. They rent billboards on the Champs Elysées in Paris and Sunset Boulevard in Los Angeles, in Times Square, New York, Piccadilly Circus, London, and the center of Tokyo, Japan. The poster is carried as far as the border between Hong Kong and Red China.

The world press, though often cynical, nonetheless runs the stories and interviews from John and Yoko. Like the Beatles before them, John and Yoko prepare to invade America, to carry their message to the very heart of the beast. It is then that John Lennon's visa is denied. The Ono/Lennons keep at it. They fly to Canada and visit Prime Minister Trudeau instead.

But John Lennon comes to love New York and America and in 1971 he and Yoko decide to move there. The war in Vietnam still rages. Richard Nixon, who was elected on a promise to get the United States out of Vietnam, bombs Cambodia instead. In reaction, demonstrators gather outside the White House. The song they sing is "Give Peace a Chance." Richard Nixon personally orders government officials to "harass [Lennon] and 'kick him out of America.'"* In the kind of language that would later become all too familiar to Americans, the Internal Security Subcommittee of the Senate Judiciary Committee submits a memorandum to Strom Thurmond

Italic Above left: John and Yoko in hospital.

*From *John Lennon: One Day at a Time,* by Anthony Fawcett. New York: Grove Press, 1976.

[202]

headed "John Lennon." It says, "If Lennon's visa was terminated it would be a strategy counter-measure."

John Lennon, lacking his own government bureaucracy, strikes back through song: "No short-haired, yellow-bellied, son of tricky Dick's gonna mother-hubbard soft-soap me . . ."

Senator Thurmond writes to Attorney General John Mitchell, "This appears to me to be an important matter, and I think it would be well for it to be considered at the highest level . . . as I can see many headaches might be avoided if the appropriate action were taken in time."

John Lennon sings, "I'm sick and tired of hearing things from up-tight, short-sighted, narrow-minded hypocritics, all I want is some truth. Just gimme some truth."

In February 1973, the Vietnam War — the longest war in American history — is drawing to an end. More than any war before it (except the Civil War), it confused and divided the American people, forced many to disavow their government, become cynical of its intentions. It led to the beatings in Chicago, the killings at Kent State. The war's end is forced upon the American government by the concerted effort of a broad coalition of Americans. Discounting this entirely, Richard Nixon intends to take full credit. "We finally achieved a peace with honor," he says. "I know it gags some of you to write that phrase."

On the podium he initiates an attack against any and every American who opposed the war, revealing once again his almost pathological insecurity about the "so-called better people in the media and in the intellectual circles." They were the problem, complains Nixon. Most Americans supported the war, "despite the fact that they were hammered night after night, day after day, with the fact that this was an immoral war."

"What really aroused his ire," reports *Time* (February 12, 1973), "was a question on whether recent calls for a healing of the nation's wounds might lead to an amnesty for draft resisters. Nixon glowered, gripped both sides of the lectern and hunched low over the microphone. 'Well,' he says, 'it takes two to heal wounds.'" Nixon, apparently, is not going to be one of them: "'It is a rule of life, we all have to pay for our mistakes. Those who served paid their price. Those who deserted must pay their price, and the price is not a junket in the Peace Corps or something like that.'"

The same issue of *Time* that reports this and tells of Nixon's electoral triumph, and speculates on the nature of Nixon's second term, carries an article on the Watergate break-in, which had taken place the previous June. Judge John Sirica says, "I hope the Senate gets to the bottom of this case."

In an interview at the White House, Nixon, with his usual forthright honesty, says, "My political enemies don't get under my skin at all. You can't be in this business if you have thin skin."

John Lennon sings,

Instant karma's gonna get you.
Gonna look you right in the face.
Better get yourself together, darling,
Join the human race.

John says, "I am not in the group of people who think that because all our dreams didn't come true in the sixties, everything we said or did was invalid. No there isn't any peace in the world despite our efforts, but I still believe the hippie-peace-love thing was worthwhile. If somebody stands up and smiles and then gets smacked in the face, that doesn't invalidate the smile. It existed."

In the face of continuous political harassment, John sings:

How in the world you gonna see?
Laughing at fools like me? . . .

But we all shine on
Like the moon
And the stars
And the sun.
Well we all shine on
Everyone!
Come on! ♪

Left: The collage that was the centerpiece of the Plastic Ono Band, onstage at the Chelsea Town Hall for the opening of "Give Peace a Chance."

CHAPTER

16

LOS ANGELES, 1973.

The billboard over the Sunset Strip showed Tom Wilkes and his new partner, Craig Braun, arms interlinked, eyes bulging, both wearing T-shirts on which was an illustration of a bulldog with a cartoon bubble with a light bulb in its center emanating from his head. There was no copy with this billboard, nothing to identify to the general public what they were meant to glean from this ad.

Such was the hip, low-key approach to the record packaging business in the early 1970s. It wasn't an ad for a record, it was an ad for record packagers. Wilkes and Braun, the company name, was to combine the talents of Tom Wilkes, who for many years had been the art director for A&M Records, with the business acumen of Craig, who came out of New York.

Packaging was part of rock and roll now, and Tom and Craig meant to enter their business at the top. Hence the billboard. I had met Tom when he was at A&M. Since then we'd often spoken of working together. This was one of our first opportunities. In the hushed tones that often accompany the signing of a major star to a new picture, Tom intimated that Wilkes and Braun were on to something big, very big, in fact, a bigger and better package than had ever been done before. He wanted me to be involved, but he couldn't tell me anything about it yet.

Tom was a big, blond fellow who might easily be mistaken for Grizzly Adams. His slap on the back could send you reeling. It was strange to see this huge fellow bent over a water-color pad, struggling with the intractability of his paint, helplessly swearing as the delicate colors refused to stay put.

The "big package," it turned out, was the Ode production of *Tommy*. Indeed, as a product it was a bit like the rock equivalent of *Ben Hur* with an all-star cast. The original *Tommy,* the brain child of Pete Townshend and the Who, was the self-proclaimed first rock opera. It was the Who's first million-seller in America, and they successfully toured the country with *Tommy*. The most prominent performance was at the Metropolitan Opera House in New York, which netted them a vast amount of media coverage. In rock terms *Tommy* was almost as acclaimed as *Sgt. Pepper.*

The combination of Lou Adler (of Carole King and Ode Records fame) and Lou Reizner, producer, resulted in the decision to re-record *Tommy* with the London Symphony Orchestra and an all-star cast. The rock 'n' roll biz had never seen an event like this. "Starring" were, among others, Ringo Starr, Rod Stewart, Richie Havens, Stevie Winwood, Richard Harris, and, of course, Pete Townshend and the Who.

"Don't tell anybody, Ethan," said Tom. "Here's the idea: Craig is going to line up a selection of the very best illustrators in New York. They're going to produce these fantastic drawings of pinball machines in a variety of bizarre settings. You and I will go to England — you know studios there, right? — and we'll photograph Ringo and Rod Stewart and everybody, and then we'll strip their faces into the drawings."

Tom was excited. I was excited. But somebody — Lou Adler, one presumes — didn't have any intention of flying Tom and me and who knows who else to London to sit and wait for Rod Stewart to show up.

In a feat of nimble creativity Tom flops the entire concept. The illustrators in New York will deal with the celebrities. "We'll get the pinball machine here, take it around California." If it made somewhat less sense, what did it matter?

So the search began for the most absolutely cherry pinball machine (one that just had to have wooden legs), which was finally discovered in some remote corner of the San Fernando Valley and loaded into the back of Tom's Japanese pickup. We proceeded to drive the length of California, unloading the machine, bolting its legs back on, dragging it into redwoods, out onto beaches, and into urban alleys. It was an undertaking so surreal it beggared description, leaving speechless and semidisgusted the Big Sur locals who had guided us to the top of a spectacular mountaintop only to be told it was not quite right. Everything was done rush! rush! rush! as is always the

Left and right: From the Tommy *libretto. "Higher," we called to the turkeys.*

case with show business until, having left my turf of northern California, we raced through Tom's territory, wiring stuffed buzzards on weathered tree trunks at Big Bear Lake, tossing stuffed alligators into fire-ravaged canyons in Ojai, until finally, speeding on some little white pill Tom had, we arrived at a turkey farm out in the middle of some God-forsaken spot and unloaded our star pinball machine. We placed it in front of these thousands of turkeys and then leapt on the back of the pickup, my hand clutching the shutter release, as Tom and I shouted "Higher! Higher!" in imitation of Sly Stone singing before the five hundred thousand at Woodstock, and all the turkeys answered us, "Gobble-gobble-gobble," their heads erect, paying strict attention.

Such was the state of cynicism rock and roll was coming to engender.

The finished package drew a lot of attention. Tom and Craig submitted it to every design and art director's show, and it won a lot of awards, including the Grammy for best album package of the year.

"You did that?" said Pete Townshend when I met with him in England. "Do you know what it costs just to produce the package? Nineteen and six, each one" (roughly two dollars and forty cents in those days). Townshend tossed his head in disgust. Used to be able to produce the whole record for a unit cost less than that, he implied. What had it all come to?

I was in England to work with Townshend to produce a cover for *Quadrophenia,* the Who's latest work and the result of more than two years of Townshend's efforts. Townshend had called me in L.A., where I was living in one of those small canyon homes, sampling southern California, trying to make sense of it. (I read in *Rolling Stone,* after I arrive, of a young screenwriter vain or foolish enough to admit that he intends to "capture the imagination" of Los Angeles. "The only person able to capture the imagination of *this* town," says the jaded reporter, "was Charles Manson.")

Quadrophenia, Townshend explains, is another rock opera. It tells the story of Jimmy, an adolescent who suffers the severe effects of having four conflicting personalities ("twice schizophrenic," it is explained; hence "quadrophenia"). Pete has conceived that each member of the Who — a quartet — represents one-quarter of Jimmy's personality. Each aspect of the personality is represented by a different musical signature, which is introduced and kept separate until the climax of the opera where, as Jimmy is symbolically drowned and reborn, the four musical signatures are revived and woven into one. It is an ambitious and impressive work that somehow never attracts the audience it hoped for.

But now it is before the release, and all expectations are high. Extensive thought and anticipation have gone into the marketing of *Quadrophenia,* which also plays off the word *quadraphonic* (four-channel) sound, which is being touted to replace stereo as the audio system of note. *Quadrophenia* will be the first major pop record to be released in quadraphonic sound.

The record needs a cover, maybe something more. There is urgency attached,

for, as ever, the record has been expected for some time. Townshend is still mixing. MCA Records, in America, wants an album in hand in time for Christmas release. The Who's first opera since *Tommy* is, unquestionably, a momentous event.

So once again I jump into the cycle that is the progression of the record biz: first write the music, then record, then mix, then look for a cover, then tour.

It was not a strange idea, the idea to produce a book. Double record sets, as *Quadrophenia* was to be, often included something additional, if only expanded lyric sheets. The original *Tommy* had one, the re-recording of *Tommy* still another. Operas, even rock operas, seemed to require a libretto.

As much as *Quadrophenia* was about the tangled psyche of its main character, it was also about "mods" and "rockers" and a dimly understood (by Americans) era in England, from which roots grew a lot of English identity, which, in turn, was exported to the United States as part of the British Invasion. (As I was to learn, what Americans thought of as mod — Brian Jones and Edwardian jackets — was not the case at all.) "Mods" were peculiarly English; "rockers," on the other hand, were English copies of the American juvenile delinquents of the 1950s, leather jacketed, with jellyroll hairdos and a lot of attitude (the young John Lennon was one). Rockers were hybrids of Elvis Presley and James Dean, copied and reproduced as only the English can when they become enthusiasts.

Mods were a combination of very different styles: they wore army parkas and Fred Perry shirts (with just the right collar), and rode Vespa scooters, chromed and decorated with a maze of mirrors, myriad lights, long antennas with fox tails.

Pete Townshend said, with his highly developed sense of the specificness of it all, "We were never mod," though early pictures of the Who — with Townshend in his gold lamé jacket and frilly cuffs, and Daltrey with his bouffant hairdo — were to Americans what "mod" was.

But, to me, it was the Englishness of it all that finally appealed. The mods were spawned during the virtual depression that marked bombed and wasted postwar England. Their identity was created through the clothing they wore and the scooters they rode. In contrast to the rockers, who were essentially recycled American, the mods (in the nonpurist state — if you were a fanatic — that the Who and Brian Jones came to represent) eventually took over as the Beatles and everything else English swept over the American landscape, and for a short time it was as if even Elvis couldn't find work.

But, as with my sister and me walking through Piccadilly Circus looking for the psychedelic explosion only to find the procession of pubs and theaters, I discovered that nothing much subtler than the Industrial Revolution really changes the face of England, and mod was something that lived and thrived in the same back streets of row houses and cafes (rhymes with "laughs") to be found in Battersea in 1973, which is when *Quadrophenia* was shot.

In 1973 the Who were building a studio in Battersea, over the bridge from Chelsea and the King's Road, the visible indicator of swinging London. Battersea was a short distance from London's East End, near the docks, bombed into rubble during the war, home of the dropped "h" — "'Ere's to 'im, mates."

Very quickly I became submerged in the details, some directly mod, others just the England of the period, everything that I hadn't photographed earlier when it was all the Beatles and pictures of Mick Jagger: the plates of chips, and chips and eggs, and chips and beans, and Spam and chips. I recalled from my early travels in the Midlands seeing a man placing huge french fries (chips) between slices of white bread. They call it a putty sandwich.

Educated and assisted by Richard Barnes — brought into the project by Pete — I began the process of finding and restoring the correct scooter, assembling an accurate period wardrobe, casting the kids who were to play the characters. They were all locals from the East End (with the exception of Townshend's younger brother, who had to have his shoulder-length hair shorn, and a professional female model who bore a marked resemblance to Queen Elizabeth, cast as Jimmy's mum).

Chad, who played Jimmy, was our star. He appeared the essential East End tough. By age twenty, his wife had already left him, he was living in his parents' Council flat, and he had the word *love* tattooed across the fingers of one hand and

Pages 211–217: Stills from the Quadrophenia *book. A mod odyssey, starring Chad.*

hate across the other. Chad didn't tell me he was in trouble with the law until at the end of the month of shooting, when exhaustion had everyone in its grip, and the details and production problems associated with creating a forty-page book ("I thought you said it would be eighteen pages, Ethan?" says Pete later. It just grew. Who knew?) were at their peak. I was standing on top of a ladder at six A.M., taking the only photograph that includes the Who in the entire book, when one of the Who's managers arrives and hands a piece of paper up to me. "That okay?" he says.

"For what?" I ask.

"It's the paper for the book."

"Yeah, seems all right."

"Good, I just ordered six trainloads of it."

As the deadline presses ever tighter I worry that the production problems of the book will slow the release of the long-awaited record. Then Chad comes up to me and says he can't shoot the next day because he has to go to court.

"Court? Why?" I ask.

"I stole a bus," says Chad.

"You did what?"

"Stole a bus."

Chad had seen a London double-decker just sitting there one day, so he thought

he'd take it for a spin. He was caught and arrested.

"Could they put you in jail for this, Chad?"

"S'pose so," says Chad.

In his own small way Chad is the star of our book, only half of which is shot. Chad in jail would be the end of the project. I accompany him to court and sit there nervously, listening to the cases that precede us, the judge sentencing a man who had struck a ticket salesman to two weeks in jail.

When called, Chad does not challenge the facts, just asks that he be given a second chance.

"What do you do now?" asks the judge.

"I'm a male model," says Chad.

"Excuse me?" says the judge.

"I work for the pop group the 'Oo," (rhymes with "moo") says Chad in a voice both proud and insolent, taunting the judge ("Wrong, Chad," I think to myself), feeling for the first time some chance of impunity, as if the vaunted reputation of the Who is certain to protect him.

[216]

"Is this true?" the judge asks me, and I affirm that it is, explaining that Chad is essential.

So Chad is released, and we leave for Cornwall to shoot the final sections of the book, where Chad has to jump, fully clothed, off the side of a boat, for the drowning sequence. This he does, in blue suit and parka, the motor-driven Nikon firing four frames a second, and we go and fish out a Chad who is shivering and adamantly refusing to go back in the water so I can get a shot of him fully submerged. Only later, when we go to do this shot in two feet of water in the small river running by Townshend's country home, when Chad once again demonstrates the same reluctance, does he reveal that he cannot swim at all.

In the end the book is finished. I have lost twenty pounds from day after day of waking at five in the morning to get an early start, producing and shooting all day, arriving at the printer's at night, working on prints until midnight, and then going back and doing it again. Quite by chance, as I'm boarding the plane to return to L.A., I see Pete carrying with him the boxes of tape, the prized masters for *Quadrophenia*. I am too tired to say much of anything, but upgrade my ticket to first so we can talk. I sleep most of the way to Los Angeles.

At customs the people from MCA Records meet Pete. The customs man reaches for the tapes held under Pete's arm. Townshend jerks them back and starts stamping his boots at the customs man's feet. "Not leaving my hands, mate. Not for a second."

Nice what you can get away with if you're famous.

"Ethan." I hear a voice and turn. It is Anthony Fawcett, who had been John and Yoko's assistant at Apple when I was there, and had stayed with them through their Peace Initiative, their move to New York, almost until John suddenly left for Los Angeles in 1973.

Anthony seems intrigued and wants to know what I have been doing. Just outside customs, waiting for my connecting flight to San Francisco, I sit at a bar and stare into a beer, the bubbles taking on an unnatural sharpness. The time change and my exhaustion are closing in on me.

"Stay out of show business," I tell Anthony, who hadn't asked. "Just don't get near it. It'll chew you up and spit you out."

I get back to San Francisco early that evening, and my father says, "You look good," but I know it's far from true.

Soon I take a plane into the heartland of the United States, joining friends who are crossing America in a battered '62 Buick, their possessions filling every spare nook, the dog's nose hanging out the open window. We drive through blizzards in a deserted Yellowstone, fish for trout by yellowing aspen in the Colorado Rockies, watch farmers paint the word *cow* in red on the sides of their cattle as the deer season opens. The sound of rifle shots echoes through the hills, as the papers are full of meat shortages. We swoop over the Continental Divide, Beethoven on the tape deck, down into the old cow towns. Bob Dylan's country voice bounces off the stratosphere, late at night, way out in the Midwest, knocking on heaven's door. We stop off in Fargo, North Dakota, to visit four generations of a family living in the same town. The kids still get married at twenty and have their own kids. Then it's up into Canada, east and then south toward New York, and smack into the height of the autumn New England blaze, the rigors of rock and roll diminishing day by day.

———◆———

We don't get fooled again.

— Pete Townshend

In a huge valley in the Catskill Mountains, the changing leaves crept over one ridgeline to slowly transform the entire valley. On the television, Richard Nixon continually affirmed his innocence while we sat around and guffawed. With the malicious glee of an Ebenezer Scrooge, I watched the unraveling of the Nixon presidency, noticing very early on Nixon's incredible mistake of pitting his word and his presidency against the entire American political system, legislative and judicial, thinking to myself, now he's done it: it's the system or him.

There was no better place to be that year than the East Coast, following the day-by-day revelations reported in depth by the *New York Times*, which dutifully carried transcripts of entire press conferences. Along with my friends I sent off an angry telegram upon the firing of Archibald Cox, awaited with anticipation the formation of the Senate Special Investigating Committee headed by Sam Ervin, sat glued to the television throughout the proceedings, a drama the likes of which the modern nation had never witnessed.

Richard Nixon, who never even had a remote inclination to pardon those who had protested the war, was now pinned and wriggling. It was a triumph for America, though opaque to the rest of the world.

That year in the East, traveling back and forth from the Catskills and the Berkshires to Manhattan, I had written, with another filmmaker, a treatment for a television special of *Quadrophenia,* employing a performance by the Who and a narrative that would have told the story of Jimmy. I had flown to England to pitch the project to Pete Townshend. A car drove me and my partner to Townshend's house overlooking the Thames near Eel Pie Island. Pete and his wife, Karen, sat quietly as I started my pitch. The house was old and the ceilings were low. From the middle of the ceiling in the small front room hung a metal chandelier. I was wound up, walking and talking, when I ran into the chandelier. Bam. I kept moving. Talking, selling. Bam. I hit the chandelier again, and then again. Finally I knocked it completely out of the ceiling. It crashed to the floor. "That's okay," said Pete, very kindly. "We've been meaning to have that removed."

To my knowledge the television presentation of *Quadrophenia* would have been the first attempt to bring a cinematic use of rock music to television, and it was hopelessly ahead of its time. Though Townshend gave us the rights to *Quadrophenia,* they were contingent upon our ability to line up a prime-time broadcast, something that ultimately proved impossible despite a sustained interest by ABC.

When that happened I returned to San Francisco. Sitting on the edge of the bed with my father, we watched as Nixon made his tearful resignation. I felt terrible for my father since he, like so many others, had stood by Nixon, believing him through the endless series of lies. Dad had voted for him, supported him, railed against all who would speak against him, citing "hard political realities" and saying how Kennedy, Johnson, even Roosevelt had been as bad or worse. Nixon, through his unbelievable arrogance and pettiness, had dragged the country my father loved and had fought for through the mud, until the once unquestionable virtue of loyalty to the president became meaningless because the president appeared to hold the American system of government in complete contempt. What a thing it must have been to accept, for all his life my father had believed in America.

Not that rock and roll really had anything to do with this anymore, except that earlier, back when people were on the streets, they seemed to get the idea that they could actually *do* something if they set their minds to it, and apparently they had no intention of forgetting that.

Imagine. ♪

Left: Fall in the Berkshires.

Below: Mom and me in Paris. On the same trip I was in England to sell Quadrophenia *as a television special.*

Welcome to the Hotel California.
Such a lovely place.

— Don Henley, Glenn Frey, and Don Felder

HOLLYWOOD, CALIFORNIA, 1975.

In the corners of the large all-white room ferns cascaded from pots on pedestals. Sand-blasted wood provided background for gleaming photographs of Japanese trucks. I was in an advertising studio in the center of Los Angeles's film district. Tom Snow — a graduate of Princeton University — repeatedly climbed four rungs up a ladder and then jumped the few feet to the studio floor. Behind him hung a sixteen-by-twenty-foot painted backdrop of an urban skyline, upside down, so that, when the actual photo was itself turned upside down, Tom appeared to be falling earthward from a great height, head first. The occasion for this apparent suicide attempt was the album cover session for Tom's first record, titled *Taking It All in Stride*.

The music business had moved west, as some said civilization had, to settle in Los Angeles. I had returned to L.A. quite simply because I had run short of money. From Los Angeles came the "new music," the singer-songwriters, all American. They had been young men and women when the Beatles first appeared. Now, with the Beatles gone, they wrote the music that, as always, spoke to us and our concerns, about the things we were going through. But there was a difference. The once passionate certainties, all the cries for "further," the huge spiritual and political ambitions, had faded, replaced by variously guised concerns about how and why we had all gone wrong. About "us" Jackson Browne sang: "Some of them were dreamers and some of them were fools. . . And for some of them it was only the moment that mattered." We were being busted for hedonism.

In 1972, Don Henley and Glenn Frey of the Eagles recorded their first album, *Desperado,* a portrait of the American Wild West, of gunfights and broken love, of youthful dreams and disillusionment, with the clear implication that we had inherited the same spirit as these romantic outlaws. Then, just one album before they, too, broke up, the Eagles wrote "Hotel California," which was about those of us in the (wild) West, 1975.

With an uncanny facility to tantalize and moralize at the same time, Frey and Henley described the insatiable appetites that drew so many of us into one kind of trouble or another. "What kind of love have you got?" they asked of a favorite character of theirs, a young woman just starting to worry about her age. "A room full of noise and dangerous boys still make you thirsty and hot."

Theirs was a world filled with Mercedes-Benzes and lithe, tanned California bodies wired to the gills on cocaine. "Life in the fast lane," they sang, "surely make you lose your mind." And they stated the concern that underlay it all. "You're afraid it's all been wasted time."

If the legacy of the sixties and its psychedelics looked to be that Timothy Leary's "tune in, turn on, drop out" had simply turned out to be "freak out, fuck up, crawl back,"★ now people seemed to be determined not to be caught out again. There was a new drug in town to keep everybody tight, wired, and alert. The drug reflected a new attitude: everyone was going to *take care of business*. Though no one ventured to describe clearly what this business was all about, it appeared to have quite a lot to do with making money.

Back in the advertising studio everyone — Tom Snow, the art director, Tom's career manager, the personal assistants — gathered around the Polaroid and reveled in the effect, talking about how the cover will stop customers in the aisles, leap off the rack at them. The emphasis was on startling, and people got pepped up and snapped their fingers and talked about — wow — *impact*.

———◆———

By 1975 it seemed as if there were as many Englishmen in Los Angeles as there had once been Americans in London. Even John Lennon had spent time in Los Angeles,

Above right: The Eagles before their first album, in Bernie Leadon's house.

Below: Tom Snow.

★As Charles Perry recounts in *The Haight-Ashbury: A History* (New York: Random House, 1984).

though he was to wither on the vine there. Tales were reported of drunken nights with Harry Nilsson (the most notorious when Lennon emerged drunk from a bathroom wearing a Kotex on his head. He said to the waitress, "Do you know who I am?" And she said, "Yeah. You're some asshole with a Kotex on his head."). Recording sessions with Phil Spector disintegrated into drunken stupors, with Spector running off to his house in the hills, guarded behind locked gates, rivaling Howard Hughes in his insanity.

Like many foreigners, these Englishmen seemed fascinated by L.A. without, apparently, having to reconcile its often inexplicable taste (as Americans often do). Far from it. It appeared as if one art director was attempting to promulgate a single-handed resurgence of the American fifties. It was apparent in his designs and in the fifties cars he was buying. "Look at that," he would say, slapping the side of his '56 Buick. "Steel. Pure, solid steel."

Whatever recollections all this stirred up for him, it was difficult for me to forget the images that the fifties, with our lovely absolute nuclear superiority, spawned: *Dr. Strangelove* and *Fail-Safe* and, ultimately, Vietnam. It was a time when gas cost less than a quarter a gallon and there was enough to power the ton or so of metal that was every American's birthright. And gas would always be cheap and plentiful because, hey, who was gonna stop us?

And if now was the mid-seventies and people were burnt out on the sixties, well that was one thing, but what were we going to replace it with? The fifties?

Whatever. Los Angeles didn't care. The palm trees, some thick and hunkered down with dinosaurlike skin, some incredibly long and thin with just a few fronds at the top, stood sentinel. In Mexican restaurants I ate enchiladas rancheras washed down with pitchers of margaritas, built up a little steam, and prepared to crank out photographs. For, as Rod Stewart might have said, "Every record needs a cover, don't it?"

I leased a studio on Sunset Boulevard, next door to a taxidermist who was always in trouble with the health department. It was a grand old building, with forty-foot ceilings and massive double doors. It had once been the garage for trolley cars back when trolley cars had traveled up and down Sunset.

My assistant, Jim Shea (a refugee from the eastern winters), and I bought gallons of white paint, rollers with eighteen-foot extension handles, and set to work refurbishing. Jim and I opened the doors and waited to see what L.A. had to offer.

She was naked. She was fat. Out in the middle of the desert dry lake she sat atop one of those high-handlebarred motorcycle hogs and scowled at camera. Tom Wilkes and I spit and cackled. CBS had commissioned Tom to produce a cover for a group called Sweathog, and Tom had hardly had to pause before this image spilled into his brain. The rest was just production, so that in a short time we found ourselves confronted with I-can't-remember-what-her-name-was. She was not the least bit flus-

Above: Jim Shea painting the walls of the L.A. studio while an assistant cuts a palm tree out of plywood.

Right: Sweathog.

[222]

tered by our cackling, nor put off by the exaggerated deference Tom used when speaking to her, before turning toward me and rolling his eyes back into his head. She came up to me, slurping fries and a Coke, and said, "Fat women are the best, Mr. Photographer. You should try me. The very best." I started frantically adjusting my equipment.

With the English Art Director, on the very same lake bed, at a later date, I found myself faced with the much lither figure of Pamela, stripped to the waist, her hair piled on top of her head in a fifties do, wingtipped sunglasses shading her eyes. Pamela modeled for us, a series of cheesecake poses, standing between a bright-red fifties El Dorado and the English Art Director's green and white '56 Buick. A single cloud floated in the desert sky.

When the English Art Director arrived in Los Angeles, his company hired a red London double-decker bus and invited representatives of all the record company art departments to attend. They toured the Los Angeles area, drinking beer and wine, chatting each other up. Young people playing the old corporate game. Packagers, they were now defined in the classic tradition: record companies housed art departments, some with their own photo departments. Theirs was a world of purchase orders, requisition forms, and accountability to heads of other departments. Throughout Los Angeles were freelance art directors and photographers with their

Left and right: Pamela.

Below: The author enjoying himself.

own studies. Theirs was a world of overhead, uncertain futures, and endless self-promotion. All in competition, the old-fashioned way. Every record needs a cover, don't it? Set up the camera, point, focus,

— CLICK —

To the guard at the gate, I gave my name, and then drove into the Malibu Colony and found Linda Ronstadt's white-shingled, green-shuttered new home. The windows facing the ocean were open and the breeze blew through. Linda kept giggling embarrassedly, excited by her purchase.

"It cost *so* much," she'd say. Then she'd realize where she was now living, the girl who once posed with a pig, once sang with wonderful conviction, "If you give me weeds, whites, and wine, then show me a sign, yeah, I'll be willing," and she'd giggle, again, anxiously, as if she were worried she would offend her constituency. Then, seriously, she said, "But it's just not safe for me to get a house by myself alone, out on some hillside."

She couldn't have been nicer, this daughter of a hardware store owner. Her new album, produced by Peter Asher, was called *Prisoner in Disguise*. She wanted to shoot as quickly as possible, she told me, since her weight tended to balloon up and down. Now she was thin.

I listened to the record. The title song was slow, anguished. I thought about the title and about Linda. I thought about Linda as America's sweetheart. This brought to mind the image of a dozen long-stem American Beauty roses. Then I thought how, as this was show business, we would get the roses made out of neon. It seemed to evoke a lot of qualities: like the flashing sign at some Arizona roadside diner but a little empty, too, like a prisoner in disguise, since these weren't real roses, after all. ("You just keep thinking, Butch. That's what you're good at," said Sundance.)

So the session was postponed while the search commenced for someone who could actually make the roses. Somewhere in the San Fernando Valley such a person was found, but, as with so many of these things, there was a snag (other than time; there is *never* enough time). You could bend the one-eighth-inch tubing to represent the roses, but the amount of voltage necessary to energize the neon gas would be massive, seriously dangerous to life and limb.

Undaunted, I proceeded, praying silently not to be the man who killed Linda Ronstadt. Two weeks later the roses were completed. They arrived at the studio, accompanied by their handlers. Six rosebuds (we had trimmed the number from twelve) whose stems blossomed into a tangle of wires and transformers surrounded by a glass cylinder to insulate Linda from electrocution. The handlers looked worried. Linda arrived.

The handler's anxiety must have transmitted itself to Linda, for when she was handed the roses she stood there uncomfortably. To make matters worse, all the electricity needed to activate the neon gas crackled like at the birth of the monster in a sci-fi movie. The whole contraption started to take on the air of some sinister beast. In the end it didn't work. The glass cylinder was too ungainly for Linda to hold naturally, despite her best efforts. So I went on to shoot her without them, in wide-shot and close-up.

When I delivered the photographs, the record company art director and the English Art Director averred that the session was a failure, for there was no "pop" and no "zap." But to me they were low-key and subdued, as they had always been intended. They promised a reshoot, talked of "saving" the cover. Suddenly I became aware of the political machinations. The English Art Director had long been angling

for the commission, the latest Ronstadt cover to be a feather in the cap of his new job. There was much moaning over the mess I had gotten them into until Linda and Peter saw the photographs, liked them, and the project went forward.

The politics, the surreptitious phone calls, the posturing, and particularly the lies were a new element that had suddenly arisen in the music business, at least for me, as competition replaced the idea that we were all in this together. I tried to shake it off. Point. Focus.

— CLICK —

Andy Caulfield (another refugee from the eastern winters) and I were offloading boxes of equipment onto the hot L.A. sidewalk. It was Sunday, and Los Angeles was

Left: Linda Ronstadt, the back cover portrait for Prisoner in Disguise.

Right: The cover photograph for Prisoner in Disguise.

[227]

blanketed in orange smog. I'd gotten a last-minute call that Jerry Lee Lewis was in town and to get to the recording studio, since Jerry Lee was too crazy or too unorganized to make it to a photo session.

Inside, the producer sat waiting with the assembled studio musicians. I could see them through the control-room window, twirling drumsticks, tuning guitars. Professionals, paid by the hour, they were all on time. But there was no Jerry Lee.

I spoke briefly with the producer. He seemed unhappy. Lewis is uncontrollable, he says. Everyone waits.

"KILLER!" yells a voice. "THE KILLER IS HERE!" and in strolls Jerry Lee, announcing himself.

He is wearing a gray business suit, complete with tie, looking every inch the prosperous Memphis businessman. I think this is terribly hip, beyond hip, as if he'd gotten dressed up for his mom. While Jerry and the producer say good morning to each other, rather guardedly it seems to me, I look around. There are not a lot of interesting photographic choices in a recording studio. While we are trying to figure out what to do, Jerry leaves the producer and walks into the studio, puffing on a cigar, saying, repeatedly, "The Killer is back!" He sits at the piano, riffling through some boogie, four bars of "Chantilly Lace." Then suddenly he slams shut the piano lid, threatening to disintegrate his knuckles, yelling, "SHIT! THE KILLER!"

"How about a little eye opener?" he asks. And a dark cloud crosses the producer's face. Jerry Lee's manager says, "There's none here, Jerry. Take it easy."

"Ah, shit!" says the Killer.

Meanwhile, Andy and I have decided to take advantage of the only distinctive quality the studio seems to have, which is that it looks a bit like a piano lounge. We draw shut the red velour curtain and stand Jerry Lee in front of it, placing a stand-up ashtray next to him. The Killer obliges by puffing away on his cigar, P. T. Barnum

Above and below left:
Jerry Lee Lewis.

Right: Roger McGuinn. Photos
by Jim Shea.

style. He seems pleased to pose, not a glimpse of the troublemaker everyone fears. Shortly we leave, overhearing the Killer ordering his manager to go and get a bottle of bourbon. Rumor has it that he goes out that night to some redneck bar in Topanga Canyon and closes the joint down.

In 1984 the Killer announces he's found Jesus. . . . Album covers. Point. Focus.

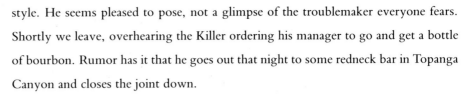

From Ron Coro (then the art director at CBS) came the phone call. Roger McGuinn needed a cover and would I be interested? Though not as radically as, let's say, Lew Alcindor or Cassius Clay, Roger McGuinn had changed his name (God knows why) from Jim. Jim McGuinn had been the lead guitar player for the Byrds whose break in the middle of "The Bells of Rhymney" used to take me traveling every time I listened to it. He was also famous from the line "McGuinn and McGuire just kept a-getting higher / in L.A., you know where that's at" from the Mamas and the Papas.

McGuinn arrived, parked his Mercedes convertible at the door, and walked into the studio with a wicked grin on his face, prepared to have fun. He carried a briefcase, which contained a telephone and a radio that provided a continuous scan of all police and fire short-wave broadcasts.

The initial part of the session was taken up posing Roger by an empty picture frame, water with glycerine sprayed on his face, and a slight bit of wind blown through his hair. Ron would later strip (that is, physically impose) an eighteenth-century illustration of a sailing schooner into the frame. (It was a typical Ron Coro idea. His tastes were broad, eclectic, and usually highly and subtly — not a contradiction — visual.) McGuinn stood patiently, guzzling anything that was put near him. I had him teach me "Eight Miles High" on the guitar.

"Can't teach you the lead break, though, Ethan. Took me six hours to do that."

"That's okay," I said.

While Jim Shea photographs McGuinn for CBS's publicity stills, Roger falls gleefully through a paper backdrop, bringing it down around him.

Many bottles of beer later, Roger McGuinn staggers out to his Mercedes. "Shokay, Ethan," he says to my offer to give him a lift. He swings the car around and heads up Sunset Boulevard, spinning back toward the Mali-boo, as Henley sang. I stand and watch worriedly as the taillights diminish. My psychedelic hero boozed out. The next day I am scared to open a newspaper, afraid to encounter a story about a car wreck.

— CLICK —

It didn't seem to matter who I was speaking to. When I mentioned that I was going to photograph Debby Boone, the reaction was identical: a cynical laugh, followed by a sneer.

In person, Debby Boone could not have been nicer. That she was sincere and conscientious was apparent. That she was a hard-working professional with reasonable concerns about her career was equally evident. Working with her was not dissimilar to working with many other entertainers: there was concern over make-up, over which clothes to wear, over the fact that her previous covers had made her look like plastic-covered furniture.

Her sin seemed to be her sincerity. She perhaps had never taken drugs, and might reasonably be expected to believe in Jesus. In the City of Angels this was apparently worse than statutory rape, which might be received with a giggle and a nudge. Or

Left: Debby Boone.

Above: Andrew Gold's What's Wrong with This Picture? *There are over 25 things wrong with the picture, not including the manager's head peeking through the window. In the fat days of the record business, the company gave away a case of Dom Perignon to the employee who submitted the correct answer.*

maybe it was simply that she wasn't hip. Well, there was certainly no question about that: in terms of hipness Debby Boone just wasn't it. Too bad.

— CLICK —

Since I was a child I had been fascinated by the newspaper game "What's Wrong with This Picture?" and for a long time I carried the idea around with me, hoping one day to recreate it. It finally became an album cover for Andrew Gold.

"Best cover you've ever done," said the English Art Director, who had taken to speaking entirely in superlatives, either best or worst. "Why'd you waste it on some-one like Andrew?" (The Los Angeles disease: save it for a "star.")

"Andrew was the only person I found who would call his album *What's Wrong with This Picture?*"

"Oh."

Los Angeles. Sprawling and elusive. New Yorkers arrive at the Beverly Hills Hotel telling Woody Allen jokes. Uncomfortable in the palm frond hallways, they try to subdue L.A.'s Slick and Cool with New York Nasty Mouth. It is a mysterious town, hard to pin down, not surprisingly when the same block in Beverly Hills has an English Tudor mansion next to French Château next to Cape Cod Summerhome next to Arabian Refurb next to Fifties Indescribable. Where — somewhere, in a canyon, in a beachhouse, in North Hollywood, in Orange County — live out-of-work actors and would-be rock 'n' rollers alongside people as diverse as George Putnam, Kareem Abdul-Jabbar, Cary Grant, Monty Hall, and even Tom Waits, hiding in the Silverlake keeping alive the time of Kerouac and the Beats, committing suicide by Viceroy. And scattered throughout the same valleys and canyons live all the makeup-wardrobe-lighting-camera-people, including photographers, whose job it is to present the famous and would-be-famous to the world.

Back to work. Album covers. Point. Focus.

— CLICK —

Buffy Sainte-Marie walked into the studio. I had been studying Edward Curtis portraits of American Indians taken in the late 1800s and early 1900s. As with many

photographs of the time, there was a peculiar quality, a kind of fixedness, attached to them. It seemed to me to be a combination of the fact that photographs were so new and unusual at the time that the sitters didn't have an easy familiarity with the process ("Who's that?" you ask a two-year-old today, pointing to a snapshot. "Me!" he/she responds). Additionally, due to the photographic constraints of the time, an exposure could take several minutes, and the sitters had to hold rigorously still, their heads sometimes supported by mechanical braces.

I elected to shoot long exposures, ranging from eight to thirty seconds. Buffy Sainte-Marie's apparent interest in this was zero. It wasn't until later, when she put on her red dress (baby) and was dancing in front of the background paper, that she seemed to feel we had gotten down to business. But the Curtis-style photograph is the one we use.

— CLICK —

A pick-up truck, its bed filled with sand, backed through the double doors of the studio. In one corner, a harried, overworked painter was creating a Tahitian beach scene on the white background the carpenters had constructed overnight. The sand was unloaded and spread out as the painter cursed. I examined a large rubber mask specially commissioned to look like a huge coconut. It had no opening for either eyes or nose, but instead a huge crack where the meat of the coconut was visible, its milk dripping down its sides, around the strands of imitation coconut hair.

All of this was conceived by Ron Coro for Dave Mason's new record, *Split Co-conut*. We all awaited Dave Mason (once of Traffic; he had performed on "Dear Mr. Fantasy"). Yet *another* Englishman living in L.A., Mason soon walked through the door, breaking into peals of laughter when presented with his mask. He placed it over his head and then sat atop the artificial sand dune, guitar in hand, a rough approximation of the headless horseman if the horseman had had a coconut in place of his void. I took pictures while the rest of the band lobbed coconuts, camera left to camera right.

The cover was immediately rejected by the powers-that-be at CBS even though their own art department had come up with the idea. Mason's face absolutely *had* to appear on the record cover (not an insignificant decision, since CBS must re-employ everyone for the reshoot, at no small expense). Other covers had suffered a similar fate. With Tom Snow, the visual joke was shunted to the back cover and replaced by a portrait I'd taken at the same session. As for poor Ms. Sweathog, she was never even considered.

Though produced in the spirit of outrageousness that, it would appear obvious to anyone who paused to think, had been the lifeblood of a good portion of rock and roll, these images appeared to be rejected for being too outrageous and not satisfying the perceived needs of "artist identification." The heart of southern California — if it can be said to have one — had taken hold, and the nature of the work I was doing

Left: Buffy Sainte-Marie.

Below: Dave Mason and the original cover.

was finally made clear to me. My images were to a record what Reggie Jackson was to Wheaties. It was a thought that, at first, I didn't want to linger over.

◆

For two years I continued. I photographed Deniece Williams. I photographed the Mormon Tabernacle Choir. Every picture had its story, didn't it? For Earth, Wind & Fire seven truckloads of sand were spread across a sound stage floor. Forty thousand watts of light were used, arcing and firing mysteriously. I pretended I was Field Marshal Rommel. I photographed Phil Everly in about fifteen minutes. I had a manager

Above: Deniece Williams.

Right, album covers (clockwise from top left): Karla Bonoff. Paul McCandless. Earth, Wind & Fire. Pablo Cruise. Dave Mason (with head retouched in). Journey.

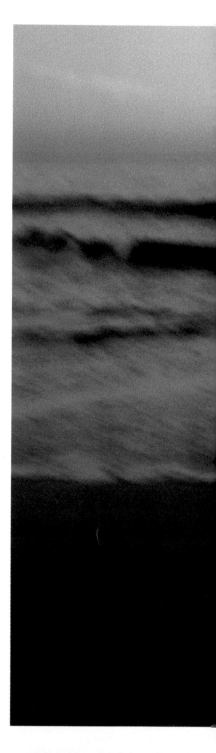

Linda Rondstadt from the
Hasten Down the Wind
*sessions. Left: Linda telling me
not to take the picture that
became the cover. (The horse
was not arranged.)*

*Pages 238–239: Rickie Lee
Jones. Phil Everly. Valerie
Carter. Gene Rodenberry. Hank
Williams, Jr. Flo and Eddie.*

in Nashville tell me to be sure to include a country singer's crotch in the photograph. "The women go crazy," the manager said. Linda Ronstadt said to me, "Don't shoot. You'll scare the horse," seconds before I exposed the cover frame of *Hasten Down the Wind.*

One day, some time later, when I was living on my father's farm, Bill, a horseman who worked for us, called me up and said I should come down because one of the mares was foaling. Though I had been around horses all my life, I had never seen one foal, so I grabbed my camera, and in the dim light I photographed the fetus slowly emerging. Standing as quietly as I could, I saw the foal born, the mother lick and smell it, and finally, within that incredibly short space of time, the little fellow raise its legs, looking every bit like a daddy longlegs spider, and hobble slowly to his feet, then fall, and then get up again. Like any true life experience, it was heart-rending. But I had a secondary, strange reaction. I felt that by having taken photographs I had somehow missed the central spirit of the event. More and more, photography seemed to get in the way.

I had a dream. I was out in the ocean off Carmel. In front of me were kelp beds. I had to make my way through them to get to shore, which I did. Once ashore, I looked up the hillside, and there was a chapel-like building, a smaller version of the Carmel mission. I walked there. When I peered inside I saw an apparent replica of *The Last Supper,* except seated at this table, instead of Christ and the disciples, were the four Beatles, Stevie Wonder, several nuns, and a chimpanzee. There were lilies all around. The scene was vibrant and full of energy. I thought to myself, "This is important. The Beatles have come back together again, and I must get a photograph," so I went running off to find a camera. I could find only my old Nikkormat. It was dinged and beaten up by many hard years of use. The lens on it was an equally old 35mm, my least favorite lens with which to work. When I rushed back to the scene, all four Beatles were gone. The scene had shifted to black and white. All of the energy had dissipated.

I took this dream to mean (among other things) that I should give up rock and roll photography.

So I did.

———◆———

I lived in Carmel Valley, renewing old friendships. I seriously considered opening a restaurant. It felt wonderful to be around people for whom show business was not the entire universe. I drank a lot of wine and spent a lot of time down the Coast. Carmel Valley has these endless, forgiving days of sunshine.

Then Glyn Johns called from England. He was working on a project called *White Mansions,* an Englishman's (Paul Kennerley's) musical appraisal of the Civil War.

"Jerry Moss [the "M" of A&M Records in America] is here," said Glyn. "And Derek Greene [head of A&M England] and Paul. Get on a plane and come over."

"I can't for a few days," I said.

"Why not?" said Glyn.

"My shirts aren't back from the laundry."

"I'll *buy* you new shirts, for Christ's sake," said Glyn, suitably disgusted.

So I went to England and, with the friendly and inestimable help of Michael Ross and his staff at A&M England, threw battles and ballroom dances, shot in England, of the American Civil War.

Right: The opening shot of the book for White Mansions. *The young Confederate lieutenant about to leave for battle, with his intended.*

Below: The author directing the attack.

I came back to America and stayed in the country. Then one day I heard that Keith Moon had died. It haunted me. I pictured him as I'd last seen him in London where he had looked old and beaten: huge stomach and baggy eyes. But he told me he was giving up drinking and that he was fine. For weeks after I learned of his death I felt helpless, as if all the early madness only ended with habits that were going to take us all to an early grave. By then I was drinking pretty steadily myself. Kind of crept up on you.

But back to work. I would fly to Los Angeles and do covers, mostly for Ron Coro. Then Jo Bergman, who had been aware of the *Quadrophenia* film project and the amount of production required by *White Mansions,* called to say that they needed someone to do a promotional film for Leon Redbone. Thereby I got to test out some of the ideas originally developed for *Quadrophenia.* They worked. Everyone loved the film, and shortly I did another with Rickie Lee Jones that people liked even better. That was followed by a piece with Emmylou Harris. Bitten by show business once again, I was soon surrounded by agents and lawyers, and I spent a lot of time going to lunch. I started to feel that maybe it *was* important that I own a Mercedes when Jo called about a film for John and Yoko. ⚓

Left: After the defeat of the Confederacy, the lieutenant becomes an outlaw.

Above: A Confederate camp scene shot on the grounds of an English country estate in January 1978.

Right: Interior of the stately home, the ballroom scene.

[242]

THE MOVIES (Director of photography: Paul Goldsmith)

Leon Redbone

Joni Mitchell

Emmylou Harris

Leon Redbone

Emmylou Harris

Rickie Lee Jones

Rickie Lee Jones

Joni Mitchell

18

NEW YORK CITY, NOVEMBER 26, 1980.

John and Yoko walked along the curving path through Central Park. They were followed by Don Lenzer, the cameraman, and his assistant. The soundman, Harry Lapham, hovered close to them. I walked with Jayme Lubarr, the production manager. All together we made up a small crowd noticeable even in New York's Central Park. As we rounded a corner, I noticed several construction workers sitting down to eat their lunch, the site on which they were working surrounded by a chain-link fence. One of the workers was young, maybe in his late twenties, with long, curly hair, wearing overalls. As we approached, he looked up.

"Look," he said, pointing. "There's TV cameras." And then, "Hey, would you look at that. That's John Lennon . . . It's John . . . John Lennon! I DON'T FUCKING BELIEVE IT'S JOHN LENNON," his Brooklyn voice rising, and he stood up and started to walk toward us, dropping his sandwich.

"I FUCKING SEE . . . I DON'T FUCKING BELIEVE . . . IT'S JOHN LEN — I DON'T FUCKING BELIEVE IT'S JOHN LENNON."

By now the guy has reached the fence and thrown himself against it, still yelling at the top of his lungs. He sticks his fingers through the three-inch hole of the chain link, straining to touch John.

We stop. The guy just stands there, riveted, while his voice maintains its screaming, as if disembodied. "JOHN FUCKING LENNON. THEY'RE NEVER GONNA BELIEVE THIS. JESUS! JOHN LENNON!" He is now not three feet from John.

"How you doin', man?" says John in a soft voice. As the guy continues his attempt to touch him, John raises a hand in greeting, and we all move on, the camera rolling, gathering indiscriminate footage for use in the promotional film for "Woman," the second single from John and Yoko's new record, (*Just Like*) *Starting Over*.

It had not been easy getting everyone together in the park. I had been in New York now for two weeks and had booked crews several times in anticipation of filming, but every time Yoko had canceled at the last minute, never giving very specific reasons, saying with her clipped Japanese accent, "Okay, Ethan. We'll do it tomorrow. Bye."

I hadn't spoken to John until this day of the shoot. I had asked to, since Yoko kept changing her mind, and it was difficult to produce without some direction, but according to Yoko, John was always unavailable. When outlining a shooting sched-

Above: John and Yoko start their walk in Central Park.

ule, I had mentioned to Yoko that we would meet them at the Dakota, where they lived. We would then walk around the park and pick up some footage there, and later drive downtown where Virginia Field, the art director, was overseeing the construction of an all-white-walled bedroom in the Castelli Galleries in SoHo. There John and Yoko would climb into bed, naked, for the camera. This was Yoko's idea, and she wished to use the material to promote her own song. Yoko seemed to believe that all the footage was modular, and that you could use any footage anywhere.

When I had mentioned to Yoko that after the shoot in the park we would drive downtown for the balance of the filming, she had seemed worried.

"He's not like he used to be, Ethan, you know."

It was not a particularly demanding schedule, so I asked her what she meant, but she didn't elaborate.

So it wasn't until the day of the shoot that I'd seen John, sitting quietly in a coffee shop with Yoko and a photographer.

"How are you?" said John, immediately friendly.

"Okay," I said, but really I was immensely uptight. Dealing with Yoko, all the cancellations, had long since taken any easygoing quality out of the production.

From the day I arrived in New York, when projected plans for shooting, then only a few days hence, had ranged from the simple (as the walk in the park) to complex productions of three to five songs, it became obvious that additional personnel might be necessary. As a result, another producer and his assistant were on their way to the L.A. airport. I told Yoko.

"Stop them," said Yoko. Emergency calls went out. They were stopped at the gate.

When I asked Yoko to sign a standard form used by Warner Brothers to indemnify the company against the possibility of cancellations, Yoko refused. "You prob-

Above left: John and Yoko on
"a beautiful fall day."

[246]

ably don't know this, Ethan, but if we sign that, then it's as if we are working for them." And she then called the record company to sort out ownership of the film. Crews were again canceled, again without notice.

One day I am summoned to the Dakota, and Yoko takes me, through endless rooms, upstairs through the back corridors, and finally into a kitchen. On the walls are various memorabilia from John and Yoko's past.

"Tomorrow, this is where I want to shoot. You see. John will be making breakfast and looking after Sean, and I will be dressed up as if I am going to the office. Okay."

I looked around, figuring angles. Whatever Yoko wanted. Then she said, "Don't tell John. Okay? I'll see you tomorrow."

The prospect of somehow surprising John into performing his house-husband role, as Yoko portrayed the breadwinner, made me uncomfortable. But, as usual, it was Yoko's gig. I booked a crew. The next day Yoko called and canceled.

◆

But finally a shoot wasn't canceled. The crew was waiting outside, along with two New York policemen assigned by the city to keep watch. In the coffee shop Yoko sat frozen in a corner. She appeared to be easily as uptight as I was.

John must have sensed this, so he stood up and we all followed him out onto Seventy-first Street and then into the park.

There was no script. The park walk arose when I asked Yoko what she wanted to do. "Well, I don't know. We could walk in the park, you know." (Yoko always said "you know.")

It was, thankfully, a beautiful day, late in the fall, and the early afternoon sun came shining through the leaves. Don Lenzer set the camera, and I spoke briefly to John and Yoko, suggesting a path for them to walk along.

John said to me how glad he was to be back, glad to have made a record, glad to be filming again.

"It's just like *Rubber Soul,*" he said, "only me face has dropped." In truth, John looked frailer, almost translucent, as if to prove the stories about the ravages of the lost weekend were true.

In the park, the shooting took about half an hour. John and Yoko would walk up a slight hill, appearing over the crest. Passers-by, noticing the camera, would turn and look, always recognizing John. When we had covered them from several angles, the crew packed up and left to go downtown. I stayed with John and Yoko. We climbed into their limousine. With Thanksgiving weekend upon us, the traffic crawled, threatening to seize up at any moment into impenetrable New York gridlock. The driver headed to the West Side Highway, trying to find an opening, but it was jammed, and we crawled downtown.

John and I talked. He spoke about films, and about how he'd seen a certain shot

[247]

that he'd liked. "It was like it opened as an aerial shot and then closed in on this train, until, at the end, it was right close up on the headlight on the front of the train."

"Those are great. They take a long time to do, though," I said, rather defensively.

As John spoke, he grew more animated. Yoko sat huddled in a corner, looking out the window. As John grew more excited, Yoko seemed to grow subtly concerned, as if she was afraid of John's enthusiasm, afraid to see him go off on one of his tangents.

I spoke to John about possibly singing some portion of "Woman," even if it had to be lip-synch. It was something I had mentioned to Yoko on the very first phone call from Los Angeles, trying to persuade her that John singing was interesting. I'd rather see John performing than just walking in the park, or getting in and out of bed. Or — rather — I was glad to see John walking in the park or getting in and out of bed, but I wanted to see him perform, too. But the idea never seemed to get picked up.

"I dunno," he said. "I like Yoko's idea. I don't want to be like Mick, you know, prancing about at forty."

And it wasn't to be. I couldn't seem to convince either of them that John singing was interesting, and it was dropped.

The limo entered downtown and started through the lower Village. John was gazing out the window. It seemed as if it had been a long time since he'd been out.

"Look, honey," he said excitedly. "There's that building we used to live in."

"Don't worry," said Yoko.

———————◆———————

At the gallery, the small crowd had grown somewhat. The lighting crew, make-up people, and camera crew were already there, of course; now they were joined by gallery employees who gathered to watch as John and Yoko walked through. In one

Left: John and Yoko.

[248]

corner of the gallery the floor had been overlaid with white, and any other object that had at one time been other than white was now white, for all-white rooms were a favorite of Yoko's. In the center of the room was a white bed, resting on top of a white platform. There were scattered other objects, a set of white stairs leading nowhere, white pedestals, a white apple, white Beatle boots. I had asked Yoko beforehand what else she might like in the room. She seemed mostly noncommittal and said I should use my imagination.

Yoko looked around. "What is that?" she asked, pointing to the white apple.

"It's a prop," I answered.

"I don't like it," she said in a voice that showed she *really* didn't like it.

"Fine," I said, and ordered it removed. "This is just for you to do whatever you want with."

Screens were erected, and all nonessential people were asked to leave, as John and Yoko disrobed, then put on hand-painted Japanese gowns.

The lighting crew scrimmed and focused lamps where John and Yoko would be lying on the bed, creating a three-quarter back light.

Yoko explained what she wanted, very close up shots of John and her: close-ups of lips, and hands touching backs, close-ups of eyes.

They took off their gowns and stood, naked, back to camera, next to the bed. When I called "Action," John reached over and kissed Yoko and, together, they leaned back onto the bed.

Don filmed the descent into bed and then switched to shoot in extreme close-up, as John and Yoko lay there. The camera ran for many minutes, following her hand on his back, his face as he kissed her. Behind us the crew waited.

On a cut, John would look up and smile. He seemed to be having a good time, and his love for Yoko was still very much evident.

When we broke for a meal (which, I explained to Yoko, was required for the crew), John sat surrounded, the film crew gathered at his feet. John told stories. He seemed so much calmer than the rest of us. Maybe so much had passed through the mind and body of the man that it had just left him spent. Maybe after too many encounters like the one in the park that afternoon, he knew it was just better to lie back and let it be. His calmness seemed to be made more dramatic by the obvious awe in which he was held. In the end we filmed until almost eleven-thirty that evening, until Don was satisfied that we had done all that could be done in that environment, and then we broke as the crew started to dismantle the lights.

John and Yoko went to the back room to get dressed, emerging shortly.

"When's the film gonna be ready?" asks John.

"Should be the day after tomorrow," I answer.

"Well, see you then," says John.

"No, no," says Yoko. "Ethan's going to Los Angeles."

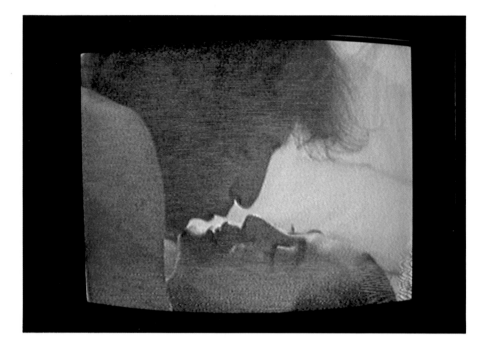

Yoko was right. I had another job and had to get back.

John looked surprised. "Okay. Bye then," says John, and they walk downstairs and are driven away.

I sat down, glad finally to have shot something, and noticed that it was midnight and my birthday was over and today was Thanksgiving.

—————◆—————

It was night when I arrived back in Los Angeles, and driving home, I could see a thirty-foot can of spinach being tugged down Hollywood Boulevard, spotlit, surrounded by limousines. There really is no place like it.

Early evening almost two weeks later, I was walking around my front room smoking a joint and listening to Bruce Springsteen's *Point Blank* when the phone rang. It was Holly Wertheimer, the film editor, calling from New York, and she was crying.

"Have you heard?" said Holly.

"Heard what?" I thought something had gone wrong with the production. People get tired and emotional.

"They've shot John."

"What?"

"They shot John."

"Is he all right?"

"I don't know, I don't know." There was silence. Over the phone line I could hear the radio, and out the window the never-ending sound of New York horns blaring, and ambulances.

"It's on the radio . . . They're saying something. Oh, no! Oh, God! He's dead." Holly crying on the phone.

"These things happen all the time," I said. I don't know what I meant. So many dead people. I said good-bye to Holly, told her I'd call her back.

It didn't sink in. It didn't mean anything. All I could think of was the film. That we had the last film of John and Yoko, and that now it was precious and had to be protected. The negative was with the lab in New York. Yoko had to have it. I called Jayme Lubarr, who was now handling the production. The negative had to be released and then placed in safe-deposit until it could be transferred to Yoko. Lawyers were called, flown to New York. Releases were gotten, the negative taken from the laboratory and finally gotten into Yoko's possession. It seemed all I could do.

The next few days were grim; even Hollywood seemed subdued. In the newspapers there appeared the awful picture of Yoko, grimacing, as the flash bulbs freeze her and David Geffen as they leave John's body. More pain than any person should be asked to bear.

I walked into the hills of Carmel Valley six days later and sat silent for the ten minutes that Yoko had requested, as did many of my friends, each separately and alone, part of the hundred thousand in Central Park and who knows how many around the world. Mark David Chapman had come all the way from Hawaii and taken it upon himself to shoot John Lennon, standing and watching as John had taken the time to autograph a record for a fan earlier in the day. Imagine.

I couldn't. It took about a year to sink in.

———◆———

Unbelievably, Yoko finished the film "Woman." She used stills from their past. She superimposed John's face from the *Imagine* album cover over the (equally unbelievable) photo that a *New York Post* photographer had somehow managed to steal of John lying in the morgue. She used the film of them walking in Central Park. Shortly thereafter she would have herself filmed, alone, in Central Park in the winter and used that, cut with the film of the two of them in bed, for her song "Walking on Thin Ice."

———◆———

At the end of the filming in the gallery in SoHo, I told John that I would like to get a picture with him and how I always regretted I didn't get one with the Beatles. He said, "Sure. You should hang on to your memories, they're all you've got." ❧

EPILOGUE

In the back of the cab driving down Seventh Avenue, all you could see through the scratched Plexiglas shield was the scruffy head of the cabbie, who was bopping to some heavy metal station blasting over his radio.

"YOU GOT TICKETS TO THE CONCERT, HUH? FAR FUCKING OUT, MAN!" He yelled to be heard above his own radio.

I didn't say anything, since I was in the early stage of a New York cab ride where you determine whether the driver is on drugs, or drunk, or just been-driving-a-cab-in-New-York-too-long, all of which can make him too dangerous to ride with. This guy seemed a candidate for drugs.

"MAN, THEY GOT JEFF BECK THERE. AND BILL WYMAN. CHARLIE FUCKING WATTS, MAN. HE'S A STONE. AND JIMMY PAGE, MAN. FUCKING JIMMY PAGE. IT'S HEAVY, MAN!" He was turning back toward me, not watching the road, maybe wondering what was going on because I was sitting back there in my Aquascutum raincoat, wearing a blue blazer and tie, a New York East Side uniform, with my girlfriend who sold art and had never been to any kind of rock show at Madison Square Garden.

"GONNA BE FUCKING HEAVY, MAN!" And he started bopping and pounding his hand on the steering wheel. The heavy metal AM station, over-amped, wrannh-wrannh, boom, boom, blaring on the radio.

"Could you turn your radio down, please?" I said.

The concert at Madison Square Garden was the ARMS concert, the Ronnie Lane benefit, which was finishing up its American tour in New York. The purpose of the tour had been to raise money for a British-based charity that was doing research into multiple sclerosis. Ronnie Lane, who had once been a member of the Small Faces, and whose music had brought pleasure to hundreds of thousands, had gotten multiple sclerosis, and the benefit was (as far as I knew) the first time in a very long time that the music community had organized a charitable event. The line-up was impressive and unique to this tour, featuring, in particular, some of the most famous lead guitar players from the sixties.

Jill and I were seated only fifteen rows back. As the players came on, Madison Square Garden went wild, major roars for Charlie and Bill of the Rolling Stones.

The music was good, with great percussion, with three drummers — Charlie Watts, Kenny Jones, and Ray Cooper. On guitars, Andy Fairweather Lowe (a fellow of no small wit) was followed by Jeff Beck. Then Eric Clapton. Finally Jimmy Page, the most reclusive of the bunch, who as lead guitar for Led Zeppelin had been rock 'n' roll's Red Baron to his generation, came out on stage.

The fans went crazy. But Page appeared with that perfected angel-of-death look, shaky, thin, wasted. He wore a long white aviator's scarf that almost hid him. I found it suddenly depressing, picturing in my mind the headline (if I was right) when he might join that seemingly endless list of dead people from the sixties, and a lot of the joy went out of the show. Page was up there with Beck and Lowe, later to be joined by Ronnie Wood (a new Rolling Stone), and the crowd just kept getting wilder. But, to me, it now seemed like a long time ago and far away, and my attention drifted.

I looked around. Way up in the third balcony, behind the stage and to the right, where you could hardly see, up in the cheap seats where the young kids sit, I saw the fans who just have to be there, who were young enough and crazy enough to keep carrying the flame. Over the edge of the balcony they had hung a sheet, like ones you see at sporting events. The sheet said, "We miss you John Lennon."

John sang, "You may say I'm a dreamer, but I'm not the only one." ☙

THANKS AND ACKNOWLEDGMENTS

Michael Lydon wrote, "I now see why authors say it is impossible to thank by name all the people who helped them: It's the truth." With that in mind, I wish to say:

Anyone who likes this book should thank, with me, Gerard Van der Leun, my great friend and editor, for in ways both practical (he said, "Ethan, you should do a book," and then proceeded to commission and edit it) and coincidental (it was through Gerard that I met Jon Cott, who, in turn, asked me to photograph Mick Jagger), Gerard is responsible for the existence of this book. Sincere thanks also go: To Richard Osborne and Mary Shaw, who helped me get started. To David Freund, who first explained to me the fundamentals of photography. To Jo Bergman, Ron Coro, Glyn Johns, and Gerard (again) for believing in me through the years. To Pete and Bobby Kaminsky, Peter and Pat Andersen, and Glyn (again) for lending me their houses to write in. To Pete for helping me with the manuscript. To Sarah Flynn for her inexhaustible efforts as manuscript editor. To Andy Caulfield for his patient aid in organizing the photographic materials, and to John Tribulato for his last-minute help. To Baily Wong for the black and white prints. To Nancy Donald and Tony Lane for their wonderful design. To Carl, in advance. And to my family and all my friends.

This book is, obviously, a memoir and does not pretend to be a history. That is to say, it relies on my memory. It is commensurately suspect. Facts have been checked where possible, and there are no known misrepresentations. Still, I would be surprised if the book managed to avoid errors of fact. Apologies are offered in advance.